CRIME SCENE DOCUMENTATION:

A Realistic Approach To Investigating Crime Scenes

Criminal Investigations Series

Jean Goodall, Ph.D.
Carol Hawks, B.S.

LawTech
Custom Publishing

pp. 334

LawTech Custom Publishing, Inc.

(949) 498-4815

FAX: (949) 498-4858

e-mail: info@LawTechCustomPublishing.com

www.LawTechCustomPublishing.com

v 04-15-05

ISBN: 1-889315-17-6

DEDICATION

This book is dedicated to my family, Jerry, Janet, Melony and BreAnna and to the memory of my mother, Roxie. Without their love and support, nothing would be worth it.

ACKNOWLEDGEMENT

My sincerest thanks go to Jerry J. Guy for all her help and devotion to this project. It couldn't have been completed without her. I also want to thank my co-author Carol Hawks for her devotion and Daniel Byram for all of his continued help and support.

Jean Goodall

DEDICATION

This is for Mom and Dad, my brothers; Paul and Neal, and to Dan for his encouragement and making anything possible.

ACKNOWLEDGEMENT

Deep thanks go to my friends; Don Howell, Richard O. Davis, Wayne Moorehead, and Daniel Byram, for sharing their experiences and to Jean Goodall — without her I couldn't have done it. Also, thanks to Joe and Glenn.

Carol Hawks

Contents at a Glance

Contents

Contents

Table of Articles and Figures

Chapter 1

Crime Scene

CHAPTER OVERVIEW

In the overall investigation of a crime scene, anything and everything should be considered as evidence. The search, recovery and collection of that evidence are critically important and cannot be left to mere memory. To be usable in Court, the evidence must be obtained properly, handled correctly and preserved appropriately.

OBJECTIVES

At the end of this chapter, you will be able to do the following:

1. Explain the concepts of Observation, Chain of Custody, and Warrants.
2. Identify the proper ways to acquire necessary evidence.

OBSERVATION

Crime Scene graphics and documentation provide a realistic approach to the preparation of a crime scene in a variety of areas, with emphasis on the use of guidelines, boilerplate material, charts, graphs, photographs and checklists. The standards for preparing these documents must be high to ensure accuracy. Accuracy of documents is critical to the investigation of the crime and prosecution of any suspects. These requirements may include establishing major steps to be followed by anyone investigating a crime scene.

It is the responsibility of the first officer arriving on the scene of a crime to preserve and protect the area. Actions taken by the officer are generally considered to be the preliminary investigation of the scene. To many veteran law enforcement officers, establishing the elements of the crime and identifying witnesses and/or additional victims, evidence or issues is second nature.

Although the general principles of searching, recovering and collecting evidence are somewhat similar, regardless of the nature of the crime, there will be instances in which they are different and may have special requirements. Because the legal admissibility of evidence and the processes by which it was collected and analyzed can continually become an issue for debate, those processes must be exact. The physical evidence, often referred to as the "unimpeachable witness," must be unquestionable.

CONSTITUTIONAL CONSIDERATION

The process for searching, recovering, and collecting evidence is largely dictated by the Fourth Amendment to the United States Constitution, which states:

> *"...The right of the people to be secure in their persons, houses, papers, and effects, against unreasonable searches and seizures, shall not be violated, and no Warrants shall issue, but upon probable cause, supported by Oath or affirmation, and particularly describing the place to be searched, and the persons or things to be seized."*

This simply means that in most cases, police officers will need a Search Warrant to search the crime scene.

WARRANTS

A Search Warrant is an order signed by a judge that authorizes police officers to search for specific objects or materials at a specific location and at a specific time. Police officers obtain warrants by convincing a judge or magistrate that they have "probable cause" or evidence to believe that a crime either has been or is going to be committed.

Once the warrant is issued, police can search only the place specified for the items specified in the warrant. However, if in the course of their search, police officers come across contraband or evidence of a crime that is not listed in the warrant, they can lawfully seize the unlisted items. A warrant is not always legally necessary, and a police officer may have information that allows the officer to make a warrantless entry.

The clearest expression within the Fourth Amendment states that "no warrant shall be issued but upon probable cause...." The probable cause standard has been defined by the Court as "...facts and circumstances within their knowledge, and of which they had reasonably trustworthy information ... sufficient in themselves to warrant a man of reasonable caution in the belief...." ***Brinegar v. United States***, 338, U.S. 160 (1949), "in dealing with probable cause... we deal with probabilities. These are not technical; they are the factual and practical considerations of everyday life on which reasonable and prudent men, not legal technicians, act." ***Carroll v. United States***, 267 U.S. 132, at 162 (1925). For a warrant to be valid, it must be supported by facts and circumstances which amount to probable cause.

Many searches occur without a warrant being issued, for example:

- Over the years, the courts have defined a number of situations in which a search warrant is not necessary, either because the search is reasonable under the circumstances or because, due to a lack of a reasonable expectation of privacy, the Fourth Amendment doesn't apply.

- Consent searches whereby the person in control freely and voluntarily agrees to the search. The search is valid and anything found by the officers is legally admissible as evidence. The only requirement for the consent search is that it must be "freely and voluntarily" given. If the consent is coerced, the search is not valid. It is always a good idea to have the person consenting to the search sign a "Voluntary Consent to Search" form similar to the one shown in Form 1.1 below.

- The "Plain View Doctrine" allows an officer to seize contraband or evidence that is "in plain view" if the officer has a right to be present when the evidence or contraband is first spotted. This doctrine extends to allow for seizure even if the officer is at the scene of an incident for some other valid reason and spots the evidence.

- Police Officers also do not need a warrant to make a search "incident to an arrest." Once someone is arrested, the officers have the right to protect themselves by searching for weapons and to protect the legal case against the suspect by searching for evidence that the suspect might otherwise try to destroy. Assuming the officer has the right to make the arrest in the first place, a search of the person and the person's surroundings following the arrest is valid, and any evidence uncovered is admissible at trial.

- An officer may search trash that has been put out for collection without a warrant because the trash has been put out in public, thereby erasing any reasonable expectation of privacy. The Fourth Amendment therefore does not apply.

The importance of the Search Warrant in the crime scene investigation can best be understood by reviewing the case of ***Mincey v. Arizona*** 427 US 385 (1978) in which the Supreme Court cited that the police had violated the defendant's Fourth Amendment rights. In this case, Mincey, who was a dope dealer, had shot and killed an undercover narcotics officer during a drug raid. Mincey was wounded and one of his companions was killed in the subsequent gun battle. The Narcotics officers, following procedure, secured the premises and notified Homicide of the killing. The Homicide detectives conducted an investigation during which hundreds of pieces of evidence were seized over a three-day crime scene search. Mincey was convicted of the murder of the undercover officer. The conviction was, however, overturned by the Supreme Court, which held that Mincey's Fourth Amendment rights were violated and that the police should have obtained a search warrant for the evidence at the crime scene. The Supreme Court's ruling made the statement that there is no exception in the Fourth Amendment for crime scene investigations.

Once the crime scene search is complete and the evidence is collected, it must be preserved for prosecution. Evidence can only be properly preserved if a proper "chain of custody" is maintained.

Form 1.1 Voluntary Consent to Search

Voluntary Consent to Search

I, _____, do hereby, freely, voluntarily and without threat, pressure or coercion of any kind, consent to a warrantless search of my

_____

_____ (Location and description of premises to be searched), by representatives of _____ (Police Department or Agency) and individuals in their company. These representatives are authorized by me to seize any items, materials or other property which they may deem to be of possible evidentiary value.

_____
Witness   Signature of person consenting to search

_____
Witness   Relationship to Premises being searched

DOB _____ SSN _____
Date _____ Time _____

CHAIN OF CUSTODY

There is a standard in criminal law pertaining to the preservation of evidence. That standard is the "chain of custody". Evidence will likely be passed from person to person during the course of an investigation and subsequent prosecution. The chain of custody begins when an item of evidence is collected. The written, chronological record of these transfers is the chain of custody. Each person who takes physical, or constructive, control over the evidence must be identified as part of the chain.

Management of this identification is accomplished with the use of various forms specifically developed for that purpose. These forms should record all transactions from the initial collection through the final disposition of the evidence. The records must include what evidence was gathered, who gathered the evidence, how it was gathered, where it was gathered and who has touched it since it was gathered. This properly maintained chain of custody will ensure continuous accountability. A chain of custody form is usually completed in triplicate and should be typed or printed in ink. The original and a copy, along with the evidence, should be presented to the evidence custodian. The remaining copy should be given to the officer to be attached to the Police Report.

Each individual in the chain of custody is responsible for each item of evidence. The care, safekeeping, and preservation, when not in the control of others, is the responsibility of the evidence custodian. Because a detailed listing of items is critical and objects must be marked without marring or destroying evidentiary characteristics, the custodian should be an experienced, trustworthy member of the department who has experience in receiving and releasing evidence. The credibility of the entire evidence custody system rests with the custodian.

Form 1.2 is a sample "Chain of Custody" form that can be used for recording recovery and transfers of evidence.

Form 1.2 Sample Evidence / Chain of Custody Log

Item: (Description, including make, model, Serial #, identifying marks, etc.)		Case No.
		Tag/Bin Number
Officer		Badge No.
Means of Recovery		
Recovery Location		
When Recovered		
Date Placed Into Evidence	Placed Into Evidence By	Signature of Person Placing Into Evidence

Removal/Received Log

Date Out	Time Out	Taken Out By	Purpose	Date In	Time In	Received By

CHECKLISTS

Crime scene information/evidence collection requires an enormous amount of effort. Incident scenes can vary and without a checklist, information can be forgotten. Form 1.3 below is a suggested checklist for obtaining the information/evidence needed from a scene. This checklist can be used by investigators searching, collecting or preserving evidence at a crime scene.

Form 1.3 Crime Scene Checklist

- ❑ Date/Time of Call-out
- ❑ Name
- ❑ Number
- ❑ Source of Call-out
- ❑ Incident Type
- ❑ Date/Time of Arrival
- ❑ Physical Location/Address
- ❑ Type of Location
- ❑ Weather Conditions
- ❑ Lighting Conditions
  - Natural
  - Artificial
- ❑ Contact Person at Scene (scene commander)
  - Name, Rank, Serial Number
- ❑ Other Officers at Scene
  - Crime Scene Log
  - Paramedics at Scene
  - Medical Examiner at Scene
  - Media at Scene
- ❑ Victim(s)/Responsible Party
  - Name
  - DOB
  - Address
- ❑ Witnesses
  - Name
  - DOB
  - Address
- ❑ Vehicles at Scene
  - Make/Model/Color/License Plate Number
  - Location
  - Damage

Form 1.3 Crime Scene Checklist (Cont.)

❏ Evidence Finder/Recorder

❏ Search Warrant

❏ Evidence/Exterior

- Point of Entry

- Location, type, condition

- Tire and Footwear Impressions

- Description, location, direction of travel

- Expended Cartridge Cases

     Description

     Make

     Location

- Bloodstains

     Type, location, direction

- Latent Prints

     Location, orientation

     Known Samples

     Type and location

- Other

     Description, type, location

- Evidence/Interior

- Point of Entry

- Location, type, condition

- Footwear impressions

     Description, location, direction of travel

- Expended cartridge cases

     Description

     Make, caliber, location

- Bloodstains

     Type, location, direction

- Latent Prints

Form 1.3 Crime Scene Checklist (Cont.)

   Location, orientation

   Known Samples

   Type and location

  – Other

   Description, type, location

❑ Photographs

 – Photo-Log

 – Point of view/Camera position

 – Subject

 – Overall/wide-angle view

 – Medium View

 – Close-up view

 – Scale

The checklist in Form 1.3 is only a guideline and will change with each different type of investigation and evidence-gathering scenario. Experience and knowledge will only be enhanced with checklists or standard templates.

SUMMARY

Search, recovery and collection of evidence from a crime scene is an art and a science. It cannot be taken lightly and it cannot be mishandled. Chain of custody procedures are critical to the outcome of criminal investigations and subsequent adjudication. Anything and everything must be considered evidence until otherwise ruled inadmissible in Court. These critical processes cannot be left to memory but rather need to have sufficient detailed documentation.

DISCUSSION QUESTION

1. Why can warrants be used in some cases but not in others? Fully explain your response.

Chapter 2

Crime Scene Elements & Documentation

CHAPTER OVERVIEW

Crime scene investigators must have knowledge of the procedures and methods for entering, documenting, preserving and releasing a crime scene. In order for testimonial and physical evidence to be analyzed and "tell" its part of the story, it must first be located, identified and collected.

This chapter will present the duties and responsibilities of the responding investigators, the various types of evidence, crime scene management, and methods of collection and preservation of the evidence.

OBJECTIVES

At the end of this chapter, you will be able to:
1. Identify methods for evidence collection, identification and preservation.
2. Recognize the duties and responsibilities of crime scene investigators.

CRIME SCENE ELEMENTS

The "Golden Rule" for any person entering a crime scene is: first, do no harm. This simply means that one should never touch, change, or alter anything until it has been photographed, measured, identified, sketched and documented. Crime scene contamination is the biggest problem for crime scene investigators because the evidence can never be restored or reconstructed if it is moved or corrupted; and, it may not be admissible in Court.

Henry Waldorf Francis once said, "A court is a place where what was confused before becomes more unsettled than ever." Crime scene investigators must continually strive to limit confusion and make sure the evidence can speak for itself, and with that having been said, there are of course, exceptions to the "Golden Rule". A couple of exceptions would be: 1) if the potential exists that an item of evidence (such as a weapon) could be used to cause harm/death to someone at the scene; and 2) if the potential exists for an item/evidence to be lost, contaminated or destroyed (such as short-lived evidence which could be subject to damage or destruction by exposure to the elements).

Crime scene investigators should have knowledge of the criminal code and be able to obtain necessary information/evidence to support a criminal charge. As such, they must evaluate current legal ramifications and obtain all necessary documents (search warrants, etc.) prior to arriving at the scene. In addition, the following objectives must be considered.

In many cases, employees or citizens are the first persons to reach the scene of a crime. The acronym "**RESPOND**" can be used to help these individuals know who to best manage a scene to minimize contamination while waiting for officials and/or investigators to arrive. The letters in the acronym represent the words respond, elevate, secure, protect, observe, notify and document and can best be explained as follows:[1]

R = Respond
- Personal Safety – the safety of everyone comes first!
- Organize thoughts and formulate a plan of how to handle the situation
- Make mental notes of any observations

E = Evaluate
- Evaluate the severity of the situation

- Identify all involved and uninvolved individuals in the area
- Be aware of weapons and hazards
- Be aware of potential evidence
- Don't touch anything unless necessary

S = Secure
- Clear away uninvolved people
- Establish a perimeter with rope, tape, cones, etc.

P = Protect
- Safeguard the scene
- Don't use phones or bathrooms within the scene area
- Don't eat, drink or smoke in the area of the scene

O = Observe
- Write down your observations
- Record detailed information – don't rely on memory

N = Notify
- Call 911

D = Document
- Take good notes – include dates, times, people at scene, doors open or closed, lights on or off, position of furniture, etc.
- Be prepared to provide your notes/information to police

Responsibilities of Responders

Most police investigations begin at the scene of a crime. The "scene" has simply been defined as the site or location where an incident took place. It is the responsibility of the first person to arrive at that location to properly secure and protect it from contamination or destruction. Protecting and securing the location can be accomplished by simply putting rope around the location or setting up a barrier.

Management of the Crime Scene

Many schools of thought exist as to how best to manage the crime scene. One protocol that is being taught today identifies a three layer or "tier" perimeter. The outer perimeter is established as a border larger than the actual scene, to keep citizens and non-essential personnel safe and away from the scene; an inner perimeter allows for a command post and comfort area just outside the scene; and the core or scene itself.

Once the crime scene is secure, additional steps can then be established for the successful searching and preserving of any evidence that may be present. Crime scene personnel can then continue with the detailed search of the scene, the preparation of the narrative description, photographing and preparing the diagrams/sketches of the scene and the collecting and documenting of evidence.

Unforeseen or Hazardous Elements of the Crime Scene

Hazards at a crime scene can fall into two categories – evidentiary hazards and health hazards. While it is the responsibility of all persons responding to a crime scene to be aware of the important evidence that can be damaged or destroyed upon entering the scene, law enforcement and investigators should also not assume that the scene has been secured and should take precautions to protect themselves from danger.

Evidentiary Hazards at a crime scene can fall into the following varieties of classifications:
- Closed Access or Unsecured Crime Scene
  - Under the Closed Access or Unsecured Crime Scene a hazard still exits. This can include hostage situations, situations where suspects may still be on the scene or one where environmental hazards may be present.
- Limited Access Crime Scene
  - This is a scene where critical evidence may be present that has not yet been secured or environmental hazards are present. Investigative personnel should take direction from the officer in charge during these types of incidents.
- Open Access Crime Scene
  - This particular type of scene may exist where evidence still needs to be collected but personnel have access to the entire area. Consultation with the person in charge should also occur before disturbing anything. Caution must be used so that evidence is not destroyed or compromised.

- Cold Crime Scene
  - There are no evidential concerns or hazards present at a cold crime scene.

In addition to these classifications, there are possibilities of being exposed to at least three different types of health hazards at a crime scene that can cause safety concerns: biohazards, chemical hazards, or physical hazards.

These hazards generate unique and different challenges for the crime scene investigator. Standard training and experience will not always assure safe results. An evaluation of the site and the situation is critical. The outer perimeter that is established will be much larger than the actual site. In addition to the regular perimeters, a decontamination area must also be established, generally away from the initial crime scene itself. Special protective equipment will need to be available for persons entering the scene.

Another challenge will be to document moving through this process. Protective suits are generally not very flexible or easy to work in. Wearing the protective equipment makes every movement slow and more deliberate. Bending and stooping are almost impossible and taking pictures becomes much more difficult.

Through all of this, it will be the lines of communication that keep it running smoothly.

EVIDENCE AT THE CRIME SCENE

Evidence falls into two categories – testimonial and physical. Testimonial evidence includes witnessed accounts of an incident while physical evidence relates to any material items that would be present at a crime scene.

Why collect evidence? Evidence can be used to prove or disprove the facts of an issue. Several other reasons for thoroughly collecting and accurately documenting items and information at a crime scene include the fact that the information may be used to prove that a crime has been committed, as well as establish key elements or link a suspect with a scene or a victim. The evidence can also exonerate suspects and corroboration of witness testimony can be established.

Although evidence collection is tedious and time consuming, crime scene investigators must be patient and should take the proper time and care in processing the scene. Teamwork is essential and may involve individuals from many different organizations. Keep the communication lines open.

SCENE DOCUMENTATION

Many law enforcement agencies use a variety of preprinted documents or forms, designed to record different aspects of a crime scene, Most of these forms are the end product of many revisions based on actual case experiences. Although the "look and feel" of the forms may differ among agencies, they are usually identical in their purpose.

However, when using forms, there are some important points to consider. Forms can only serve as a guideline and should be used as a reminder of the minimum information needed. Each scene will require some personal deviation from the form based on the complexities of the individual case. Forms are not substitutes for individual thinking but are merely tools to assist in the thought processes of experienced personnel.

Administration of the Crime Scene, a Narrative, a Photographic Log, a Diagram/Sketch, Evidence Recovery and Fingerprint Lift Logs, and Initial and Final surveys of the crime scene are several specific categories of documentation that are normally part of the search of any crime scene.

Administration of Crime Scene

All major events, times and movements relating to the search efforts must be documented and preserved. These documentation efforts will insure that an organized search is accomplished and can serve as an accurate record should the processes of the search ever come into question. The administrator should create a crime scene log to document who has entered the scene, the time of entry, the time out and the reason for the entry. Form 2.1 is a sample of a simple crime scene log that will allow for maintaining the integrity of the scene.

Form 2.1 Crime Scene Log

CRIME SCENE LOG

Case Number:		

Type of Incident:		

Location of Incident:	Date of Incident:	Time of Incident:

Officer Maintaining Log:	Badge Number:	Date/Time Log Started:

Subsequent Officer:	Badge Number:	Date/Time Log Started:

Time In:	Name	Position/Title	Reason for Entry	Time Out

Initial Survey

Once the crime scene is secure, an initial preliminary survey of the area should be conducted. The initial survey is nothing more than an organizational stage to plan for the entire search. A cautious walk-through of the scene is completed, a delineation of the extent of the search area is established and a general theory of the crime is developed. Any problem areas that need to be resolved are discussed at this stage.

Narrative

The narrative should describe the general appearance of the scene as first observed. Describe the scene in a "general to specific" scheme. Consider what should be present at the scene. For example, is there a victim's purse or a vehicle at the scene – should there be? Be sure to watch for situational factors such as whether the lights are on or off, is the heat on or off, are the drapes open or closed. This should include all things initially visible to the eye. Although extreme detail is not normally required at this level, notice the "little things".

Several forms of media, such as written memo form, audio or video, may be used to prepare the Narrative.

Photographic Logs

The photographs taken record the true depiction of a crime scene and photographing should begin as soon as possible.

Documentation of the process of photographing, which will record the overall, a medium and close-up view of the scene is critical. A log should be produced representing the technical and descriptive information concerning each photograph taken. Information such as the date, time, location where the photo was taken and the manner in which it was taken must be included.

Recognized scale devices should be used in photographs to establish measurement and identification. However, if a scale device is used, a photograph should first be taken of the object without the scale device present. Evidence should be photographed in its original location prior to it being placed in packaging.

Diagrams/Sketches

A diagram/sketch establishes a permanent record of a crime scene. Locations of physical evidence, as well as measurements showing pertinent size and distance relationships in a crime scene area, must be completed. All parts of the diagram/sketch must be properly identified and labeled. Extreme caution should be taken to insure that measurements are correct. Inaccurate information or measurements could render the diagram/sketch inadmissible in Court.

When drawing a diagram/sketch, a preliminary, or rough sketch should be drawn at the crime scene (normally not to scale) and used as a model for the finished sketch, which will be drawn to scale later. Typically a diagram/sketch will include such things as the date, time, location, case number, and the preparer's name and signature. Also included will be such things as weather conditions, lighting conditions, scale (or scale disclaimer statement), compass orientation, measurements and a key/legend. Be sure to consider doors and windows as evidence.

Evidence and Fingerprint Logs

As the crime scene search produces evidence, the evidence must be marked and packaged properly to preserve it for further use. The chain of custody rules must be followed exactly so as not to contaminate the evidence collected. All information pertaining to the evidence and/or latent fingerprints lifted at a crime scene must be accurately recorded in the appropriate log. Logs will be maintained as a permanent source of information.

Because the future use of evidence is critical, do not handle the evidence excessively, and do not guess on packaging requirements after recovery. All evidence should be placed in crime scene containers. The containers should be sealed at the crime scene and initialed by the investigator or officer who collected the item. If vehicles are involved, VIN numbers, license numbers, position of keys, odometer reading, gear shift position, amount of fuel in the tank and whether the lights are on or off is recorded.

Final Survey/Release

The final survey is the critical review of all aspects of the search of the crime scene. Discussion should be held with all personnel to make sure that everything has been completed and all documentation should be checked for errors. An assessment should be made to insure that all evidence is accounted for, and all equipment used in the search is retrieved. One last "walk through" should be conducted of the crime scene to insure that no possible hiding places or difficult access areas have been overlooked. Lastly, think about whether the search has gone far enough for evidence, that all documentation is complete and that all assumptions that have been made can be proven later.

A release of the crime scene should be done only after completion of the final survey and then only by the person in charge. Before a crime scene is released, consideration should be given to all legal requirements and whether the scene will need to be reviewed later by other persons, such as specialists, medical examiners or analysts. Once the crime scene is released, it may take another search warrant for re-entry.

CHECKLISTS

Form 2.2 is a checklist that can be used for scene management by both First Responders and Responding Investigators.

Form 2.2 Checklist – Crime Scene Element/Documentation

FIRST RESPONDER
- ❑ Self-Protection
- ❑ Care for Injured
  - – Victims
  - – Suspects
- ❑ Secure and Protect Immediate Crime Scene
- ❑ Witness
  - – Locate
  - – Identify
  - – Remove
  - – Separate
- ❑ Arrest
  - – Suspect
- ❑ Establish/Maintain Control
- ❑ Re-establish or Maintain Contact with Headquarters
- ❑ Collection of Initial Information
- ❑ Record Initial Observations
- ❑ Brief Responding Investigators
- ❑ Relinquish Formal Control of Scene
  - – Time/Date
  - – To Whom

RESPONDING INVESTIGATOR
- ❑ Contact First Responder for Briefing
- ❑ Determine Extent of Scene
  - – Interior Perimeter
  - – Outer Evidential Range
  - – External Limit

Form 2.2 Checklist – Crime Scene Element/Documentation (Cont.)

❑ Establish Control

❑ Protect Scene

❑ Perform Preliminary Survey

❑ Determine Objectives and Needs

  – Personnel

  – Equipment

❑ Assign Duties to Others at Scene

❑ Prepare Notes

❑ Review Information

❑ Direct Search of Scene

❑ Deal with "Fires"

❑ Direct Final Survey

❑ Review Goals

❑ Check Completeness with Personnel

❑ Check Documentation

❑ Photograph Final Condition of Scene

❑ Check Evidence Inventory

❑ Gather Equipment

❑ Release Crime Scene

  – After Completion of Final Survey

❑ Complete Documentation

  – Date/Time

  – Released to Whom

  – Released by Whom

❑ Provide Copy of Inventory of Items to Responsible Party

❑ Evaluate Information/Evidence Collected

SUMMARY

Developments in technology and improvements in the analysis and interpretation of physical evidence recovered from crime scenes places even greater importance on properly documented and preserved evidence. An important factor influencing the ultimate legal significance of this scientific evidence is that investigators follow an objective, experienced approach. The goal of this process is to recognize and preserve physical evidence that will yield reliable information to aid in the investigation and eventual prosecution.

Investigators should approach the crime scene investigation as if it will be their only opportunity to preserve and recover these physical clues. They should consider case information or statements from witnesses or suspects carefully in their objective assessment of the scene. Investigations may change course a number of times during such an inquiry and physical clues, initially thought irrelevant, may become crucial to a successful resolution of the case.

It is recognized that all crime scenes are unique. It is impossible to propose a single, step-by-step procedure to approach every type of situation. There are, however, fundamental principles of investigating a crime scene and preserving evidence that should be practiced in every case. The judgment of the investigator on the scene, with the assistance of other responders, should however, outweigh any checklist or template. A checklist is not a comprehensive or rigid scheme of activities, but rather merely a guide. Care must be given to recognize the authority of Federal and State statutes, case law, and local policies and procedures.

DISCUSSION QUESTIONS

1. What are the major responsibilities for Crime Scene Investigators at the scene?
2. How can a Crime Scene Investigator protect evidence?
3. Why is it so important that evidence be preserved and not contaminated?

Endnotes

1.   Crime Prevention Publication, School Crime Scene Management, New York State Troopers. http://www.troopers.state.ny.us/Publications

Chapter 3

Records/Evidence Management

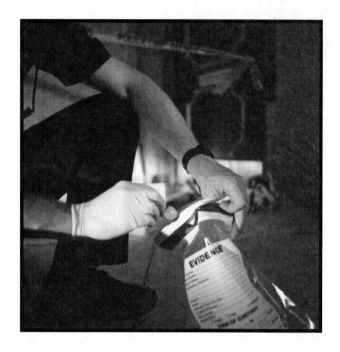

CHAPTER OVERVIEW

Major scene documentation is the responsibility of not only the first responder but also the entire experienced crime scene unit working in conjunction with other agencies. Because different types of evidence may need to be processed differently before being entered into evidence, those who possess the knowledge, experience and training to properly deal with the evidence should process major crime scenes.

OBJECTIVES

At the end of this chapter, you will be able to do the following:

1. Understand the proper methods for documenting evidence.
2. Identify the various processes for preserving evidence.

PACKAGING AND SHELVING

Standard practice dictates that most evidence seized or collected is placed in a standard paper envelope, bag or box. If the item cannot be placed in one of these containers, it should be properly tagged and labeled.

When evidence is packaged or bagged, it should be marked with the collecting investigator's initials and badge number. However, nothing should be marked if the potential is present that by doing so it will destroy or contaminate the evidence.

When packaging or shelving evidence, investigators and evidence custodians should always wear latex gloves. This is particularly important for investigators who handle chemical or drug evidence.

Shelving

Although it may vary from agency to agency, some specific procedures exist for packaging and shelving evidence items such as clothing, firearms, bullets and cartridges, gunshot residue (GSR), money, jewelry, chemicals, drugs, blood, latent fingerprints, paper documents and other miscellaneous items, including hair, fibers, etc.

Clothing

Items of clothing can usually be placed in a standard paper bag or envelope and marked with the collecting investigator's initials and badge number. Unless it will destroy or compromise the evidence, the collecting investigator should also place his or her initials or badge number on the item itself. There is nothing to dictate where on the item the initials or badge number should be placed, but consistency is important.

Information relating to the collection process, date and time, incident and case number should be documented on the bag or envelope. In order to preserve additional evidence, increased special management must be taken when handling clothing that may also contain additional evidence such as hair, fibers or gun shot residue. Each additional item of evidence should be removed from the clothing and packaged separately.

When clothing contains body fluid or blood, it must be allowed to air dry before being placed in a sealed package. If the body fluids and blood are to be analyzed at a later date, the package must be placed in a freezer and marked as "bio-hazard" to alert anyone coming into contact with the item that it could be potentially harmful to them.

When clothing is to be folded before placing it into the package, paper should be placed between the folds to prevent the transfer of fluids or other evidence.

Firearms

The handling of firearms must be conducted so as to minimize contamination or destruction of any evidence, especially fingerprints or trace residue. Special attention should be taken when transporting small guns or pistols. The proper method for transporting the weapon is to tie a string through the trigger guard of the gun so that the gun is suspended and connect the ends of the string to the sides of a box. This will prevent the gun from rubbing against or bumping into anything that could cause the loss of any physical evidence.

Weapons should be diagrammed and cartridge type should be documented. Weapons should be marked with the investigator's initials or badge number and unloaded. Never place a loaded weapon into evidence.

There are, of course, exceptions. Firearms that need to be processed for additional evidence such as blood or fingerprints should NOT be unloaded, the magazines or bullets should not be removed and they should not be entered into evidence.

Bullets/Cartridges

Bullets and cartridge casings are found at the scene of a shooting. Investigators will find the bullets or spent casings and must document the location of the bullets and/or casings prior to moving any of the items. Investigators may also be required to sketch or diagram the scene prior to removing the casings. Once these steps are complete, the bullets or casings can then be placed into an envelope for transporting. The investigator should mark the envelope with all pertinent evidentiary information. Investigators should not mark the individual bullets or casings with initials or badge numbers unless specifically directed to do so by department policy. When policy dictates the items be marked, a bullet should be marked at the base and a cartridge should be marked at the mouth of a cartridge. Marking these locations will help eliminate the possibility of losing important evidence.

Gunshot Residue (GSR)

Gunshot residue (GSR) is easily lost if caution is not practiced. Once samples are obtained, they should be packaged in a standard paper envelope, sealed with transparent tape and marked with the investigator's initials or badge number. The envelope should be documented with all pertinent information, including but not limited to, the date and time of the shooting, the location of the shooting, the type of ammunition used, how many shots were fired, and whether the shooting took place inside or outside. Form 3.1 on the next page depicts a sample data sheet for logging a firearm, ammunition and GSR information.

Form 3.1 Firearm, Ammunition and GSR Data Information

FIREARM INFORMATION

[ ] Revolver [ ] Pistol [ ] Rifle [ ] Shotgun

Make _____

Model _____

Caliber _____

Barrel Length _____

****

AMMUNITION INFORMATION

Brand _____

Caliber _____

Bullet Style

    [ ] Round nose [ ]Hollow point [ ] Wadcutter [ ] Other

Bullet Type

    [ ] Full metal jacket [ ] Semi-jacketed [ ] Other

****

GSR DATA INFORMATION

Subject's Name _____   Case No. _____

Classification of Case _____   Date _____

Investigator Name _____   Badge No. _____

INCIDENT INFORMATION

Subject:

    [ ] Right handed [ ] Left handed [ ] Unknown

Occupation _____

Activity prior to shooting _____

Dead at the scene [ ] Yes [ ] No

    If yes, where was gun found in relationship to body

_____

Incident:

Location of shooting

[ ] Indoor [ ] Outdoors [ ] Unknown

Number of shots fired _____

Date/Time of shooting _____

Date/Time evidence taken_____

Money

Money should be placed into an envelope. The money should be counted and the amount, including the dollar and coin amounts, should be placed on the outside of the envelope. The amount should be written in both numbers and words. It is always a good idea to "double bag" money by putting the first envelope into a second one, especially if there are large amounts of money.

Chemicals

Chemical evidence is the most dangerous. This type of evidence is usually found where there has been a hazardous material spill or where a clandestine lab has been discovered. In most of these cases, the initial investigator on the scene is not properly trained to collect or preserve this type of evidence. The proper authorities should be called to handle the situation.

When collecting chemical evidence it should be placed in an airtight container, then sealed and marked appropriately. It should be shelved in an appropriate location where temperatures and surroundings are safe.

Drugs

When suspected drugs or narcotics need to be packaged, they should be placed in a container and clearly marked as drugs. Most of the evidence present at crime scenes has been found to be small plastic bags containing such things as marijuana, heroin, cocaine or crack. Occasionally, larger containers are also discovered.

These smaller bags should be placed in larger envelopes and the larger samples should be placed in boxes. All should be appropriately marked as drugs. The investigator's name and badge number should also be placed on the tag.

Once taken to the evidence repository, the suspected drugs/narcotics should be placed in a location where they can remain safely until needed for future analysis or use.

Investigators should use extreme caution when handling these items. Often the narcotics and the chemicals used for processing them are very strong and can be absorbed through the skin or inhaled.

Blood

When blood is involved at the crime scene, many different things must happen. The investigator must decide whether the blood should merely be photographed and diagramed or whether samples should actually be taken. This decision will rest largely with the circumstances of each case. For example, if there is only one victim who merely has a bloody hand, samples will generally not be taken. On the other hand, if there is a murder scene where the victim was shot and blood is present everywhere, samples will be taken.

Blood, like fingerprints can identify someone. Trained crime lab personnel take most blood samples. These individuals will not only take blood samples but they will also "read" and document the blood using a process known as "bloodstain pattern analysis". This process is done with a combination of photographs, sketches and notes. The crime lab individuals have been trained to view not only the immediate scene, but surrounding areas as well for bloodstains. Bloodstain pattern analysis can be used later to reconstruct the sequence of events that led to the crime.

There are several ways to collect the blood samples but the two most common are by swab or swatch. Simply dipping the swab or swatch in wet blood will produce the sample. After collection, the blood must be allowed to air-dry before placing it into a suitable paper container for labeling. It should be labeled as "Biohazard" and "Freezer" and placed in the appropriate location.

Latent Fingerprints

This could be the largest base for evidence. Latent fingerprints have the potential to be anywhere. Because fingerprints can be identified as belonging to a particular individual, properly collected fingerprints are the one type of evidence that can "stand on its own" in proving a crime. Identification can be made with even a partial fingerprint.

Investigators look for items that may contain fingerprints. Once obtained, the fingerprints can be identified through a process known as AFIS (Automated Fingerprint Identification System). This system consists merely of a sophisticated computer that searches a database for fingerprint patterns similar to the ones being identified.

As a general rule, smooth, glossy, nonporous surfaces are the best place to find latent prints. However, latent fingerprints can be found in such places as on the bodies of victims, doors, windows or paper. Investigators should not allow anything to be touched until it has been examined for fingerprints and released.

Once obtained and examined, the fingerprinted item should be placed in a box or paper envelope, marked appropriately and stored for future use. Caution must be taken not to handle the item or destroy any fingerprints left on the item.

Paper Documents

Paper evidence such as checks, credit card receipts, extortion letters, robbery notes, suicide notes, etc. should be handled carefully so as not to destroy or contaminate any evidence which may be present on the item.

Much can be learned from these documents. Therefore, no one should be allowed to handle the document and it should not be written on or marked in any way. The document(s) should be stored in an envelope that is large enough to hold the document without the need for folding. Investigators should leave the document in the condition in which it is found and never attempt to reconstruct it if it is torn or damaged. Shelving of documents should be in a place away from excessive light, heat or moisture.

TAGGING/LABELING

Some items must be tagged and labeled as opposed to packaged or bagged. An evidence tag serves to identify the item. For example, vehicles cannot be packaged or bagged and therefore must be tagged.

ACCOUNTING/TRACKING

All evidence obtained at a crime scene must be accounted for and tracked. The Chain of Custody should be followed rigorously to insure that evidence is not tampered with, destroyed or compromised. It is generally the duty of the evidence custodian to maintain this accountability.

Barcodes

Evidence tracking through the use of barcodes was developed to accurately and quickly record the movement of evidence in and out of inventory. Barcode labels are printed and applied to the container in which the evidence is stored or to the evidence itself. The system records the type of agency and agents that are responsible for checking evidence in and out. A user ID is scanned and a receipt is printed for each of these transactions. In addition, there is a section on the receipt for a signature of the party that received the evidence. Two specific evidence receipts are generally used. One receipt is designed for checking evidence in and another for checking evidence out. These receipts are signed and saved to provide an accurate chain of custody.

Transportation

Transport evidence in a safe, non-contaminative place such as the front seat of your car. Take care when transporting evidence in the trunk of a car. Gasoline, petroleum or other products or items commonly found in car trunks could mix with the evidence.

Computer Documentation

Computer evidence is unique when compared with other forms of "documentary evidence". Unlike paper documentation, computer evidence is fragile and a copy of a document stored in a computer file is identical to the original. The legal "best evidence" rules change when it comes to the processing of computer evidence.

In addition, computer evidence has the potential for unauthorized copies to be made of important computer files without leaving behind a trace that the copy was made. This creates problems for investigators and can destroy the chain of custody for critical documents. Extreme caution must be used when generating information that may be privileged or proprietary.

DISCUSSION QUESTIONS

1. Discuss why latex cloves should be worn by investigators and others handling evidence.

2. Explain the Chain of Custody.

Chapter 4

Note-Taking

CHAPTER OVERVIEW

Taking notes in an investigation is a fundamental investigative task. The rest of the case is built upon the initial field notes. This process is not dissimilar from the way scientists record observations and outcomes when doing an experiment. Good science requires that the experiment be documented in such detail that the process can be recreated perfectly by others. In law, the recorded observations are the basis for recreating the investigation for a jury.

This chapter will address the fundamentals of note-taking, and how the investigative notes are critical to the outcome of the final report. The student will be able to understand the theoretical aspects of note-taking and apply them in a practical situation.

OBJECTIVES

At the end of this chapter, you will be able to do the following:
1. Explain the purpose of note-taking at a crime scene.
2. Identify who takes notes at a crime scene.
3. Understand and apply the mechanics of note-taking.

WHO TAKES NOTES

Everyone involved in a crime scene investigation takes notes. This can include first responders to the scene, supervisors, lead detectives, coroner/medical examiners, forensic examiners or crime scene technicians. In some cases, for example, if you are working for a small rural department, you may be the first responder, the detective and the crime scene technician. You will interview witnesses, take photographs, draw sketches, and process and collect the evidence. In this situation the case is completely dependent upon your notes. In large municipal agencies, there are personnel who specialize in specific parts of the investigations. Their individual notes may cover only small parts of the case investigation.

The notes from the scene are then formatted into a formal departmental report usually referred to as a *"DR"*. In order for the lead detective in the larger agency to write a final report, he will need the reports/notes from each specialist. It is much like putting a puzzle together; you must have all the pieces in order to see the full picture.

PURPOSE OF NOTE-TAKING

What information should you document in your notes? To better understand the "what" let's look at the "why". The purpose of crime scene notes and documentation is two-fold: to assist in investigations and aid in the trial preparation and presentation.

Investigations

The crime scene is the very start of an investigation. At this point all one has are questions. Proper note-taking should document the facts and observations needed to enable investigators to find answers.

Who

Who is the victim, who is the perpetrator? Sometimes the victim is able to talk to you and give their identification. Other times you may only have a dead body. Discovering the perpetrator can be simple, such as arriving at a scene to find the battered wife standing over her dead husband's body with a gun in hand.

What

What happened? If there is a dead body involved, are we looking at a robbery, homicide, suicide, accident, or natural death scene? What if there is no body? Is it a kidnapping, runaway, or has the perpetrator attempted to dispose of the body? If there are no deaths involved, what type of crime are we looking at? If there is fire damage was it an accident or arson? Has someone been assaulted, etc.?

Where

Where did the crime take place? You may get a call about a dead body in a shallow grave by the interstate. When you arrive you notice the victim has multiple stab wounds but no blood is at the scene. This should lead you to believe the murder itself occurred elsewhere.

When

When did it occur? Is the dead body still warm or has it decomposed? If it is a case of sexual assault maybe you meet the victim while getting treatment at the hospital. In some cases the victim may be reporting a crime that happened to them years ago.

When documenting the crime scene you should be aware of these questions in order to understand the importance and purpose of your work. But remember, your responsibility in documenting a crime scene is not to figure out the "why". Your goal is to only document the facts. Your notes and reports should only include facts, not your opinion, analysis or conclusions of what you think happened. Document what you see, not what you think. As Joe Friday in the television show Dragnet used to say, "Just the facts ma'am, just the facts."

Ideally the investigator or detective working the case would be able to view the crime scene. But this is not always the case. In a large agency it would not be feasible to have the detectives process all the crime scenes. Technicians that free up valuable time for detectives can do much of the crime scene processing. In addition, it is not always initially known what division will be investigating a case. As we stated above under "what" type of crime occurred will negate who is assigned to investigate. A robbery or assault could turn into a homicide investigation if the victim later dies from their injuries.

When documenting and taking notes of a crime scene you also should think beyond the immediate investigator and/or detectives of your agency. A murder or assault case may turn out to be the work of a serial criminal. There may be multiple victims across the state or states. In that case your agency may become part of a task force involving other law enforcement agencies. If the case involves drugs, guns, fraud, kidnapping, etc., Federal agencies may become involved, such as FBI, DEA, ATF, etc. In these circumstances many of the investigators will not have had the luxury of viewing the crime scene for themselves. The success of their investigation will rely on the notes, photographs, sketches and evidence collected at the scene.

DNA, along with other advances in forensic science, have made it possible to solve old cases and bring long-time fugitives to final justice. Investigators might view the crime scene notes you take today many years from now. Suspects, witnesses, or investigators may die, move away, or disappear. As time progresses, their recollection of events and details depreciates. Even physical evidence is fragile and can depreciate. Improper storage and handling may render evidence inaccessible.

Having comprehensive thorough notes that document the crime scene is imperative for the investigators who were not there. The written documentation should walk the investigator through the crime scene in chronological order documenting the facts.

Trial

Ultimately the end goal of crime scene documentation is to retell or recreate the crime scene for the courtroom. Having clear, logical and chronological written reports to reference during trial will give the investigator credibility with the jury. Reports and/or notes may also be requested in the pre-trial discovery process. Both the prosecution and defense will view and utilize the written reports to prepare their cases.

If it's not in your notes it didn't happen. What this means is that it will be difficult to convince a jury of an event or statement if it isn't written in your notes. How believable would it be to a jury if the investigator claims the victim named the defendant as the perpetrator just before dying, if it isn't in his notes? Usually in criminal cases hearsay is not allowed. But if written notes are made recording the actions or spontaneous excited utterances of a suspect, witness or victim at the time of the event, they may be allowed in court as an exception to the hearsay rule. This exception is referred to as res gestae; meaning "things done" and allows the hearsay to be admitted in criminal court.

MECHANICS OF NOTE-TAKING

Depending on the agency, the type of tools you utilize to takes notes will vary. Some departments give officers special pre-printed forms to use. Most of the time it is up to the officers' discretion to use what works best for them – spiral steno pads, index cards, notebooks or preferably a loose leaf binder. Some officers prefer to dictate their notes into a tape recorder. Make sure you follow your agency's guidelines in order to avoid issues with "discovery".

What you use to take notes is not as important as what information you take in your notes. Remember, the notes are not just to refresh your recollection but will be used in a final report that will be used in investigations and court. In crime scene work, more is better; if something catches your attention, mark it in your notes. We will expand on some of the items from the Crime Scene Checklist that was provided in the previous chapter.

- Date/Time of Call-Out
  - Use military time so as to avoid confusion of A.M. or P.M. In addition to noting the day and month, you must put the year, as cases can drag on sometimes for decades.
- Name
  - Usually your last name and badge number.
- Case Number
  - Typically the case number will be generated by the dispatch center.

- Source of Call-out
  - Document how you were notified of the scene ? dispatch, another officer, or came upon it yourself.
- Incident Type
  - Robbery, assault, homicide ? again usually dispatch provides this information, but it is subject to change upon officer discretion of facts. You could be dispatched on a domestic violence call, but when you arrive you find one spouse dead.
- Date/Time of Arrival
  - The time it takes from receiving the call until the time you arrive is important. If you discovered the scene on your own, you must document when you arrived and/or contacted dispatch.
- Physical Location/Address
  - Document the street address, cross streets and the type of structure; for example, residential home, mobile home, vacant lot, apartment, commercial building, and name of the building if available.

You won't always have the luxury of having a street address, for instance a deputy sheriff may find a body in a field off a county road. What would you do to document the spot so that others could locate it? Use as much information as possible to accurately document the location. Highway mile markers can be used, measurements from the nearest road, or from a permanent fixed object. Some agencies now use satellite global positioning systems (GPS). The object is to make sure you or others will be able to locate the scene again in days or even years to come.

Weather Conditions

Although it may seem trivial at the time, weather conditions play an important role in recollecting the crime scene. Document if it is snowing or raining, and for how long. If a foot of snow has come down in the last hour and there are no footprints leading away from the scene, would this be important?

Would it seem suspicious for a man to be standing outside of a bank in a long heavy trench coat in November? If it was an unseasonably warm 82 degrees that day, you would wonder what he had under that coat and certainly that would be worth documenting in your notes.

In court, a defense attorney questioned a detective as to why he didn't lift prints off of a vehicle. The smug attorney inferred that the detective had been incompetent in not retrieving the prints. He went on to claim that the real perpetrator's prints would have been found on the car and not his clients. In this case the detective was redeemed because he had documented in his notes that the temperature was over 116 degrees that day. In Phoenix, Arizona, the hot desert temperatures can impact the ability to recover and lift fingerprints from an automobile. Fingerprints are left from the transfer of oily residue from our hands. When you are cooking and don't want things to stick to your metal frying pan, what do you use? What happens to the oil, does it melt?

A rookie investigator attempted to lift a shoe print from a dusty vehicle trunk on a 115-degree day in Phoenix. Not only did the investigator fail to retrieve the print, but she ticked off the car's owner. The adhesive from the lift strip melted and stuck to the vehicle's paint.

Do you think freezing temperatures could slow down a body's decomposition? The medical examiner will need to factor in temperatures when approximating time of death.

Good notes made the difference in a homicide case in an east coast city. When a man was discovered dead in his car, it appeared by the condition of the body he had just recently died. The medical examiner was intrigued when he read the investigator's notes that stated although the outside temperature for that autumn day had been in the high 80's, the body temperature felt colder than usual. The investigator noted that he estimated the body temp around 45 degrees. Further investigation revealed that the body had been hidden in a walk-in freezer at a nearby restaurant through the summer.

Temperatures and weather conditions can play a big role in traffic accidents as well. Snowstorms, dust storms and fog can impair a driver's visibility. It is well to note if it is a bright sunny clear day.

Lighting Conditions

Natural conditions: "Officer, the sun was in my eyes and I didn't see the stop sign!" Document what position and direction the sun was in. Is it near sunrise or sunset? Note cloud conditions.

Artificial lights: note if the lights in a building are on or off, inside lights as well as outside. Are the blinds or curtains open or closed?

Other Conditions

If medical or fire department personnel have been at the scene, document what changes they have made to area and people. Note if there appears to have been a struggle (chairs knocked over, lamps broken) or if the place was ransacked (files strewn across the room, drawers dumped out, etc.).

Take a look at the doors, windows and entryways; note if they appear to be locked, unlocked, open, or closed. Notice if the heat or air-conditioning is on or off. Pay attention to mail inside as well as in the mailbox. Check for newspapers inside or on the driveway.

A suspect in a homicide admitted to investigators that he had cocktails at the victim's home, but he insisted that it was hours before she died. However, crime scene notes documented that there were still ice cubes in the cocktail glasses when investigators arrived.

Keep your eyes open as well as your mind. Don't just document what you see, make sure and notice what you don't see. Are there any odors present? Some examples are perfume, gasoline, natural gas, cigar and cigarette smoke. What isn't there that should be there? The place has a heavy odor of cigar smoke but there are no cigars, ashtrays or butts. The victim's purse and car keys are on the counter, but no car.

Contact Person at Scene (Scene Commander)

Depending on the situation and size of your department, there maybe someone on scene before you arrive. Assuming you are a detective at a large agency, the scene commander (usually a sergeant) will be in charge. Document their name and badge number along with what they know about the scene so far. The scene commander will be in charge of other officers at the scene.

Other Officers at Scene

Again, the size of the department and type of crime will dictate how the scene will be handled, but in general, there will be several other actors involved in the scene. In order to keep who did what and when straight, there must be a crime scene log. Usually a lucky officer will be in charge of documenting everyone who comes in and out of the scene. Each individual's name, badge number, agency, department or other identifiers will be noted along with the date and time they entered and left.

This list is not exclusive to officers; paramedics, medical examiners and media personnel must also log in.

Victim(s)/Responsible Party

Always get the basics: name, date of birth (DOB) and address. Write down their statements and description of events. If the victim is injured and it appears he/she may not make it, document anything he/she has to say; this will be considered a "dying declaration".

Witnesses/Suspects

Again, get the basics; name, DOB and address. Keep witnesses separate from one another; document what their accounts are of the incident. Also put in your notes your observations of them (slurred speech, odor of alcoholic beverage, nervous, calm, irritable, and general appearance).

Vehicles at Scene

Note the make, model, year, color, and license plate number of vehicles along with any other distinguishing marks. Document the location, whether it is parked or the direction it was going. In traffic accidents also note the damage.

Evidence Finder/Recorder

If you have a large department and it is a big case there will be crime scene techs/evidence techs that will be collecting the physical evidence. The investigator will document the items collected, and the evidence techs will document in an evidence log the items processed and collected.

Photography, sketching and evidence collection documentation will be addressed in further detail in other chapters. At the final phase of documenting a crime scene it should be noted at a minimum the date and time at the scene and to whom and by whom it was released.

SUMMARY

No matter how good your memory is, no matter how thorough a report you can write, the mark of a good detective is effective, contemporaneous notes. The technique is not critical, but being consistent in the technique you choose, may be critical.

Notes are the basis for recording the who, what, when, where and how during the investigation. They are the tools for recollection of light and weather conditions. They record summaries of the observations of the investigator and provide a platform for writing a formal report.

DISCUSSION QUESTIONS

1. What does DR stand for?
2. Who takes notes?
3. What are the basic facts you should document from witnesses and victims?

PRACTICAL EXERCISES

Read the following narrative from a crime scene investigator notebook and use the crime scene checklist in Chapter 1, Form 1.3 to evaluate whether or not the basic areas are covered.

Officer Barnes, #3505.

On April 25, at approximately 3 o'clock I observed a female at the corner waving frantically in my direction. When I pulled over she told me her house had been robbed and she wasn't sure if the perpetrator was still inside or not. She informed me her name was Terry Ferguson and her birth date is October 1966. Terry had just returned home from work and had not entered the house yet.

I followed the woman a few houses down to her home. I called dispatch to inform them I was at 611 East Roosevelt at the home of Terry Ferguson. As I approached the front entrance to the home I noticed the front door was open and damaged. There appeared to be pry marks around the frame.

When I entered the home there were no interior lights on and the shades were drawn. There were several cabinets in the kitchen open as well as open drawers, cabinet and closets. I cleared the home and found no one inside. The back door was closed and locked.

Civilian crime scene tech Sylvia Parson arrived at 3:47 and began photographing the scene. I had her take photos of the scene that are noted in the attached photo log. She took a picture of the entertainment center in the living room that did not have a television on it. In the place were a television would be there was a large square section avoid of dust.

I allowed Ms. Ferguson to enter the home and guide Ms. Parson and I through the home. Ms. Ferguson pointed out items that were missing. The following items were noted;

1. Bank of America checkbook in brown leather case. (Don't know check no's)

2. Gold ring with 1-karat diamond.

3. DVD player

4. Approximately $400.00 dollars in cash.

Terry Ferguson's neighbor Ted Phillips came over, DOB: 4-11-32, Address: 609 East Roosevelt, Phone No: home 555-7937, business 555-2636. Mr. Phillips informed me that he saw two suspicious men parked in front of the Ferguson home about an hour earlier. He said they were in a light blue Ford minivan. The men were both about 5'9 and slim. Mr. Phillips believes the plates were from California. Mr. Phillips also wears thick glasses due to being near sited.

At approximately 5 o'clock Sylvia Parson and I wrapped up our investigation of the scene. I left my card for Ms. Ferguson to contact us I she discovered any other items missing.

Chapter 5

Crime Scene Photography

CHAPTER OVERVIEW

Photographs of a crime scene create a permanent record of the scene as it was first observed by law enforcement. They serve two different purposes but with the same goal. They are used by investigators to facilitate the investigation and by the court to re-create the scene for juries. The goal of each is to seek justice and truth. All crime scenes are unique and do not always call for photographs, but for purposes of this book we will be working on the premise that our crime scenes require photo documentation. Photography is a specific skill and is usually a course in itself. Crime scene photography is even further specialized and requires detail beyond the scope of this chapter, but we will cover the basic concepts to understand its purpose as an element of crime scene documentation.

OBJECTIVES

1. Outline of the purposes for photo documentation of a crime scene.
2. Identify where in the process of crime scene work the photos are to be taken.
3. List the basic crime scene photography terminology.
4. Recognize the three types or series of photos taken at a crime scene.

GLOSSARY OF TERMS

Angle of view is the area or size the scene that fits in the frame. When looking into the view finder of the camera, the angle of view is the largest angle of recognition that the lens is able to produce of an image for functional quality on the film. Angle of view is determined by the focal length of the lens; more of the scene is included when a wide-angle lens is used, it has a shorter focal length.

Aperture is an opening or hole in a camera lens that allows light to pass through for film exposure. The aperture is typically calibrated by the f –stop. The smaller the f-stop the larger the opening.

Bracketing is a photography method of ensuring the correct exposure by taking several photos of the subject at a variety of (lighter / darker) exposures.

Close-Up Lens is a lens attachment that allows the camera lens to focus and take pictures at a much closer distance.

Depth of Field is the area between the closest and farthest points in the subject area that provides a workable sharp focus for the exposure. The depth of field or focus area can be varied by the distance between the camera and subject, focal length (lens) and aperture.

Digital camera records or captures visual images without film by using a computer chip to record the images.

Exposure is the amount of light that makes contact with the film. How long the shutter is left open (shutter speed) and the size in which the lens opening is set (aperture) determines how much light is let in.

Exposure meter or light meter is a device that determines the amount of light reflected from or on an object and assists in determining to proper exposure setting.

Film is a material (celluloid) usually formed in a strip that has been covered in a silver halide grain emulsion that makes it sensitive when exposed to light.

f numbers or f-stops a method designating a number to the size or aperture opening of the lens. The smaller the f-number the larger the lens opening. Common f-stop numbers are f/1.4, f/2, f/2.8, f/3, f/4, f/5, f/8, f/11, f/16 f/22. When in doubt f/8 is a safe place to start.

Film Speed is often referred to as ISO. ISO stands for the International Standards Organization. Film is given an ISO number that rates it by how sensitive the film is to light. If it is highly sensitive it will expose quickly, giving it its speed or ISO number. The higher the ISO the faster or sensitive the film is.

Filter is a transparent colored section of glass is placed over the camera lens. The filter modifies the photograph of the scene by either by highlighting, eliminating, or exaggerating a color.

Flash supplements the lighting at the crime scene by providing a burst of light from the flash unit filling in the low light areas.

Focus is the most important element for achieving quality photos. The focus is affected by adjusting the lens distance (focal length) between the film until the image appears sharp and clear. If a photo is 'out of focus' it will appear blurry.

Measurement scale is an object showing standard units of length (e.g., ruler) used in photographic documentation of an item of evidence.

Lens is a curved piece of optical glass that bends and focuses light to shape a precise image onto the film.

Shutter/ Shutter speed is the mechanical mechanism that opens and closes the blades or curtain in a camera thereby controlling the amount of time that light strikes the image sensor (film) and exposes the image.

Tripod is used to hold the shot steady by supporting the camera on a stand made of three legs.

Wide-angle lens (short focal lens) allows for the widest angle of image or view

PURPOSE OF CRIME SCENE PHOTOS

Investigations

For investigators, photographs from the crime are vital. Not only do the photographs serve to refresh the memory of the crime scene investigator, but they are also a valuable tool for those not present at the scene; such as specialized investigators and crime scene analysts. For example, analysts or "profilers" use the information or clues in the photos to gain insight into the lives and personalities of the perpetrator and victim. Ballistics experts, interviewers, and even defense attorneys will be able to do their job more effectively using the photos.

Use at Trial

Photographs help the jury visualize the scene as it was when the police arrived. A clear and concise depiction of the scene can be created for the jury by supplementing the officer's testimony with photographs, serving to refresh memory and call attention to details.

Just as officers do not remember every detail about a case, eyewitnesses don't always either. Sometimes their recollections can become distorted and tainted; occasionally they have reasons to lie. Skilled defense and prosecutorial attorneys can raise doubt as to the accuracy and motive of witness testimony, but photographs of the crime scene provide accurate depiction of factual evidence and cannot be swayed by emotional factors. Photos are a powerful tool for representing the physical evidence and can affect the outcome of a trial.

Admissibility of Photos in Trial

Although we will go into admissibility of evidence in a later chapter, it is important to note some of the requirements. Sometimes understanding why we are doing something helps us understand the value of what we are learning. For a photograph to be useful in court it must first be properly exposed, undistorted, focused, and clear. In addition, the items or objects pictured should be accurately represented in size and relation to the scene. This is done with the support of the crime scene sketch and use of measurement scale in the photograph. Documenting the description of the items and other technical data in a photo-log will provide additional support in getting the photos admitted at trial.

PREPARATION FOR PHOTOGRAPHING A CRIME SCENE

Recall the steps for processing and documenting a crime scene from the Crime Elements chapter; Narrative, Photography, Diagram/Sketch, and Evidence Recovery. The photography is done before sketches or evidence collection begins.

Trained technicians will perform the photography at a major crime scene but there are instances when a patrol officer will be required to take photos as well.

Important

Figure 5.1 First Responder Standard Operating Procedure (SOP)

GENERAL GUIDELINES FOR A FIRST RESPONDER SOP
(A)

(A) The only images taken are those by the first responding officer(s).

Title: First Responder Photography SOP.

Purpose: To document conditions found at an incident by the first law enforcement officer(s) on the scene where a crime scene photography unit or specialist will not be requested.

Note: Examples may include domestic violence incidents, traffic accidents, minor property crimes, and other incidents as defined by agency-specific policies. Photography generally is not the first responder's primary responsibility, and the first responder may have only a minimal amount of photography training.

Equipment: (Image Capture Devices)
- Silver-based media film camera. The minimum recommendation is a 35-mm camera with flash and close-up capability.
- Digital still imaging. The minimum recommendation is for a camera with more than 640 x 480 pixels, on-camera viewer, close-up capability, flash, and removable storage media.
- Video imaging can be used in a supplementary capacity. S-VHS, Hi-8, or better quality formats are recommended. It is suggested that cameras have the ability to incorporate external or wireless audio, to disable on-camera audio, and to incorporate in-camera image stabilization. (See Video Cameras, Fig. 5.3)
- Other standard photographic equipment as necessary.

Procedures: Agency-specific step-by-step instructions for documenting the scene.

Note: Images from separate incidents should be clearly delineated through a change of storage media or through proper documentation.

Figure 5.1 First Responder Standard Operating Procedure (SOP) (Cont.)

Calibration: If considered necessary, agencies should develop procedures specific to their needs.

Calculations: If considered necessary, agencies should develop procedures specific to their needs.

Limitations: Successful capture of close-up images will require adhering to manufacturers' specifications. Images captured digitally typically have a limited enlargement capability that is less than those captured using 35-mm film. (See Advantages and Disadvantages of Major Image Capture Technologies in Field Applications, Fig. 5.3) Successful capture of images also requires using fresh media (e.g., film that is not past expiration and has been stored properly) and well-maintained equipment .

Safety: Agencies should develop procedures specific to their needs.

References: Agency-specific documentation and manufacturers' manuals.

General Guidelines for a First Responder SOP (B)

(B) Images taken by the first responding officer(s) prior to arrival of a crime scene photographer.

Title: First Responder Photography SOP.

Purpose: To document conditions found at an incident by the first law enforcement officer(s) on the scene prior to the arrival of a crime scene photographer.

Note: This guideline is directed toward documenting transient conditions that might be lost prior to the arrival of crime scene photographers. Examples include situations in which evidence must or might be moved, lost, or altered. Photography generally is not the first responder's primary responsibility, and the first responder may have only a minimal amount of photography training.

Equipment: (Image Capture Devices)
- Silver-based media film camera. The minimum recommendation is a 35-mm camera with flash and close-up capability.

Figure 5.1 First Responder Standard Operating Procedure (SOP) (Cont.)

- Digital still imaging. The minimum recommendation is for a camera with more than 640 x 480 pixels, on-camera viewer, close-up capability, flash, and removable storage media.

- Video imaging can be used in a supplementary capacity. S-VHS, Hi-8, or better quality formats are recommended. It is suggested that cameras have the ability to incorporate external or wireless audio, to disable on-camera audio, and to incorporate in-camera image stabilization. (See Video Cameras, Fig. 5.3.)

- Other standard photographic equipment as necessary.

Procedures: Agency-specific step-by-step instructions for documenting the scene.

Note: Images from separate incidents should be clearly delineated through a change of storage media or proper documentation.

Calibration: If considered necessary, agencies should develop procedures specific to their needs.

Calculations: If considered necessary, agencies should develop procedures specific to their needs.

Limitations: The successful capture of close-up images will require adhering to the manufacturers' specifications. Images captured digitally or with video typically have a limited enlargement capability that is less than those captured using 35-mm film. (See Advantages and Disadvantages of Major Image Capture Technologies in Field Applications, Fig. 5.3) Successful capture of images also requires using fresh media (film that is not past expiration and has been stored properly and new, unused videotapes) and well-maintained equipment.

Safety: Agencies should develop procedures specific to their needs.

References: Agency-specific documentation and manufacturers' manuals.

Source: FBI. (2003). Handbook of Forensic Services Revised 2003. Retrieved January 21, 2004 http://www.fbi.gov/hq/lab/handbook/intro16.htm

Once the scene has been assessed and a plan of action set, photographs of the crime scene are taken. Before you begin shooting, visualize the photos and images you want. Photographs need to be taken as soon as possible to preserve the scene as it was first observed. As the identification, processing, and collection of evidence takes place, photographs and notes will continue to be taken. Photographs not only provide an impartial and accurate representation of the scene as it was found, but may also document the actions of the crime scene personnel as they process the scene.

Figure 5.2　Crime Scene Photography SOP

GUIDELINES FOR STANDARD OPERATING PROCEDURES (SOPS)

General Guidelines for a Crime Scene Photography SOP

Title: Crime Scene Photography SOP.

Purpose: To permanently document, by qualified personnel, evidence and other details at a crime scene for future reference.

Note: Crime scene photography generally requires the ability:
- To record information that crime scene personnel may not know was important at the time the images were captured,
- To deal with varying lighting and physical conditions,
- To accurately represent the details and colors at a crime scene, and
- To get close-up and wide-angle images with accurate spatial relationships.

Crime scene photography is usually a time-limited activity in which there is only one opportunity to correctly complete the task. Depending on the nature of the crime or incident, conditions at a crime scene may dictate the selection and use of equipment and techniques.

Equipment: (Image Capture Devices)
- Silver-based film cameras are recommended for use as the primary image capture device. The minimum recommendation is a 35-mm (SLR) camera capable of manual override, interchangeable lenses, off-camera flash, and tripod mount.

Figure 5.2 Crime Scene Photography SOP (Cont.)

- Digital still imaging can be used in a supplementary capacity. (See Digital Cameras, Fig. 5.3.) Digital still imaging can be used when the performance of the equipment can be shown to meet anticipated needs.

- Video imaging can be used in a supplementary capacity. S-VHS, Hi-8, or better quality formats are recommended. It is suggested that cameras have the ability to incorporate external or wireless audio, to disable on-camera audio, and to incorporate in-camera image stabilization. (See Video Cameras, Fig. 5.3)

- Other standard photographic equipment as necessary.

Procedures: Agency-specific step-by-step instructions for documenting crime scene evidence.

Calibration: If considered necessary, agencies should develop procedures specific to their needs.

Calculations: If considered necessary, agencies should develop procedures specific to their needs.

Limitations: See Advantages and Disadvantages of Major Image Capture Technologies in Field Applications. (Fig. 5.3)

Safety: Agencies should develop procedures specific to their needs.

References: Agency-specific documentation and manufacturers' manuals.

Source: FBI. (2003). Handbook of Forensic Services Revised 2003. Retrieved January 21, 2004 http://www.fbi.gov/hq/lab/handbook/intro16.htm

---

MECHANICS OF PHOTOGRAPHY

Depending on the type of crime and purpose of the photos, crime scene photography has numerous specialized pieces of equipment. Digital cameras are used successfully in crime scene photography, however, according to the FBI (ref1.) "Silver-based film cameras are recommended for use as the primary image capture device. The minimum recommendation is a 35-mm (SLR) camera capable of manual override, interchangeable lenses, off-camera flash, and tripod mount".

The crime scene photographer and lead investigator will decide the use of color or black and white film depending upon the circumstances of the scene. Oftentimes both color and black and white are used.

Figure 5.3 Major Image Capture Technologies Compared

ADVANTAGES AND DISADVANTAGES OF MAJOR IMAGE CAPTURE TECHNOLOGIES IN FIELD APPLICATIONS

The selection of an acquisition device (camera) is driven by the purpose and requirements of the end product. Therefore, the final use of the image should determine the choice of the camera.

Silver-Based Film Cameras

It is strongly recommended that conventional silver-based film be the primary capture media for evidentiary photography or imaging in field applications.

Advantages of Silver-Based Film Cameras in Field Applications:
- Highest resolution.
- Highest dynamic range.
- Best color range.
- Most flexibility of currently available image options.
- Most durable storage medium.
- More readily available in the field than video or digital storage media.

Resolution is the amount of sharpness or detail in the image and is dependent on the amount of pixels or grain in an image. Generally, the quality of the final image is determined by the amount of grain or pixels contained in the primary image.

In digital imaging, resolution is a function of the number of pixels across the width and the height of the charge coupled device (CCD). The pixel count is established by multiplying these numbers:

Camera resolution of 640 x 480 = 307,200 total pixels.

Pixels must be capable of recording three colors to make a traditional color photograph. Each color is typically recorded as a byte of information. To determine the file size of a 640 x 480 pixel image, multiply 640 x 480 x 3 (3 colors) = 921,600 bytes or 900k.

Figure 5.3 Major Image Capture Technologies Compared (Cont.)

Two hundred pixels per inch (ppi) are generally used as the divisor to determine the acceptable printing size from a given image resolution. (This value is considered to be conservative by some.) In general, dividing the number of pixels by 200 ppi will provide the optimum printing size for an image captured by a digital camera.

For example, a camera with a resolution of 640 x 480 pixels would be calculated:

640 pixels/200 ppi = 3.2 inches and 480 pixels/200 ppi = 2.4 inches.

Therefore, the best photographic result produced by this camera would be a 2.4 x 3.2-inch image which is approximately a wallet-sized photograph. Although it is possible to print an 8 x 10-inch photograph from an image captured by this camera, the quality of the photograph will be degraded. In order to produce an acceptable 5 x 7-inch photograph, a digital camera with a resolution of 1280 x 960 pixels is required, and a resolution of 2000 x 1600 pixels for an 8 x 10-inch photograph is required.

Due to the extremely small size of the silver crystals used to make a film image, the resolution of film is dramatically higher than images produced with digital cameras. The average 35-mm negative has an approximate resolution of 5500 x 3600 pixels. This number changes with the ISO of the film because faster film uses larger silver crystals. By comparison, a digital camera with a resolution of 640 x 480 contains only 1.6 percent of the information capable of being recorded on a 35-mm negative.

Additional Comparisons

Sensor	35-mm film	High-end digital cameras (at least 1500 x 1000 pixels)	Low-end digital cameras (less than 1500 x 1000 pixels
Pixel count	5500 x 3600	3000 x 2000	1280 x 960
Print size	27.5 x 18	15 x 10	6.4 x 4.8
Average cost (at press)	$20,000		$1,000

Figure 5.3 Major Image Capture Technologies Compared (Cont.)

Dynamic range: The difference between the brightest highlight and darkest value that a sensor (film or CCD) can detect and record in a single image. Negative film provides from two to four more f-stops than most digital cameras. This increased dynamic range allows capture of both shadow detail and highlight detail in a single frame of film. These details may require several different images (at different capture settings) when recorded with a digital camera.

Color range: The range of colors that can be detected by a sensor compared to normal human vision. Negative film has a color range that is superior to CCDs.

Flexibility: Silver-based photography provides a wider selection of film speeds and types than digital cameras. Film can be selected for specific applications in the field, and the film speed or type can be changed on-site to meet specific needs.

Disadvantages of Silver-Based Film Cameras in Field Applications:
- Need for separate processing and printing facilities.
- Relatively long processing time.
- Environmental hazards generated by processing byproducts.
- Preprocessing fragility (e.g., temperature, humidity, X-ray effects).
- No means of immediate image evaluation (with the exception of instant film).Digital Cameras

Advantages of Digital Cameras in Field Applications:
- Immediacy of image (instant viewing and verification of image).
- Ability to transmit and disseminate image with minimum of intermediate steps.
- On-site image management.
- On-site image printing.
- Operational security (all processing is in-house).
- More environmentally friendly than film.

Figure 5.3 Major Image Capture Technologies Compared (Cont.)

Disadvantages of Digital Cameras in Field Applications:

- Battery or power supplies (environmental impact, availability, power conversion).
- Limited availability of storage media (available only from specialized stores).
- Storage media subject to damage from electromagnetic fields.
- Image acquisition subject to electromagnetic interference.
- Automatic compression in some digital cameras.
- Hardware and software frequently proprietary and incompatible between manufacturers.
- Requires increased technical support compared to film-only systems.
- Legacy file problem (evolution of technology, including hardware and software, may impact ability to access archived images over time).

Notes on Digital Cameras:

- High-end digital cameras are designed for the professional market and typically have sensors with at least 1500 x 1000 pixels. These cameras have imaging versatility including interchangeable lenses, macro-to-telephoto capabilities, off-camera flash, full-manual override, focus override, and through-the-lens (TTL) viewing and focus.

- Low-end digital cameras are designed for the consumer market and typically have sensors with less than 1500 x 1000 pixels. These cameras do not have the versatility of high-end cameras and may be referred to as point-and-shoot cameras.

Advantages of Video Cameras in Field Applications:

- Real-time motion record capability.
- Immediacy of image (instant viewing and verification of image).
- Ability to transmit and disseminate image with minimum intermediate steps.
- More environmentally friendly than film.
- Ability to print in the field.

Figure 5.3 Major Image Capture Technologies Compared (Cont.)

- Ability to synchronize and capture audio.

Disadvantages of Video Cameras in Field Applications:

- Battery or power supplies (environmental impact, availability, power conversion).
- Limited availability of high-quality storage media (all formats available only from specialized stores).
- Storage media subject to damage from electromagnetic fields.
- Image acquisition highly subject to electromagnetic interference.
- Resolution of still images is less than that of digital or silver-based capture media.
- Limited color fidelity.
- Reduced media lifetime.
- Hand-held video frequently lacks image stability.
- Automatic compression in some formats.
- Weight and portability of equipment may be a problem.

Notes on Video Formats:

- VHS and 8-mm formats are the most commonly available formats but have the worst signal-to-noise ratio of any video format (greatest amount of noise).
- Super VHS and Hi-8 formats are the second most commonly available formats and have somewhat better signal-to-noise ratio than VHS.
- Beta SP and MII formats are professional broadcast quality and are the best analog format available.
- Digital video quality varies, and the high-end is better than analog systems.

Hybrid Imaging Systems

A hybrid imaging system is a combination of silver-based photography and digital imaging technology that typically involves the conversion of silver-based film or print images to digital images through the use of scanners. Hybrid imaging systems incorporate some of the benefits of both film and digital image technologies and are recommended for agencies and organizations seeking to add digital imaging technologies to their photographic resources.

Figure 5.3 Major Image Capture Technologies Compared (Cont.)

Advantages of Hybrid Imaging Systems in Field Applications:
- Shortened darkroom time for producing prints.
- Maintains high-quality original film images.
- Flexibility of digital image processing.
- Enables easy electronic transmission of images.
- Enables image analysis.
- Simplifies case-file management.
- Ability to use a variety of output devices.

Disadvantages of Hybrid Imaging Systems in Field Applications:
- Separate processing and printing facilities.
- Relatively long processing time.
- Environmental hazards generated by processing byproducts.
- Preprocessing fragility (e.g., temperature, humidity, X-ray effects).
- No means of immediate image evaluation (with the exception of instant film).
- Requires increased technical support compared to film-only systems.

Source: FBI. (2003). Handbook of Forensic Services Revised 2003. Retrieved January 21, 2004 http://www.fbi.gov/hq/lab/handbook/intro16.htm

Basic Equipment

For now the basic components you should familiarize yourself with are:

- Camera(s)
- Film (color and/or black and white)
- Lenses
  - Normal 50mm
  - Wide Angle 28mm
  - Close-up
- Tripod
- Scale/Ruler
- Level
- Gray Card

Pop quiz hotshot: What did we state earlier regarding the criteria for a photograph to be useful in court? Right, very good if you answered "properly exposed, undistorted, focused, and sharp." This is where it gets a bit technical. You may want to study the Glossary section before going further.

Proper exposure can be achieved by reading the light meter, adjusting flash, lens aperture and shutter speed. By bracketing the exposures you give yourself leeway or a margin of error. To avoid distortion of objects and items, keep the camera level and shoot from eye level if feasible. If it is suitable, a normal lens works best.

To achieve focused and sharp photos, hold the camera steady, use a tripod whenever the situation allows. "Frame" the scene by focusing on the object or item of evidence and bring it into the maximum depth of field.

At the start of each role a photo should be taken of a gray card. The gray card is to provide a frame of reference for the colors of items taken on the roll. When the technicians process the film they use the photo of the gray card to precisely replicate the colors of items at the crime scene.

The color scale is a piece of paper usually about 8" x 10" and should note the number of the roll, photographer's name, date, crime scene location and report number.

Types of Shots

For the sake of simplicity, let's say our crime is a burglary and it happened inside the bedroom of your home. Keep in mind that those viewing the photos may never have and never will be inside your home. Your photos need to tell the story of your home and the how it relates to the crime. Traditional story telling always starts at the beginning, and that is where you should start your photos. There are three series of photos taken at a crime scene – overviews, mid-range and close-up.

Overviews

Start by taking photographs of the general area to establish an overall view of the scene. These would start outside the home; the use of the wide angle lens would be beneficial here. You should take a photo of the exterior of the home, and include a shot of the address numbers if available. The series of photos should also document the doors, windows and any other entrance or exits.

Now head inside taking a photo of the entrance, and then a photo of the view inside; turn around and take a photo of the entrance from the inside looking out. Take photos in a clockwise direction overlapping each other, thus getting an overall view of the room. Another method is to take photos from each corner of the room.

Proceed to take photos of the hallway and pathway to the bedroom where the crime took place. If the lead investigator feels other rooms may be relevant to the crime they should be documented as well (because you can't go back later). When reaching the bedroom repeat the process of overlapping photos and corners. Jewelry box, dresser drawers, broken window, shoe print, anything that could be construed as evidence should be included in the overalls.

NOTE: The crime scene technician works in conjunction with the lead investigator to determine the number of photographs to be taken. The factors in determining the amount of photos to be taken are scope of scene, seriousness of offense, and quantity of evidence. Keep in mind there is only once chance at a pristine crime scene.

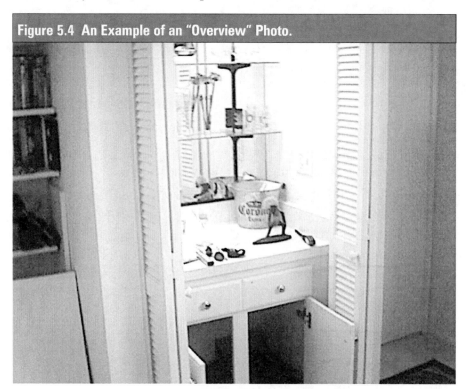

Figure 5.4 An Example of an "Overview" Photo.

Mid-Range

Photos are then taken of items that are considered evidence. The mid-range photo shows the item in context to the scene but at a closer view.

Figure 5.5 An Example of a "Mid-Range" Photograph.

Close-Up

Close-up photos are just that, photos taken at a close range filling the frame. Depending on the size of the evidence and its distance from the camera, a close up lens is used. Close-up photos are used for examination purposes and should have a scale/ruler next to it for measurement. The first photo is always taken without the scale to show how the scene looked originally and the second with the scale. [See Figure 5.6 for an example of a "close-up" photograph.

You should be taking notes of the photographic process. These notes will create the photo-log. Some of the information listed in a photo-log may include:

1. Name of photographer
2. Date and time
3. Case number
4. Address or location of crime scene
5. Type of camera or camera used
6. Type of film used
7. Shutter speed
8. Lens aperture
9. Light source/flash
10. Environmental conditions

11. Type of lens used

12. Camera distance from subject

13. Description of images and location photographed

Figure 5.6 An Example of a "Close-Up" Photograph.

VIDEO CAMERA

Video is sometimes used to record a crime scene, however it should never be in place of still photos. Videotape serves to enhance still photography, as does the crime scene sketch. It gives a better perspective of the distance between items of evidence and their relationship to the structure of the surroundings. The same three-step photo process is done – overviews, medium range, and close-up.

Whether the audience is a jury or other investigators, a video puts the scene in a three-dimensional perspective giving the viewer a "real life" look. A few important pointers for videotaping a crime scene are: move slowly (so the view doesn't blur), keep the tape rolling (stopping and restarting can be questionable when used in a trial), notify and advise all crime scene personnel that videotaping is to take place and that they should remain quiet and out of sight (keeps the scene image pristine and avoids picking up inappropriate commentary).

SPECIAL EQUIPMENT NEEDS

Photos of fingerprints, shoeprints, tool marks and other specific evidence are often taken at crime scenes. Each requires special techniques and equipment. Some of these will be addressed in further chapters.

When completed with the photo documentation of the crime scene, photo negatives are impounded as evidence. The same procedure of labeling – case number, date, time, location, type of crime, photographer, roll number, etc. – should be performed as with any other piece of evidence. This keeps the chain of custody intact. If the scene is finished and there are still exposures left on the roll, turn the roll in anyway. It is important that only one crime scene be documented per roll. Officers should be aware that the negatives will be considered as evidence and if there are other personal pictures on the roll with the crime scene photos, the defense will see them. Defense attorneys have been known to attempt to embarrass officers on the stand by showing the family vacation pictures the officer took on the roll of film.

Figure 5.7 FBI Crime Scene Photography Summary and Checklist

Photography

- ☐ Photograph the crime scene as soon as possible.
- ☐ Prepare a photographic log that records all photographs and a description and location of evidence.
- ☐ Establish a progression of overall, medium, and close-up views of the crime scene.
- ☐ Photograph from eye level to represent the normal view.
- ☐ Photograph the most fragile areas of the crime scene first.
- ☐ Photograph all stages of the crime-scene investigation, including discoveries.
- ☐ Photograph the condition of evidence before recovery.
- ☐ Photograph the evidence in detail and include a scale, the photographer's name, and the date.
- ☐ Take all photographs intended for examination purposes with a scale. When a scale is used, first take a photograph without the scale.

Figure 5.7   FBI Crime Scene Photography Summary and Checklist

☐ Photograph the interior crime scene in an overlapping series using a normal lens, if possible. Overall photographs may be taken using a wide-angle lens.

☐ Photograph the exterior crime scene, establishing the location of the scene by a series of overall photographs including a landmark.

☐ Photographs should have 360 degrees of coverage. Consider using aerial photography, when possible.

☐ Photograph entrances and exits from the inside and the outside.

☐ Photograph important evidence twice.

- A medium-distance photograph that shows the evidence and its position to other evidence.

- A close-up photograph that includes a scale and fills the frame.

☐ Prior to entering the scene, acquire, if possible, prior photographs, blueprints, or maps of the scene.

Source: FBI. (2003). Handbook of Forensic Services Revised 2003. Retrieved January 21, 2004 http://www.fbi.gov/hq/lab/handbook/intro16.htm

---

SUMMARY

Crime scene photography tells a visual story to those investigating a crime and those rendering a verdict in trial. Photos capture the scene as it first appeared when investigators or first responding officers arrived.

DISCUSSION QUESTIONS

1. When and why would a patrol officer be required to take crime scene photos?

2. Why is it imperative that the photos be taken before any alterations are made to the scene?

3. What are the three types or series of photos that are taken at a crime scene?

4. List at least 3 things that should be documented on the photo-log.

5. How many pictures should be taken at a crime scene?

6. Describe Bracketing and its purpose.

PRACTICAL EXERCISES

Recreate the burglary crime scene of your home using any type of camera you choose – Silver-based (standard) 35 mm, Digital, Polaroid, or disposable. Create a gray scale with basic identifiers and shoot this first. Keep a photo-log numbering each exposure, the subject matter, distance, lighting conditions and camera settings (if applicable). Use all the exposures by taking all three types of photos – overview, mid-range and close-up.

After getting the film developed or downloading the images, study the results. Compare the quality shots with those blurred or out of focus. Refer to your photo-log to note the conditions of the shot. Analyze what factors caused the poor photos over the good ones.

REFERENCES

1. FBI, U.S. Department of Justice. (1999, June 8). Guidelines for Field Applications of Imaging Technologies: Scientific Working Group on Imaging Technologies (SWGIT). Forensic Science Communications, January 2000. Volume 2, Number 1. Retrieved January 21, 2004 at:
http://www.fbi.gov/hq/lab/fsc/backissu/jan2000/swigit.htm

Chapter 6

Measurements & Sketches

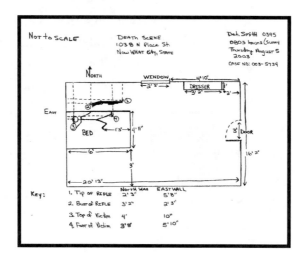

CHAPTER OVERVIEW

Sketches are part of crime scene documentation and complement the written reports/notes and photography. After the initial assessment of the crime scene, the investigators decide what type of documentation will be needed. If it is deemed necessary to have sketches, they are done after the photography and before evidence collection. Crime scene sketches are a method of documentation that should contain all relevant details to the scene. "The sketch establishes a permanent record of items, conditions, and distance and size relationships. Sketches supplement photographs" (FBI).

OBJECTIVES

At the end of this chapter, you will be able to do the following:

1. Explain the elements of a crime scene sketch.
2. Identify the tools and methods used in crime scene sketching.
3. Outline the importance of accurate measurements.

SKETCHING IN RELATION TO PHOTOGRAPHY

There are many advantages to sketching the crime scene. Even with a fish eye or wide-angle lens, the camera can only take sections of the crime scene at a time. The sketch can depict the entire scene in one visual. Sometimes evidence blends into its background or is hidden by shadows, making it difficult to view in a photograph, but a sketch can record the detail of the item. Cameras capture all objects and items in the frame causing the photo to appear cluttered. A sketch on the other hand, can be selective and eliminate distracting confusion.

A very important advantage of a sketch is the ability to record the spatial relationships between items. A sketch can capture proportional measurements relating to bullet trajectory, angles and distance between objects. Because photographs are only two-dimensional, they lack the ability to show depth and can cause items to appear closer together or farther apart than they really are. Sketches and photographs each have their limitations, but used together they can provide a clear and accurate representation of the scene to support investigators and courtroom demonstrations.

ELEMENTS OF CRIME SCENE SKETCHING

Basic Tools for Sketching in the Field

- Pencil w/Eraser
- Paper (preferably graph)
- Clipboard
- Measuring Tape
- Compass
- Ruler/Straightedge

There are of course more exotic tools such as T-squares, protractors, French curves, and assorted templates. Some departments have computerized and architectural tools that can be used in the field.

Four Types of Sketches

1. Overhead
2. Cross Projection or Exploded View
3. Elevation
4. Perspective

Overhead

This is the most common and basic style. This type gives a view of the floor plan as if you were hovering above looking straight down.

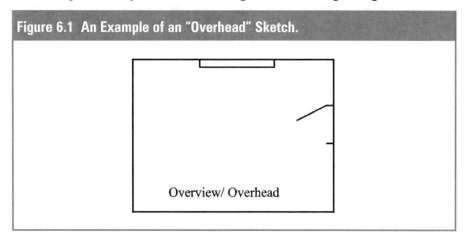

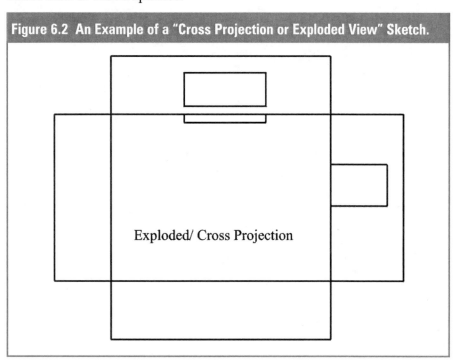

Figure 6.1 An Example of an "Overhead" Sketch.

Overview/ Overhead

Cross Projection or Exploded View

Imagine if you were to cut along the sides of a cardboard box and lay all four sides out flat as if the room exploded. This is very useful if there is evidence on the walls that needs to be documented, for instance, a bullet hole or blood spatters.

Figure 6.2 An Example of a "Cross Projection or Exploded View" Sketch.

Exploded/ Cross Projection

Elevation

This method gives a view of a room or scene from straight ahead or eye level.

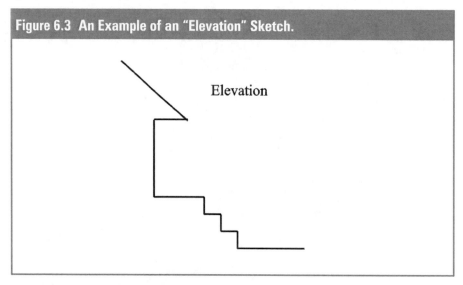

Figure 6.3 An Example of an "Elevation" Sketch.

Elevation

Figure 6.3a – Is another example.

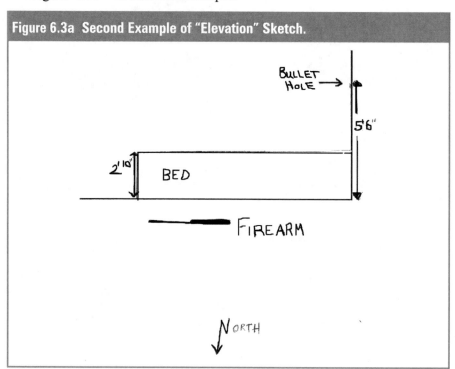

Figure 6.3a Second Example of "Elevation" Sketch.

BULLET HOLE →

5'6"

2'10"   BED

FIREARM

NORTH

Perspective

This type requires some artistic skill, as it depicts vanishing points and/or horizon lines. It resembles a view like a photograph.

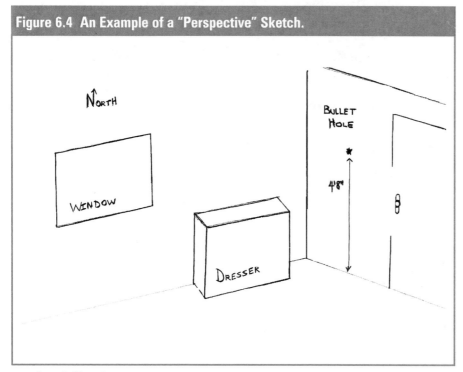

Figure 6.4 An Example of a "Perspective" Sketch.

Rough Sketch

As with photography, you will need to assess the scene to determine what type of sketch or sketches will be done. The rough sketch is just that, a rough drawing. The person rendering the sketch does not have to have artistic talent, but they do need to have patience and an eye for detail. Depending on the crime and its components, sketches can be quite comprehensive. Some complex scenes may require more than one sketch. There may be a sketch representing measurements, another to complement the evidence log by documenting locations of evidence collected; also there may be one to support the photo log showing the different camera positions used. Some scenes are just too big to try to fit onto one sheet of paper or some need a detailed breakdown of a smaller area.

The rough sketch will be completed at the scene and used later as a guide for the final sketch. The rough sketch must contain accurate measurements but is not drawn to scale. It is important that you note on your rough sketch that it is "Not to Scale".

Basic contents of a rough sketch:

- Preparer's Name
- Case Number
- Type of Incident
- Date & Time
- Location
- Weather/Lighting conditions
- Compass Direction
- Objects/Evidence
- Measurements, including:
  - Dimensions of rooms, windows, doors, furniture
  - Distances between objects, bodies, persons, entrances/exits
- Key/Legend

Figure 6.5 Crime Sketch with Key/Legend

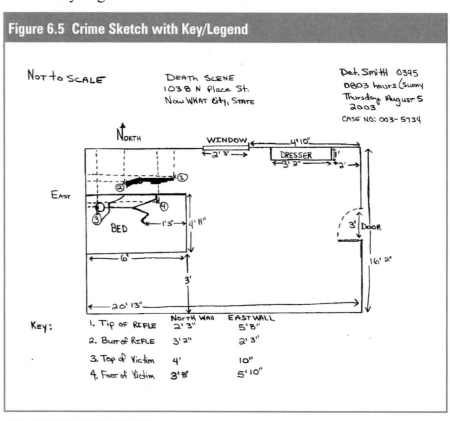

OBJECTS/EVIDENCE

After photographs and before evidence is moved and/or collected, a sketch should record the location of each item. Evidence markers are placed next to items and help identify each piece as they are entered in the evidence log. The sketch should show the number and location of each marker. "Sketch-number designations should coordinate with the evidence log number designations" (FBI).

Sketches should also document the surrounding area: cross streets, plants, trees, landmarks, and entry/exit ways, such as windows, doors, paths, gates, or roadways.

MEASUREMENTS

Two people should do the measuring at a crime scene. One person can hold the tape and record data while the other runs the strip. The rule is that measurements should be taken twice to ensure they are correct. Having two people observing and recording the measurements also eliminates hearsay evidence by allowing two investigators to testify about the accuracy.

Tools for measuring can be as simple as a retractable tape measure (at least 100 ft length). A metal tape measure is beneficial because it doesn't stretch. Then there are walking wheels that are great for large areas such as traffic accident scenes. Maybe you have seen these in use; an officer stands upright and walks while pushing the handle. Other helpful devices use electrical ultrasonic measurements. They send a pulse to a fixed surface and compute the distance. There are a vast variety of these and other measuring devices. Whether you use English or metric measurements, be consistent and don't mix. With standard measurements, use feet and inches; metric use meters and centimeters.

Starting with the interior of a crime scene, the measurements of the room are taken; walls, windows, doors, then measurements of the size of objects such as furniture, people, guns, shoe prints, etc. Next the distance of these items from a fixed point should be measured. Keep in mind this is done so that if the scene was to be re-created, every item could be placed back in its exact original location. If a crime scene is large or outdoors, measurements should be taken between adjacent buildings and/or landmarks. The importance of finding a truly "fixed" object becomes more important. The triangulation method is often used indoors and almost always used for outdoor scenes.

Methods of Measurement

Triangulation Method

The triangulation method should be used for outdoors and can be used for indoor sketches. There are three points of measurement in this method: 1 is the item of evidence; 2 and 3 are fixed objects. A triangle is

created when measurements are made from each of the two fixed points to the item of evidence.

For outdoor crime scenes the triangulation method is best. It is imperative that the objects chosen for reference are stationary and will be there for a long time to come. If you are in an inhabited area good objects to use are corners of buildings, light poles, street signs, fire hydrants, etc. Uninhabited or remote areas prove more challenging to find permanent or fixed objects for reference.

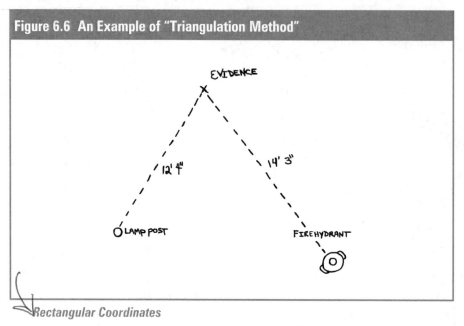

Figure 6.6 An Example of "Triangulation Method"

Rectangular Coordinates

This method is commonly used indoors. A rectangle is made when two measurements are taken at right angles from the evidence item. "Each object should be located by two measurements from non movable items (e.g., doors or walls,)" (FBI).

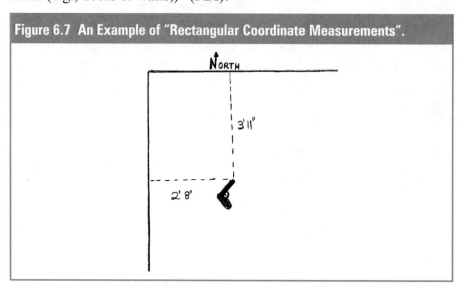

Figure 6.7 An Example of "Rectangular Coordinate Measurements".

Cross-Projection/Baseline Method

This method is useful indoors as well as outdoors. It can be helpful if the scene covers a large open area. A tape is laid between two fixed objects and each item of evidence is measured from this baseline. Two measurements are taken; one documents where the item is located along the length of the baseline, the other measures the distance from a 90-degree angle from the baseline.

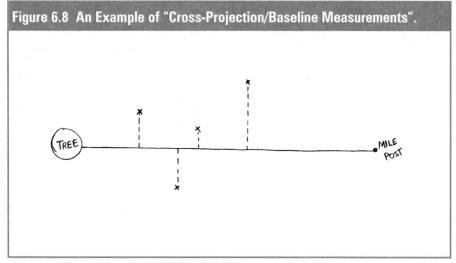

Figure 6.8 An Example of "Cross-Projection/Baseline Measurements".

Key or Legend

The key or legend is usually at the bottom or side of the sketch in a box. It gives an explanation of what each letter or symbol on the sketch represents.

FINAL SKETCH

Components of the Final Sketch

The final sketch is done to scale. This is another reason why it is important to have two people take measurements. Typically the scale for an indoor crime scene is 1/8 inch equals one foot. For exterior crime scenes the scale is usually 1 inch equals 20 feet. Of course the scales can vary depending on the needs and purpose of the sketch.

Basic Tools for Completing a Finished (to scale) Sketch
- Table or Drawing Board
- Draftsman Pencils
- Ink Pens (variety of colors)
- Drawing Paper and Tracing Paper, and/or Clear Overlays
- Pencil and Ink Erasers
- T- Square

• Templates and/or Architect Triangles

The final sketch can be simple or complex. A simple sketch can be created with a few tools – pen, pencil, paper, and rulers. To communicate more detail to a jury or judge, different colored inks may be used. Certain points of reference, such as direction of the fleeing suspect, could be marked in red. If a large amount of physical evidence was collected and documented on the sketch it maybe cluttering or distracting; the use of transparent overlays could help organize the display of evidence.

Computers have changed the way we do many things; crime scene sketches are no exception. There are many different software programs that take crime scene sketching to a whole new level. In short, the measurements can be plugged into the computer and voila; the floor layout is created to scale. Instead of drawing items by hand, the designer can choose from hundreds of templates – knives, tables, chairs, desks, bodies, etc. Again, the designer inputs the measurements of the item and the computer calculates it into the sketch proportionately.

Utilizing the Crime Scene Sketch

An accurately done sketch along with notes and photographs depict and "recreate" the scene for investigators who were not there. The sketch supplements the photographs by giving exact descriptions of where evidence is located at the crime scene. They refresh the original investigator's memory, and serve as a frame of reference when interviewing suspects or witnesses. A properly prepared sketch also supports the investigator's final and formal report. The rough draft should always be kept in addition to the final sketch.

In addition to being helpful to investigators, the sketch is valuable to attorneys handling the case. Sketches are often entered into trial to provide the court with a clear and concise portrayal of how the scene appeared. This gives the jury a "sense" of the scene and guides witnesses in their testimony. The sketch is also used as a base for 3-D models or blowup visuals in court presentations.

The final sketch must have accurate measurements, relevant facts and be intelligible and clear in order to be effective in court. The better the ability of the investigator and prosecution to convey the crime scene in a concise manner, the easier it is for the jury to comprehend the scene. A good thorough sketch documenting the scene gives credence to the case and the investigator, thus influencing the jury.

SUMMARY

The crime scene sketch is an integral part of the documentation process; it helps place items from the evidence and photo log into place visually and supports the notes for the final report. The sketch will be used as demonstrative evidence in court to aid in depiction of the scene. There are several methods and tools available to create a crime scene sketch; however they rely on accurate and complete measurements to be successful.

DISCUSSION QUESTIONS

1. What are the reasons you should have a second person help you with taking measurements at the crime scene?
2. List the four types of sketches noted in this chapter. Provide rough drawings demonstrating the different styles.

PRACTICAL EXERCISES

Take measurements of a small room you have access to. Plot out the simple floor plan. Review the methods for measurement and select one for this project. Pick an object in your room and use your chosen method to document on a rough sketch where the items relate to the room. Keep this simple, try to pick a small room with room to move and measure.

REFERENCES

FBI. (2003). *Handbook of Forensic Services Revised 2003. Crime Scene Search*. Retrieved January 21, 2004 at: http://www.fbi.gov/hq/lab/handbook/intro16.htm

Chapter 7

Final Reports

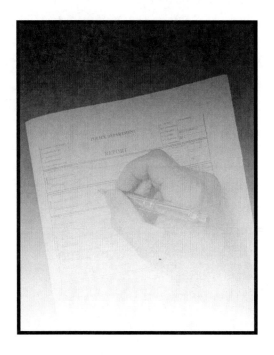

CHAPTER OVERVIEW

There are many courses and books that address report writing; this is not one of them. Most law enforcement and investigation agencies have their own manuals, training courses, and preferred standard formats for reports. Agency or company specific guidelines will outline in great detail the proper grammatical and stylization of reports. What we will cover are the basic nuts and bolts that make up a final report. Our focus will be to define the final report, examine its components and identify its functions.

OBJECTIVES

1. Explain the purpose and definition of the final report.
2. Understand and apply the mechanics of report writing.
3. Identify the ABC's of report writing.

DEFINING THE FINAL REPORT

A report is the written description that documents the work done by a law enforcement officer and represents the formal procedure rendered by his or her agency to other departments within the agency and in the criminal justice system. In defining a final departmental report (DR), we must remain open minded as to our outcome. In a major homicide case with an extended crime scene, the final report may be marked by the closure of weeks, months, or perhaps years of investigation. In a minor theft, or assault, the final report may be closed by the first responding officer who completes the interviews, sketches, and makes the arrest or issues the summons.

Even though this chapter is called "Final Reports", keep in mind that nothing is ever final. At any time new evidence or information could be developed that may result in further investigation being required. For example, in a serial murder case, upon conviction, it is possible for a deal to be cut with the defendant to reveal information concerning additional victims, missing evidence, or unknown co-defendants, in return for leniency in sentencing, thus re-opening a "final" investigative report.

THE PURPOSE OF THE FINAL REPORT

These departmental reports (DR's) need to be well organized, accurate, appropriate, and self sufficient, as they will reflect the officer's credibility and integrity. Inaccurate, misleading or omitted information can cause detrimental repercussions for the officer and the case at hand. The police department will use the reports to issue warrants, record and report crime statistics, and conduct investigations. The courts will use them for probation, pre-sentence reports, prosecution, and defense.

The report should provide follow up investigators information on what has been done and what needs to be done. If something has not been done the reasons why should be noted in the report; for instance, the officer did not take a statement from a witness at the scene. When the follow up investigators locate her in an attempt to interview her, they discover she speaks only German. Had the report stated this information, the follow up investigators could have saved time and effort by bringing an interpreter along the first time.

Listing all pertinent information regarding emotional and physical demeanor of suspects and witnesses is necessary to convey the events for the reader. For example, in 1997 Newport Beach, California, a man made a frantic request to authorities for help, claiming his wife was knocked off their boat by a rogue wave and disappeared into the sea. A large-scale ocean search for the missing woman was undertaken. The reporting officers at the scene noted that the husband was sobbing and needed assistance boarding the search and rescue boat. The efficient and observant officers also noted in reports that once the search boat was away from the crowd and media, he stopped crying and had no trouble walking on his own. In fact, once out at sea the husband took a nap. When the search and rescue party returned to shore and the media, the husband suddenly appeared grief stricken again.

To the follow up investigators this was crucial information. The notable changes in the husband's emotional and physical state were a big tip off to authorities who were already suspicious of the "rogue wave" story. They focused their investigation on the husband, who eventually was convicted of murdering his wife. *good asshole*

The prosecutor was not at the crime scene to witness the fear, pain or terror that took place. The details of the final report will help the prosecutor to comprehend the seriousness of a crime. The prosecutor will study the details in the final report to ensure that all the necessary elements to establish probable cause have been met to sustain the charges and guarantee a conviction.

It is important to remember that not just those in the criminal justice system read the final reports; they are considered public information and may be viewed by victims, suspects and witnesses. News reporters often review the DR's when researching a story. Insurance companies use the reports to assist in their investigation of claims.

MECHANICS OF REPORT WRITING

As mentioned earlier in this book, not all cases warrant photos, sketches and various logs; but for this class assume "our" case is a major crime scene and there are several components of documentation the investigator is responsible for compiling before the close of the investigation at the scene.

You arrived at the scene, assessed the scene, and made a plan of action. Like a true professional you documented everything; you took notes, photos, and sketches. So now what, toss them on your Sergeant's desk and go home? Television and movies like to entertain us by depicting police work as glamorous with high- speed chases, shoot-outs, and things getting blown-up. And why not, would you really want to watch a couple of cops writing reports for an hour?

Police Lieutenant Richard Davis (retired) admits that police work can be a very thrilling and exciting career, but for every couple of moments of glory there are many more moments of report writing. The Davis equation: 3 minutes of excitement = 3 hours of report writing.

Granted, high- speed chases require precise driving skills, shoot-outs are survived by tactical skills, and blowing stuff up requires demolition skills, but cases are solved and justice is served through good documentation and communication skills. Law enforcement officers utilize a variety of skills during their shift; how well they document those activities so that those who were not present can follow and comprehend is largely how they will be appraised and evaluated.

So now what do you do with your crime scene documents? If you still think the correct answer is "toss them on the Sergeant's desk and go home", then switch your major to basket weaving. If your answer involves "promptly creating a final report that can be utilized to assist the investigation and trial" congratulations, you are moving up in rank.

Typically your written reports will be due at the end of your shift. If the case is particularly complicated and requires further processing, a preliminary report should at least be submitted at the end of duty. Time line policies for when a report is due are determined by each agency and can vary. For example, the Monroe County Florida Sheriff's Office, requires that the final report be turned in within 72 hours of arriving on the scene; Mesa Arizona Police require a 24- hour deadline. Some agencies don't have specific designated times and only state reports are due "promptly".

Each agency will have specific formatting requirements defining how the report shall look. Some agencies use face sheets that contain information such as date, time, location, suspect and witness information, and officer name, etc. Many agencies have pre-printed report forms of different categories of events such as booking, evidence/property impound, DUI, accidents, traffic, arson, death, robbery, assault, and so on. The forms usually have blank spaces or boxes for the officer to fill out. The officer can enter certain codes, numbers or abbreviations in the forms. These abbreviations, numbers or codes are defined by each department and are taught during training.

After the officer fills in the blanks or boxes they tie the information together with the narrative.

The final report is like making lasagna; you have noodles, sauce, meat and cheese, but until you combine the ingredients in just the right way, you still don't have dinner.

To make the report (dinner) you will need the proper ingredients, taking into account that each scene is unique and the items (ingredients) will vary. Some of the items that may be included are the narrative, witness statements, crime scene log, photo log, sketches, and evidence log.

Although some of the items will vary, every report will contain a narrative. Remember the notes you took at the crime scene, they will provide you with the basis for your narrative. The narrative provides a detailed description of the scene that addresses the who, what, where, when, why and how. The flow of the narrative should be written in paragraph form using a time line that begins with your first observations upon arriving at the scene. The report is told in a story format and written in the past tense.

Think of the narrative as the mixing bowl for the ingredients to be blended in. You can't just dump the noodles, sauce, meat, and cheese in at the same time. It is a step- by- step process. Describe the scene as you arrived. Include:

- Who was present?
- Were photos taken?
- Was a sketch made?
- Was evidence collected?

If so, you will need to explain these events and include the scene log, photo log, sketch, etc. You may list the information from the log into the narrative or note it in the report and add it as an attachment. Most departments find it best to have the logs referenced in the narrative and then included as an attachment. This makes it easier when requests for photos or evidence are made. The department can produce only the report or log requested and does not need to copy the entire report.

See Figure 7.1 for a Sample Narrative Report

Figure 7.1 Sample Narrative

DR: 04-156400 PAGE 001

METRO POLICE DEPARTMENT
4200 Maple Street, Anytown, USA
Phone: 555-646-5656

INCIDENT: Mark Willard Death Investigation

OFFICER: Detective Sgt. David Smart   BADGE: 3456

DATE: 09/23/04 TIME: 1436 HRS

DEPARTMENTAL REPORT NO: 04-156400

NARRATIVE:

On Thursday, September 23, 2004, at 0856 hrs. I was dispatched to 164 East Lake Blvd. to assist Ofc. Kalwaksi, Badge #7867 at the scene of a death investigation. When I arrived (0920 hours), I contacted Ofc. Kalwaski who introduced me to Mr. Jeb Smith in the driveway of the above address and informed me that Mr. Smith had made discovery of the dead body. Kalwaski handed me the driver's license of Mr. Smith.

Officer Kalwaski and other officers had secured a perimeter at the scene and separated the witness, Mr. Smith from others until my arrival. (See Kalwaski report)

I initiated my interview with witness Smith DOB 5/15/85 (identified by California DL #5234507) who told me that he is employed as Mark Willard's landscaper at the above listed address. Mr. Smith said he arrived at 8:00am (0800hrs) to mow the lawn. When he opened the door to the gardening shed he saw Mr. Willard's body. He recognized the body as Mr. Willard, who he has known for approximately two years. Mr. Smith stated he believed Mr. Willard was dead because of the large amount of blood on the floor and the color of the body. Mr. Smith told me he did not enter the shed or touch the deceased. Mr. Smith related that he used his cell phone to call 9-1-1 and report his finding. At that point he reports that he waited in the driveway by his 1980 Chevrolet truck (California license plate 3JHY393) until officers arrived at the scene. Witness Smith advised that he did not see any other people at the scene. He said the only other car on the property was Mr. Willard's 2003 Volvo (California License 7EHT523) which was also parked in the driveway with the doors locked.

Mr. Smith took me and Ofc. Kalwaski to the gardening shed. The shed was located in the far Northwest corner of the property. Mr. Smith had left the door to the shed open and I could see the decedent's body. The deceased, identified by the witness as Mark Willard, was sitting on the floor with his legs extended straight out in front of him and his back propped up against a riding lawn mower. He was wearing a white dress shirt and necktie with black dress slacks. The victim did not have shoes or socks on. The victims clothing was saturated in brownish red substance that appeared to be blood. There was a large puddle of the brownish red substance surrounding the victim's body.

I called dispatch at approx. 0910 hrs, and requested a crime scene unit and an investigator from the medical examiners office. While waiting for the requested units to arrive, I proceeded to take Mr. Smith around to the front of the house. I had him complete a witness statement form (see attached Witness #1) Mr. Smith. Mr. Smith completed the report and then signed it as a true representation of the facts.

I took no further action pending the arrival of the requested units.

You should remember the ABC's when writing a report:

- Accurate

- Brief

- Clear

"**Accuracy**" means getting the facts right; the correct address, full names, the correct date of birth, and the proper use or connotation of words. Having someone else review your report is not only efficient in many departments, it is required protocol. Very few agencies, if any, still have officers hand write final reports, most use computers. Computers save time and have helpful features such as spell check. But computer spell check alone is not enough. If you used the wrong word but spelled it correctly the computer will not catch it. How embarrassing can that be?

"**Brevity**" means sticking to facts and observations relevant to the case at hand. Documentation of observations should be addressed in a concise, objective manner. Tell the events as you believe they actually transpired. Being brief does not mean your departmental report should be short in content; all the necessary details should be provided. If your fight with a hostile suspect ends up with him in the hospital your report should contain more than "suspect stated he wouldn't go without a fight. I had fight with suspect, I won." Don't laugh, reports like that really have been submitted! On the other hand, leave out the irrelevant personal opinions; don't write "the suspect wore an ugly T-shirt and had a stupid tattoo of a duck on his arm". Simply write the suspect "wore a red and blue T-shirt and had a tattoo of a duck on his arm". Leave out "ugly" and "stupid". Those are opinions, not facts.

"**Clarity**" in report writing means the report is clear and can be comprehended by the reader. The report should be written the way we speak, but even that needs some clarification. The report should be written the way we speak, provided we speak proper English! Slang, incomplete words and sentences that get filled in with hand gestures, facial expressions and tone of voice in order to complete the point or message obviously do not translate onto paper. Make sure you message is clear.

Jargon is another problem for report writers. What might seem perfectly clear to the writer may seem to be written in secret code to the reader. For example, "I responded to the 211 audible code three" or more clearly "I answered the emergency response to the armed robbery".

A few departments require the reports be written in the 3rd person arguing it keeps the officer and report sounding neutral and unbiased. If you were to write a report in the 3rd person, you would refer to yourself as "this officer" or the "undersigned officer of this report". If an officer was to take the stand and testify to their actions would they talk that way? It would sound odd if they did. When a police officer takes the stand to relate the events that occurred, they will state things such as "I approached the subject.... He handed me his license." The way you speak is how you should write.

One other point of clarity depends upon whether your notes are handwritten or typed. If your report is to be handwritten you must write legibly and neatly. If you do use a computer to write your reports, follow your agency's guidelines for which typeface and size font to use. Departmental reports get faxed quite often and style and size of the typeface make a difference in the quality of the fax. Most agencies prefer using Times New Roman typeface in a 12 pt font; anything smaller than a 12 pt size will virtually disappear when faxed.

Figure 7.2 Thoughts & Experiences Reviewing Police Officers' Reports

At the start of my shift I would review the officers' reports given to me by their Sergeant. The officers were responsible for the accuracy of their reports and utilized spell check, plus the Sergeants were also required to review them. Even with this inspection process, errors and inaccuracies still occurred. A difference in just one or two letters in one word can render an entirely different meaning to the whole report. Let me give you an example of an actual report that had been turned into me:

"...I informed the suspect he was under arrest. I then read him his rights at which point he rested my arrest. I forced the suspect to the ground and he continued to rest. I stuck him a couple of times with my baton while giving him verbal commands to lay still. His resting became more aggressive..."

I had to ask this officer how a suspect "rests" more aggressively. Do they snore louder? If you think the officer was very embarrassed, the reviewing sergeant was even more embarrassed. What do you think a good defense attorney would do with this report on the stand? Would the jury lose interest in the seriousness of the resisting arrest case and focus on the amusing spelling error?

Retired Lt. Richard O. Davis.

FINAL REPORT AND CASE FILE

The final departmental report is part of the case file. The case file should include all documentation and reports by all departments and individuals. For example, fire department, emergency personnel, lab reports, ballistic tests, etc. As we stated earlier, nothing is ever final. A case my go unsolved and become a "cold case" or new evidence and events could re-open a case. New investigators may be assigned to the re-opened case and will need to recreate everything that had been done (and not done) in the past. Properly documented case files will enable investigators to proceed with their task.

Figure 7.3 is an excerpt from "A Guide for Law Enforcement Crime Scene Investigation," published in January 2000 by the U.S. Department of Justice, Office of Justice Programs, and National Institute of Justice.

Fig. 7.3 Excerpt from "A Guide for Law Enforcement Crime Scene Investigation

Principle: Reports and other documentation pertaining to the crime scene investigation shall be compiled into a "case file" by the investigator(s) in charge of the crime scene. This file shall be a record of the actions taken and evidence collected at the scene. This documentation shall allow for independent review of the work conducted.

Policy: The investigator(s) in charge shall ensure that reports and other documentation pertaining to the crime scene investigation are compiled.

Procedure: The investigator(s) in charge should obtain the following for the crime scene case file:

- a. Initial responding officer(s') documentation.
- b. Emergency medical personnel documents.
- c. Entry/exit documentation.
- d. Photographs/videos.
- e. Crime scene sketches/diagrams.
- f. Evidence documentation.
- g. Other responders' documentation.
- h. Record of consent form or search warrant.

Fig. 7.3 Excerpt from "A Guide for Law Enforcement Crime Scene Investigation (Cont.)

    i. Reports such as forensic/technical reports should be added to this file when they become available.

Note: The above list is limited to crime scene documentation. This should not be considered a comprehensive list of the documents involved in an investigative case file.

Summary:

This will ensure that reports and other documentation pertaining to the crime scene investigation are compiled into a case file by the investigator(s) in charge of the crime scene and allow for independent review of the work conducted.

Source: http://www.ojp.usdoj.gov http://www.ojp.usdoj.gov/nij page 31

SUMMARY

Agencies will vary in the due date, style and formatting of the final report, but all call for certain similar elements. No matter what agency you work for, proper documentation dictates proper use of English, grammar, spelling and inclusion of relevant facts. The final report is utilized by a variety of agencies and departments and must contain all the pertinent elements of the crime. Some of the readers will not be law enforcement officers and must be worded in a manner so that the message is clear. Make sure your reports are accurate, brief, and clear. The information must be correct, not contain personal opinions and be completed in a format that is comprehensible.

DISCUSSION QUESTIONS

1. What are some of the other reports or documents that might be included in a final report?
2. Explain why the final report is not always the last report.
3. Who or what entities read the reports, and what do they use them for?

Chapter 8

Documenting Assaults

OVERVIEW

Documenting an assault requires the tools and skills of note-taking, photography, sketching, and report writing. This chapter will define "assault" and expand on use of these tools to document assault crime scenes.

OBJECTIVES

1. Define the differences in simple and aggravated assault.
2. Identity the types of people who are victims of assault and how proper documentation can speak for them.
3. Outline the proper methods of photographing assault victims.

DEFINING ASSAULT

There are many types or terms associated with the word "assault", such as simple, aggravated, misdemeanor, felony, criminal, civil, and battery. Basically put, an assault is the threat or attempt to physically harm another person. The term "assault" is derived from the Latin term *assilire* which means, "to leap on" or attack. The assailant does not have to be successful in his attack; if it is reasonably believed that he has the ability to carry out the attack and causes the victim to feel personally threatened, it is considered an assault. Some states define this as a simple assault, misdemeanor, second degree, civil or tort assault.

What makes it an aggravated, criminal, felony or first degree assault can depend on whether the assailant actually struck or injured the victim, used a deadly or dangerous weapon, rendered serious bodily harm, or committed the assault in the commission of another crime such as robbery or rape. Some states define the actual bodily harm as "battery" thus creating the phrase "assault and battery".

VICTIMS

According to the National Crime Victimization Survey (NCVS) for 2002, over 5.3 million U.S. residents over age 11 reported being victims of violent crimes. Violent crimes were defined as rape, sexual assault, robbery, aggravated assault, and simple assault. Simple assaults far out number aggravated assaults; in 2002 the NCVS reported 990,110 aggravated assaults and a whopping 3,591,090 simple assaults.

Of those 5.3 million victims of violent crime the NCVS declared that 7% of them had "faced an offender armed with a firearm" while 6% were threatened with a knife and 7% by other types of weapons. (Rennison & Rand).

The NCVS collected its data from victim interviews; the report stated that "violent crimes against females were more likely to have been reported to police than those against males". The report goes on to say "males were victims of overall violent crime, robbery, total assault, simple assault at rates higher than those of females" however, women are more often victims of rape or sexual assault. In addition, domestic violence makes up a large percentage of assaults. Rennison and Rand also reported that women are most likely to be victimized by someone they know (67%) compared to men who are victimized more often by a stranger (56%).

Importance of Assault Documentation

What does the data from the NCVS mean to you regarding crime scene documentation? Your documentation and reports can aid victims in protection and compensation. Some states allow for victims to be compensated.

The State of Oregon's Crime Victims' Compensation Program uses police reports as a tool in evaluating the victims' claims. Victims who are being harassed and are in fear of their aggressors can file restraining orders. The police report is used by prosecutors in order to build the criminal case against the perpetrator.

Domestic violence and child abuse are serious assaults that depend heavily on accurate and complete documentation. Proper documentation of injuries can aid in the prosecution even when the victim won't testify. Typically the victims of domestic violence and child abuse live with their abuser and often times are fearful of testifying against them. They can be financially and emotionally dependent upon their abuser. Emotional dependence can mean they are coerced or threatened into not testifying. If the documentation is done thoroughly and properly it can be admitted at trial; in effect, it can testify in place of the victim.

Understanding the types of assaults and the victims will help you define the crime and the level of documentation required. I think it would be safe to say that many of the calls you respond to will be some type of assault. Almost all calls you respond to will require some note-taking and reporting; many will require photos and even sketches. The elements of documentation vary some between different types of crimes.

NOTE-TAKING

The depth and number of questions you ask the victim and/or witnesses will depend on the level and nature of the crime. Let's go back to the first chapter and review the documentation checklist. For assault documentation we will expand on parts of the checklist with additions.

- Victim(s)/Responsible Party
  - Name
  - DOB
  - Address
  - Social security number, phone numbers, home, job, family, cell, etc.

- Witnesses
  - Name
  - DOB
  - Address
  - Social security number, phone numbers, home, job, family, cell, etc.

When documenting the victim and or witness recollections, there are a few things to keep in mind:

- Document the victim/witness statements accurately and completely; do not leave any of their comments out.
- Whether the victim/witness interview was recorded via audio, video, or victim's/witness' own handwriting, a written version should be made.
- Allow the victim/witness to review the written documentation to confirm the information is a correct representation of his/her statement.

Documenting the victim/witness statement accurately and completely will ensure the integrity of the evidence. Asking the victim/witness certain questions about the event will help trigger their recollection, enabling you to gain a more thorough documentation of the account. This is not a complete list but it should give you an idea of the type of information to include in your documents.

- Are there any other witnesses, and if so, do you know their names and how to contact them or describe them?
- Was there more than one suspect or attacker?
- Did they say anything; if so what did they say?
- Did they take anything?
- What were their actions?
  - How did they enter or approach?
  - What direction or exit did they take?
- If the suspect is not known to the victim, the following questions should follow:
  - Did they have an accent, lisp or stutter?
- Description of Suspect
  - Male or female?
  - What color or race?
  - How old?
  - How tall were they?
  - How were they built?
  - Describe the color, length and style of their hair.

- Did they have facial hair?
- Eye color?
- Describe their complexion, smooth, clear, acne, etc.
- What were they wearing?
- Any significant logos, tatters, holes or emblems?
- Any scars, marks, tattoos or deformities?
- Any other distinguishing features or actions?

- Vehicles at scene
  - Make/Model/color/license plate number
  - Location
  - Damage
  - Bumper stickers, parking permits, luggage rack, items hanging on rear-view mirror, items on antennae, etc.

- Weapons
  - Did they have a weapon or claim to have one?
  - Which hand did they hold the weapon in?
  - What was it – a gun, knife, club, etc.?
  - Can you describe it in detail – color, size, texture, make, brand, etc.?

Lead your victim or witness to accuracy by qualifying their descriptions. For example, they state the assailant had a rifle. Ask how they know it was a rifle, what is their knowledge or experience with firearms; have they ever shot one, been around one, or have they just seen them on TV and in movies? Could they be mistaking it for a shotgun? Ask these questions now because a good defense attorney will later.

Victim or Suspect Injuries

Take notes explaining any injuries sustained by the victim, torn clothing, burns, cuts, abrasions, etc. Document the victim's account of how each injury occurred. If the suspect got away, ask the victim or witness if the suspect sustained any injuries. Did they leave any evidence behind such as blood, torn clothing, or hair? Back up these notes with sketches and photos.

PHOTOGRAPHY

The U.S. Department of Justice, the Office of Justice Programs and the Office of Juvenile Justice and Delinquency Prevention has put together a "Portable Guide to Investigating Child Abuse: Photo-documentation in the Investigation of Child Abuse". Although this is a guide for documentation of child abuse, many of the techniques described apply to all physical assault cases.

The following is an excerpt taken from that guide. The entire Guide can be viewed at:

http://www.ncjrs.org/html/ojjdp/portable_guides/photodoc/contents.html

Foreword

A picture, so the saying goes, is worth a thousand words. In the case of the investigation of a charge of child abuse, a picture can determine the eventual case result.

To do the task of documentation properly, child abuse investigators require the right tools and the right techniques. Photo-documentation is one of the most important of these tools.

This guide provides valuable pointers regarding the selection and use of camera equipment, film, and photographic techniques that are most appropriate for use in cases of suspected child abuse. Proper photographing of the child's physical condition will help provide evidence integral both to the investigation and to the courtroom presentation, should formal charges ensue.

It is my hope, therefore, that this guide will help protect children from abuse through the enhancement of investigative techniques.

Shay Bilchik, Administrator
Office of Juvenile Justice and Delinquency Prevention
June 1996
Third Printing March 2000
NCJ 160939

Photographs documenting a victim's injuries often provide key evidence in child abuse cases and convictions. To ensure effective photo-documentation, it is important to use the most appropriate camera equipment and film and to properly identify and investigate the child victim. Critical to all investigations of child abuse is the method of photographing injuries such as pressure injuries, bite marks, bruises, burns, facial injuries, amputations, neglect, and sexual abuse injuries. The following can hinder accurate courtroom evidence:

- Ineffective camera equipment and film.

- Insufficient methods of photographing the victim or the victim's injuries.
- Misinformation regarding the photographs of the case.
- Mislabeling of child abuse information, including photographs.

This guide offers important information on how to document cases of suspected child abuse through photography to enhance the investigation process or provide courtroom evidence and testimony.

Camera Equipment

To be effective in documenting child abuse cases, camera equipment should have the following capabilities:

- Be easy to use and require little training.
- Offer accurate color balance.
- Provide automatic exposure and the capability for film advance and rewind.
- Have a built-in flash with quick recharge (flash recharges within 1 to 3 seconds).
- Offer comfortable operating distance from subject.
- Be able to produce life-size reproductions of trauma sites and to show much larger areas of the body or the device believed to have caused the injury.

Camera systems for photographing abused children range from expensive and sophisticated colposcopic (a specialized camera/examination unit used specifically by medical examiners for viewing or photographing subtle abnormalities or injuries to the vagina, cervix, or anus) and 35mm close-up systems to less expensive and simpler "bridge" cameras and instant or self-developing cameras.

Film

The standard film for medical use in documenting child abuse cases is 35mm color slide film, sometimes referred to as color transparency or color reversal film. Color slides are relatively inexpensive and easy to file and can be quickly developed and converted into color prints if necessary.

Regardless of the camera equipment used, the following points concerning type and use of film are important in ensuring consistency in results and reproduction of the injury, its location, color, size, and pattern:

- Use fine-grain color slide or print film that has a film speed rating of 100 or 200 ISO (International Standards Organization). This type of daylight film allows for a greater depth of field (sharpness) with a minimum amount of grain and blurriness. Always use a flash when shooting indoors with daylight film. Sixty-second, self-developing film is not recommended.

- Keep film and camera equipment in a clean, empty, dry thermal container or picnic cooler. Do not store the film unprotected in a vehicle. Sunlight and extreme temperatures can adversely affect color accuracy, reduce the film's sensitivity to light, and in some cases result in tearing or splitting.

- Store film in the refrigerator or freezer to keep it fresh, but place at room temperature for approximately 2 to 3 hours before it is to be used (24 hours if film is frozen).

- Process exposed film as soon as possible to avoid a color imbalance or shift.

- Remember when the film was loaded, the type of film, and how many exposures a roll contains. Attach an end flap from the film carton to the camera back as a reminder. Failure to do so could result in lost evidence. Always remove rewound film from the camera and attach an identification sticker or place in an evidence bag before the film is sent for processing.

- Make sure an extra camera and set of flash batteries are available at all times.

Ultraviolet Photography

Ultraviolet (UV) photography has an established role in clinical forensic medicine and is beginning to be used in child abuse assessments. UV is a method of photography in which a standard, high-speed (ISO 800/1600) color slide film is used in conjunction with a high-powered electronic flash. The flash must be covered with a Wood's Filter (Wratten Filter 18A); another filter (Wratten Filter 2B or 2E) must be used on the camera lens. The end result of UV photography is an image that may display healed wounds, bite marks, belt imprints, and old pattern-type injuries.

There are disadvantages to UV photography. Photographing conscious subjects can be difficult and may produce little usable evidence, and the image cannot be seen until after development. In addition, the methodology is complex, the working parameters are tight, and subject movement or inaccurate focusing may alter any proof. If UV is to be used, the subject should also be recorded on conventional color slide film using a standard non-filtered flash and lens combination.

Photographing Injuries

Prior to photographing the injuries, the investigator should identify the suspected child abuse victim by completing an identification sheet and/or taking a full-face picture of the child that also displays the child's name. Separate rolls of film should be used for each case to avoid losing or mixing up evidence, which could result in dismissal of the case. Although time-consuming, it is helpful to place an identifying sign, including name or initials, date of birth, date and time of photographs, case number, and the photographer's name or initials, in front of the victim's injury for each picture. In addition, many 35mm cameras contain databack attachments that imprint the time, date, and an identifying code on each film frame.

In addition, the investigator can use a medical photography form as a tool for highlighting injury sites, description of injuries, time and date of photographs, the victim's identification or case number, and the number of photographs taken and by whom. The form is then included in the finished photo envelope as relevant to the chain of evidence.

Tips for Photographing a Suspected Victim of Child Abuse

- Take two pictures of every view and angle, one for the file and one for court.
- Photograph the injury with an anatomic landmark. The inclusion of an elbow, knee, belly button, or other body part identifies the location of the wound.
- Include two pictures of each wound or other injury, one that identifies a landmark and one that provides a close-up (fills the film frame) of the wound.
- Position the camera so that the film surface or plane is parallel to, or directly facing, the injury.

- Vary the perspective of the picture by taking various shots from different angles and distances. This is particularly important since the flash may produce unpredictable reflections. Darker complexions can cause flash reflections and loss of definition. If unsure about correct exposures, take pictures at the camera's recommended exposure and one slightly lighter and one slightly darker (bracketing). To do this, adjust the lens aperture by one-half to one full f-stop on either side of the recommended exposure. Bracketing will ensure proper color balance and brightness when documenting victims with very light or very dark skin tones.

- Place a measuring device such as an adhesive metric scale directly above or below the injury to ensure accurate representation of the size and depth of the injury. A standardized color bar may be placed in the photographic plane for comparison with the color of the injury. This ensures that if color is distorted in the film developing process, adequate color comparisons can still be made.

Methods for Photographing Specific Injuries

Punctures, slashes, rope burns, or pressure injuries

When documenting these types of injuries, take photographs straight on and at a slight angle. Photographing the injury straight on provides an overall view of the surface and extent of the injury, while shooting from a slight angle provides depth and texture to a picture.

Bite marks

Forensic bite mark photography is a specialized field of medical photography and is interpreted best by a forensic dentist or pathologist. Bite marks can be recorded by following the method described above for punctures, slashes, and so forth, but the size, shape, color, depth of indentations, and three-dimensional contours also need to be documented. Multiple views from various perspectives are important in delineating texture and shape. Parallel or direct views best depict shape and size, while slanted or indirect views and lighting highlight texture.

Bruises

Bruising goes through several stages of development—a bruise discovered several hours after abuse will become more pronounced as time goes on, and additional photographs will be needed to document the injury. If a second or third series of pictures is required, the investigator should reproduce the angles and positions that were used to photograph the first series. If a child shows evidence of having old and new bruises, repeated abuse may be suspected. Both old and new bruises should be photographed. Areas of swelling (edema) sometimes exhibit a strong reflection that is caused by the flash bouncing off the swollen/rounded injury site. This effect may obscure the photograph. To help minimize the reflections, take photographs from several different angles, and then do a follow-up series when the swelling has gone down.

Burns

In cases of burns or severe scalding, take pictures from all angles before (especially before any creams or oils are applied) and after treatment. Accidental burns usually exhibit splash marks or indiscriminate patterns of injury. Intentional submersions show distinct lines or well-defined areas of damaged skin compared with healthy skin.

Facial Injuries

If an injury is inside the mouth, use a plastic or wooden tongue depressor to keep the mouth open and the injury visible. If there is an eye injury, use a pocket flashlight or toy to distract the child's gaze in different directions to show the extent of the damage to the eye area.

Amputation

In cases where abuse involves the amputation of a body part, photograph the dismembered part alone and then in relation to the body as a whole. Close-ups should also be taken of the skin's torn edges, which may help verify the method of amputation in court.

Neglect

When there is suspected child neglect, the child's general appearance should be photographed, including any signs such as splinters in the soles of the feet, hair loss, extreme diaper rash, wrinkled or wasted buttocks, prominent ribs, and/or a swollen belly.

Photography Tips

- Establish a protocol or checklist for photo-documentation.
- Decide in advance who will be photographing the victim.
- Shoot a test roll before using a new camera system.

- Compose the picture as the injured area would normally appear.
- Magnify the picture (create a close-up to fill the film frame) as it is being taken, not during printing.
- Bracket (vary f-stop above, at, and below expected correct or recommended exposure) if correct exposures are uncertain.
- Take many pictures from different angles and distances (more is better than less).
- Review all pictures after they are developed.
- Label all the prints and slides after development.
- Keep photographs protected and techniques logged.

SKETCHES

Back in the Crime Scene Sketch chapter we discussed the types of drawings that could be used to document the crime scene area. The chapter focused on physical surrounds of the area – buildings, rooms, exterior/outdoors. Depending on the type of assault scene you document, there will be a need for these types of sketches. In addition to these sketches, you will need to sketch the physical or human injuries of the victim.

The victim sketch will support the photos you have taken. Most departments will have a form designed to assist with documentation of bodily injuries. The form has a template diagraming a human body. There are diagrams representing males, females, adults or children. The areas of the body where the victim has been injured are marked on the corresponding diagram.

FINAL REPORTS

The final report is done the same way as discussed in the previous chapter. The ABC's still apply: Accurate, Brief, Clear. What is important to keep in mind in assault cases are the victim/witness statements. Include them in their entirety in your report. Get it right the first time. Victims of these crimes often have a difficult time dealing with a criminal trial. Your report and subsequent documentation will be the victim's voice in many of these cases.

SUMMARY

Assaults can be simple or aggravated. Law enforcement deals with a large volume of assault cases. Victims don't always come forward to testify. In trial, getting victim and witness statements correct in their own words can make an important impact in the courtroom. Photo-documentation is one of the most effective methods to document and recreate the assault for a jury. Follow the proper techniques and guidelines to ensure the photos will be true representations of the scene and admissible in court.

QUESTIONS

1. What type of photography is used to document healed wounds, bite marks, belt imprints, and old pattern-type injuries?
2. What are the difficulties in using this method?
3. Identify importance of victim/witness statements.

REFERENCES

The U.S. Department of Justice, the Office of Justice Programs and the Office of Juvenile Justice and Delinquency Prevention. (2000, March). Portable Guides to Investigating Child Abuse: Photo-documentation in the Investigation of Child Abuse. Retrieved January 30, 2004 from:

http://www.ncjrs.org/html/ojjdp/portable_guides/photodoc/contents.html

Rennison, C. Ph.D., & Rand, M. (2003, August). Criminal Victimization, 2002. U.S. Department of Justice (DOJ), Office of Justice Programs (OJP). Bureau of Justice (BOJ) statistics: National crime victimization survey. Retrieved January 29, 2004 from:
 http://www.ojp.usdoj.gov/bjs/pub/pdf/cv02.pdf

State of Oregon Department of Justice. (2002, April). Crime victims' Assistance: The Crime Victims' Compensation Program.

Chapter 9

Sexual Assault

CHAPTER OVERVIEW

NO, DON'T, STOP. If you understand the meaning of these words, then you have an understanding of when an encounter becomes a sexual assault. Sexual Assault is defined as: "Threats of, or deliberate physical contact of a sexual nature which is against another person's will or without consent."

✓ Important

But what happens when the encounter does become a sexual assault? Investigators cannot treat this crime as they would many others. Assistance to the victims and timely preservation of evidence is essential. Each assault and every victim is different, and an investigator must be trained to handle the different categories of assault as well as the different classifications of victims. Documenting and reporting the evidence in these matters will vary with each case. This chapter will define the victims, the issues and the methods of dealing with each category and classification.

OBJECTIVES

At the end of this chapter, you will be able to do the following:

1. Define and list different ways of interviewing sexual assault victims.
2. Learn the importance of documenting evidence.

VICTIMS

Sexual offenses fall into three classifications.

- Serious Sex Offenses: This type of offense is considered high priority. Rape or sexual battery, as it is sometimes called, fall into this classification because they constitute the greatest physical and psychological injury to the victim.

- Nuisance Sex Offenses: Acts of voyeurism and exhibitionism fall into this classification. Normally these acts present no personal danger.

- Sex Offenses Involving Mutual Consent: There are times when there has been mutual consent for sex but it can still be illegal. For example: adultery, prostitution, fornication and certain homosexual activities. Usually it is only because of citizen complaints or the offense took place in public that these acts are even investigated.

Many people are of the misunderstanding that women are the only victims of sexual assault and that unless there was penetration the victim was not sexually assaulted. This is simply not true. Men, children and even the elderly are not immune from sexual assault. Therefore, the investigator must adapt and apply different techniques when investigating a sexual assault. Remember, sexual assault is one of the most traumatic experiences that can happen to an individual.

Female

When preparing documentation involving women, the investigation must be tempered in such a manner as to create an atmosphere of privacy. Women often find it difficult to discuss the assault without reliving it. The difficulty may stem from being embarrassed or that they have never been able to openly discuss issues dealing with sexual content. Women who have been sexually assaulted can have many different emotions. Those emotions can range from crying to screaming to angry outbursts or even extreme calmness. It is extremely important for the investigator to understand that there is not a specific emotion that fits all, therefore the interview will not always be handled in the same way.

Women often will be more comfortable if a member of the family or friend is present after being interviewed. Offering to make a call for them before they ask may make the victim feel as though her well-being is important to the investigator. Women often have concerns that are unique to them. For example: possibility of pregnancy, reaction of husband or significant other, having their name and the nature of the assault released to the media. They will also fear reprisal by the assailant. The sexual freedom in today's environment has added another concern, the fear of being infected with HIV/AIDS or another STD.

Many women will request a sexual assault counselor. If they do, their choice of either a male or female should be honored. They may want this immediately or it may be weeks, months and sometimes even years before they are ready to work through the assault.

Male

Male victims of sexual assault are the least likely to report it. This may be the result of a long-standing mentality that "Men cannot be sexually assaulted." Because of this, male sexual assault is enhanced by the stigma of weakness, cowardice and the lack of gender identification. Males fear that by reporting sexual assault they will be subjected to ridicule and will not be taken seriously. If they do report the assault they are less willing to follow through on such things as going to the hospital or preserving evidence. It is extremely unlikely that a case of male sexual assault will ever reach the trial stage.

Males tend to feel intimidated (real or imagined) by the investigator. Keeping this in mind, the investigator must demonstrate the same level of compassion toward males as toward females. The high level of professionalism must not be lowered.

CHILDREN

When a child is sexually assaulted his or her entire world has been changed forever. Innocence has been lost. The child's life has become a battlefield. Most sexual assault victims will have some psychological adjustments to make, and most of them have at least some understanding of what has happened to them. This is not the case when the victim of sexual assault is a child. The child does not have the psychological growth or mental capacity to understand the adult world in which they find themselves. With this in mind, there are many things the investigator can do that may minimize the long-term trauma later in life while still producing the needed evidentiary information.

Once the assault has been reported, it is imperative that the investigator remove the child to a secure, comfortable setting before the interview begins. Most cities have a Child Advocacy Center that has been set up with toys, stuffed animals, books and tables and painted in bright warm colors. They have separate rooms that allow total privacy. It is highly recommended that this facility be utilized. The child becomes less stressful in an environment that is familiar. Once there, the process of establishing trust and rapport with the child can begin. This sometimes can develop quickly or it may take an hour or two. Remember, the child has no concept of time so it is up to the investigator to allow as much time as needed to gain that trust and rapport.

Children respond to an assault differently depending upon their age. Following are some guidelines for dealing with children in those different age groups. These are only guidelines. Each case is different and each investigator has developed a method of interviewing and should proceed with what has worked for them in the past.

Preschool Ages 2-6

Children in the preschool ages 2-6 may be more comfortable doing the interview at home as long as the assault did not take place there. A parent, or another person the child trusts, should be nearby. This age group may need constant reassurance they have done nothing wrong. Remember, the attention span of this group is short. If the child appears to be tired, restless, or even cranky these are signs that no further information will be forthcoming. It may be necessary to have several small interviews rather than a continuous one. Keep in mind that children of this age oftentimes cannot separate fact from fiction, so do not wait an extended period of time to commence the interview. Remember however, that well-meaning parents may confuse a child by talking to them about what happened.

Elementary Ages 6-10

Children in this age group often worry about getting into trouble. Having a parent in the next room is recommended but they should not be in view of the child. This age group should be advised many times they are not in trouble and, in fact, should receive more praise for doing the right thing. This is not difficult to do. Compliment them often and tell them how helpful they are being. It is a good practice to involve this age group in decision-making. You will also recognize that this age group responds better if they are included in the decision-making process, like going to the hospital. They also need an explanation of everything that is happening and what will happen next.

Pre-Adolescent Age 10-12

This is a very difficult age. Children of this age have begun to share their thoughts and secrets with their friends, sometimes leaving their parents out of the loop. The investigator may find it more helpful if a friend, rather than a parent, is nearby.

Adolescent Age 13-17

At this age, victims of sexual assault may find it very difficult to "rat on a friend." They are so peer oriented that to identify or talk about a peer results in a feeling of betrayal. Therefore, it is recommended that the interview be conducted in a secure, private place with no peers nearby.

It is also important that the investigator use common terminology and repeat information often. Limit the number of times the child has to repeat the story by bringing together all agency personnel that will need to question the child. However, be careful that the child does not feel they are being "ganged up on" or intimidated because there are too many people present.

ELDERLY

When an elderly person becomes a victim of assault, many issues are set into motion. Usually the elderly person suffers not only physical injury but also mental and financial injuries. Elderly people most likely will have injuries that send them to the hospital. They are usually on a fixed income and the burden of paying for the hospital bill adds additional stress. Because of the aging process the elderly may or may not mend completely, thereby usually having to stay in the hospital longer and their mental state can become very confused and remain that way.

Many elderly people have a real fear that a family member will declare them incompetent and take away their freedom. They become so embarrassed that they begin to have feelings of guilt that they allowed this to happen to them. They also have a tremendous fear that the assailant will return because they reported the crime.

The elderly are not much different than children when it comes to an investigation. The investigator must have a different mind-set when dealing with an elderly sexual assault victim and must consider the following issues:

- Is the victim tired and/or not feeling well?
- Has the victim had time to collect his/her thoughts?
- Is there adequate lighting in the room?
- Do not act as though they are not there. Include them in any decision-making process unless it is very apparent they are not able to participate.

- Do not confuse the victim by asking more than one question at a time and avoid interrupting.
- Keep the questions short and simple.
- Make sure you establish eye contact and continue to hold eye contact throughout the interview.
- Make sure the print is large and dark enough on anything the victim needs to read.
- Never assume the victim can't hear and shout into their ear. You may have to speak a little more loudly but keep it below the shout level.
- Always preserve their dignity.

WITNESSES

It is the responsibility of the first responder to identify any witness and document their story. A witness is defined as anyone having knowledge or information of the crime and can be anyone the victim has told about the assault. This can include friends, parents, other family members, medical personnel, neighbors, investigators, and any other law enforcement officer that the victim may have spoken to. A witness may also be an expert or psychologist, a rape counselor, a personal doctor or anyone the victim may have communicated with personally, telephonically or through e-mail.

TIME FRAME

Normally the time frame of sexual assault begins with the first notification or knowledge of the crime. It is at this time most investigators begin their documentation and organization of the crime scene. Upon arriving at the crime scene, the investigator determines if the victim is safe and free from injury. Evidence and information gathering begin. The investigator should offer the victim the option of going to the hospital and explain to the victim that the time frame is crucial to preserving evidence that will help with prosecution of the assailant. This also is the time to explain to the victim that he/she should not shower, bathe, eat, drink, brush their teeth, go the bathroom, etc. Steps that will occur at the hospital should be explained to the victim. It is preferable that the victim go to the hospital immediately. If the victim refuses to go to the hospital the investigator should explain that usually all physical evidence can be contaminated or lost within the first 72 hours.

During the first 72 hours the investigator will need to have the victim provide information related to the assault. Although each jurisdiction has policies and procedures for collecting and preserving evidence gathered during this time, all understand the importance of the first 72 hours.

The following topics should be considered and documented by all investigators within the first 72 hours:

- How does the victim seem mentally (incoherent, fearful, etc.)?
- Are drugs or alcohol present? Make sure if present, they are bagged and tagged in the proper way.
- Survey the crime scene noting as much information as possible. This is not something to do later from memory.
- Listen and document the victim's account of the assault making sure that any description of the assailant is included.
- How did the assault begin, where did it take place (car, bedroom, garage, basement, etc.)?
- Did the victim know the assailant (friend, family member, teacher, stranger, etc.)?
- The victim's account should also include the type of assault (oral, penetration, anal, etc.).
- Does the victim know other people that can be relied on to furnish information about the assailant?
- If the assailant is known, does victim know where he/she lives, what a phone number might be, what kind of vehicle the assailant drives, where he/she might work?
- Was a weapon used during the course of the assault?
- Did the assailant take or leave anything at the crime scene?
- Did the victim see the assailant leave the scene? If so, in what direction did the assailant go?

- Did the victim run on foot from the crime scene or was someone waiting in a vehicle (what color, make, model, etc.)?

ADMISSIBLE EVIDENCE

Evidence is anything that tends logically to prove or disprove a fact at issue in a judicial case or controversy. A case can be lost or won on the merits of the evidence gathered and the manner in which it was gathered and preserved. Proper documentation proving that all Fourth Amendment protections were preserved while the evidence was collected must be available. Evidence must be properly identified. Below are some issues that must be considered when collecting evidence from the assault scene.

- Has the evidence (blood, weapons, clothing, hair, fibers, fingerprints) been properly collected and processed?
- Has the chain of custody been preserved?
- Have all persons who handled the evidence been properly identified?
- Was the scene properly secured (police tape, rope, etc.) to keep the evidence from being contaminated?
- Is the evidence collected relevant to this particular case?
- Has the evidence met all legal requirements?
- Is there an evidence recovery log that contains, in chronological order, each item of evidence, who collected the evidence, where and when was it collected, who witnessed the collection and whether it was documented using photos or diagrams?
- Has the rape kit been handled properly and all results documented by medical personnel?

DOCUMENTING

The documentation process for a sexual assault has to be done with utmost sensitivity. A victim of sexual assault may be affected by things such as the tone of voice of the interviewer or the look in his/her eyes (is there sympathy there, are the eyes accusing, patronizing, etc.). These observations by the victim could influence the answers to questions or the way the facts of the assault are related.

There are some guidelines which should be kept in mind when interviewing a sexual assault victim.

- The victim may or may not want a family member present during the interview. This is usually left up to the discretion of the investigator as to whether the request is granted. Try to locate an area that will provide the most amount of privacy for the victim.
- The victim should be allowed to tell the story of the assault uninterrupted and in his/her own words. It is also important that the victim be allowed as much time as needed and not feel rushed.
- The investigator should take detailed notes regarding the date and time of assault, what activity was taking place just prior to the assault, were alcohol or drugs involved, who was present, and where the assault took place, etc.
- The investigator should also be aware and note the physical appearance of the victim. The mental condition of the victim can be noted, but it is not generally given much weight as each victim handles a sexual assault differently (crying, screaming, calmness, etc.).

Many times, the first official contact the victim will have with anyone following an assault will generally be a 911 operator. That operator has the responsibility to ensure that the victim is safe and out of harm's way. If the victim is injured and needs medical attention, the 911 operator will send emergency personnel. The 911 operator will also dispatch law enforcement personnel to the crime scene. It is also his/her responsibility to determine if the victim is coherent enough to understand that certain actions must be followed so that evidence will not become tainted. If the victim is unable to understand what procedures need to be followed and there is a third party available, the 911 operator can relay through them what the victim must do. It is always helpful to explain to the victim/third person why you are making the request.

The 911 operator will: *Important*
- Advise the victim not to change clothing and explain that the reason for this is to preserve any trace evidence, hair, fibers, etc.
- Advise the victim not to take a shower or bath because important evidence will be lost forever.
- Advise the victim not to eat or drink anything.
- Advise the victim it is his/her option to go to the hospital.
- Explain to the victim the importance of going to the hospital and explain to the victim what will happen at the hospital.
- Advise the victim of the importance of not revealing pertinent facts of the assault to anyone other than law enforcement personnel.

SUMMARY

Developments in analyzing the issues resulting from a sexual assault have made it possible to convict persons who otherwise may have gotten away with a crime. This means properly documenting and preserving the evidence is extremely important. The goal of this process is to recognize the different methods that must be implemented to ensure that any physical evidence will yield reliable information to aid in the investigation and eventual prosecution.

Investigators should approach a sexual assault crime scene as if duplicating the incident were the only thing that matters, because it does. Sexual assault crime scenes are unique. Checklists are a "must" for investigators working in the sexual assault arena because nothing can be overlooked.

DISCUSSION QUESTIONS

1. What are the duties of a 911 operator upon receiving a call regarding a sexual assault?
2. What would you advise a victim to do following an assault?
3. Who are the "typical" sexual assault victims?

ADDITIONAL READINGS

Howell, Don and Dalberg, Susan Davidson *Interviewing Sex Crime Victims: Getting It Right!"* 2nd ed. San Clemente CA LawTech Publishing 2002. ISBN 1-930466-29-3. A step-by-step formula for interviewing sex crime victims, particularly children. Forward by John Walsh, the host of *America's Most Wanted*.

Chapter 10

Documenting Death Investigations

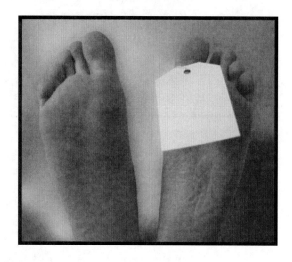

CHAPTER OVERVIEW

This chapter is entitled "Documenting Death Investigations" rather than "Homicide Investigations" because the cause of death is not always immediately known. Documenting a death scene uses the documentation components we previously covered; note-taking, photography, sketching and report writing. This chapter uses the National Institute of Justice's (NIJ) "Death Investigation: A Guide for the Scene Investigator". This guide introduces steps for documenting the decedents profile information. Keep the previous elements and check lists in mind when you read the guide.

OBJECTIVES

1. Identify the roles of those involved in a death scene investigation.
2. Outline steps for proper death scene investigations.
3. Explain the importance of ensuring these proper steps are taken.

The NIJ guide is the product of the National Medicolegal Review Panel, a multi-disciplinary group of nationally recognized experts from the medical, forensic and legal professions.

Jeanne M. Adkins, former member of the Colorado State Legislature, said in the introduction of the Guide:

> "Few things in our democracy are as important as ensuring that citizens have confidence in their institutions in a crisis. For many individuals the death of a loved one is just such a crisis. Ensuring that the proper steps and procedures are taken at the scene of that death to reassure family members that the death was a natural one, a suicide, or a homicide is a key element in maintaining citizen confidence in local officials.
>
> How local death investigators do their job is crucial to family members who are mourning a loss today and who may be seeking justice tomorrow. Most of us cringe at the idea of death investigations where important steps were omitted that might have led to arrests and ultimately convictions in those deaths. Justice denied breeds contempt for the institutions created to ensure that justice is done."

A BRIEF GLOSSARY

1. **Adipocere:** A light brownish, soft, greasy or waxy-like substance that muscle tissue and fat sometimes turn into due to decomposition. It can occur when a body has been submerged in water or buried in a damp place.

2. **Livor mortis:** The black or blue skin discoloration of a corpse.

3. **Petechiae:** Small, red spots on the skin.

4. **Rigor mortis:** Stiffness or rigidity of the muscles that develops approximately 4 to 10 hours after death. Rigor mortis can last up to 3 or 4 days.

5. **Tardieu spots:** Purplish blue patches in the skin or mucous membranes caused by effusion of blood due to strangulation or asphyxiation. Also known as Tardieu ecchymoses. Named after France physician Auguste Tardieu (1818-1879).

TYPES OF DEATH INVESTIGATIONS

Death can result from an accident, murder, suicide or natural causes. A person can die from a variety of means such as:

1. Plane, train, automobile, or boat crashes

2. SIDS (Sudden Infant Death Syndrome)

3. Electrocution

4. Drowning

5. Strangulation

6. Hanging

7. Fire

8. Freezing

9. Poisoning / Drug overdose

10. Asphyxiation

11. Falling

12. Stabbing

13. Shooting

14. Shock / Trauma

15. Bleeding

16. Disease

The point is, there are numerous means of death and the cause, either murder, suicide, natural or accident, will not always be apparent. Something may look like a natural death or accident and later may be determined to be a homicide. You just don't always know. Assume the worst and document appropriately because you only get one opportunity at the crime scene. How would you like to testify at a murder trial in front of a jury and the victim's family that you were "sure" it was suicide so you only took a couple photos and didn't even make a sketch?

Wayne Moorehead, Forensic Scientist and Educator
BS in Criminalistics UC Berkeley
MS in Criminalistics CSULA
Fellow of the American Board of Criminalistics
(F-ABC)
for4n6@yahoo.com [Consultant/Instructor]

Article 10.1 Documentation - the Difference Between Suicide and Homicide

A woman was found shot to death in the hallway of her home. Her boyfriend stated that he was trying to prevent her from committing suicide. His story was that she was standing with the firearm in the bathroom about ready to shoot herself. He attempted to prevent her from completing the act by attempting to wrestle the handgun away from her when the firearm went off accidentally.

Good photo documentation at the scene and notes made at the autopsy, permitted a more realistic assessment of the events of the crime scene.

The woman was shot with a .357 Magnum revolver in the left shoulder in an angle downward and to the right, next to the collarbone near the neck. A gaping wound was noted. No stippling or tattooing was noted around the wound with faint sooting at the margins and some powder noted in the wound tract. Sooting marks were noted on portions of both of her hands at autopsy.

In the bathroom, there was high velocity blood spatter on the wall to her left and spatter against the side of the bathtub and at least one pool of blood on the floor near the spatter on the tub with apparent blood wipe/contacts on one wall and the doorjamb in the bathroom. The blood wipe/contacts and apparent low velocity blood spatter continued down the hallway and ended at the victim.

Because of the documentation of the spatter at the scene, the evidence led to an interpretation. The woman was shot while kneeling as her boyfriend stood to the side and slightly behind her. After shooting her, he gave her no assistance. The sooting on her hands was consistent with her hands being near or on the firearm near the cylinder gap – perhaps trying to move the gun away from her and not on the trigger. The high velocity blood spatter on the wall was sufficiently high that she had to be kneeling at the time of the injury. The spatter on the tub and the blood pool nearby were consistent with her kneeling on the floor at a distance far enough from the tub that she could fall forward after being shot and still not hit her head on the tub. Both of these distances led to the same spot in the bathroom. Blood was pouring from the wound as she lay momentarily in a near horizontal position face down. She then got up, attempted to stem the flow of blood, having blood on her hands, touched one wall for support, stepped forward touching the doorjamb to the bathroom for more support and began to stagger down the hallway, using the wall for balance and support until she finally collapsed several feet down the hallway.

DEATH INVESTIGATION: A GUIDE FOR THE SCENE INVESTIGATOR

Our intent is not to beat a dead horse, but we do want to stress the key steps in crime scene processing and documentation. The outline from the National Institute of Justice Death Investigation Guide serves as a refresher to the steps we covered earlier. It also introduces new elements relevant to the documentation of death scene and investigation documentation after the scene.

Death Scene Checklist

Arriving at the Scene

- Introduce and identify self and role
- Exercise scene safety
- Confirm or pronounce death
- Participate in scene briefing (with attending agency representatives)
- Conduct scene "walk through"
- Establish chain of custody
- Follow Laws (related to the collection of evidence)

Documenting and Evaluating the Scene

- Photograph scene
- Develop descriptive documentation of the scene
- Establish probable location of injury or illness
- Collect, inventory, and safeguard property and evidence
- Interview witness(es) at the scene

Documenting and Evaluating the Body

- Photograph the body
- Conduct external body examination (superficial)
- Preserve evidence (on body)
- Establish decedent identification
- Document post mortem changes
- Participate in scene debriefing
- Determine notification procedures (next of kin)
- Ensure security of remains

Establishing and Recording Decedent Profile Information

- Document the discovery history
- Determine terminal episode history
- Document decedent medical history
- Document decedent mental health history
- Document social history

Completing the Scene Investigation

- Maintain jurisdiction over the body
- Release jurisdiction of the body
- Perform exit procedures

ARRIVING AT THE SCENE

Introduce and Identify Self and Role

- Identify and document the identity of the first essential official(s) to the scene (first "professional" arrival at the scene for investigative follow-up) to ascertain if any artifacts or contamination may have been introduced to the death scene.
- Confirm or Pronounce Death. Identify and document the individual who made the official determination of death, including the date and time of determination.

- Conduct Scene "Walk Through". Document and photograph fragile evidence immediately and collect if appropriate.
- Establish Chain of Custody.
  - Document location of the scene and time of arrival of the death investigator at the scene.
  - Identify, secure, and preserve evidence with proper containers, labels, and preservatives.
  - Document the collection of evidence by recording its location at the scene, time of collection, and time and location of disposition.
  - Develop personnel lists, witness lists, and documentation of times of arrival and departure of personnel.

DOCUMENTING AND EVALUATING THE SCENE

- Photograph Scene. Photograph the body before it is moved. If evidence has been moved prior to photographing, it should be noted in the report, but the body or other evidence should not be reintroduced into the scene in order to take photographs. Follow the photography protocol from the photography and assault chapters.
- Develop Descriptive Documentation of the Scene. After photographic documentation of the scene and prior to removal of the body or other evidence, the investigator should:

  - Diagram/describe in writing items of evidence and their relationship to the body with necessary measurements. Follow the protocol from the sketching chapter.
  - Describe and document, with necessary measurements, blood and body fluid evidence including volume, patterns, spatters, and other characteristics.
- Establish Probable Location of Injury or Illness. The location where the decedent is found may not be the actual location where the injury/illness that contributed to the death occurred. It is imperative that the investigator attempt to determine the locations of any and all injury(ies)/illness(es) that may have contributed to the death. Physical evidence at any and all locations may be pertinent in establishing the cause, manner, and circumstances of death.

  - Document location where death was confirmed.
  - Determine and document location from which decedent was transported and how body was transported to scene.

- Identify and record discrepancies in rigor mortis, liver mortis, and body temperature.

- Check body, clothing, and scene for consistency/inconsistency of trace evidence and indicate location where artifacts are found.
- Check for drag marks (on body and ground).
- Establish post-injury activity.
- Obtain dispatch (e.g., police, ambulance) record(s).
- Interview family members and associates as needed.
- Collect, Inventory, and Safeguard Property and Evidence. The decedent's valuables/property must be safeguarded to ensure proper processing and eventual return to next of kin. Evidence on or near the body must be safeguarded to ensure its availability for further evaluation. Personal property and evidence are important items at a death investigation. Evidence must be safeguarded to ensure its availability if needed for future evaluation and litigation. Personal property must be safeguarded to ensure its eventual distribution to appropriate agencies or individuals and to reduce the likelihood that the investigator will be accused of stealing property.
  - Inventory, collect, and safeguard illicit drugs and paraphernalia at scene and/or office.
  - Inventory, collect, and safeguard prescription medication at scene and/or office.
  - Inventory, collect, and safeguard over-the-counter medications at scene and/or office.
  - Inventory, collect, and safeguard money at scene and at office.
  - Inventory, collect, and safeguard personal valuables/property at scene and at office.
- Interview Witness(es) at the Scene. The documented comments of witnesses at the scene allow the investigator to obtain primary source data regarding discovery of body, witness corroboration, and terminal history. The documented interview provides essential information for the investigative process. The final report must document witness' identity and must include a summary of witness' statements, corroboration with other witnesses, and the circumstances of discovery of the death. This documentation must exist as a permanent record to establish a chain of events.

– Collect all available identifying data on witnesses (e.g., full name, address, DOB, work and home telephone numbers, etc.).

 – Establish witness' relationship/association to the deceased.

 – Establish the basis of witness' knowledge (how does witness have knowledge of the death?).

 – Obtain information from each witness.

– Note discrepancies from the scene briefing (challenge, explain, verify statements).

– Tape statements where such equipment is available and retain them.

Don R. Howell, Retired Detective
Huntington Beach, CA.
B. S. California State University, Los Angeles
30 years Law Enforcement Experience
Author of *Interviewing Sex Crime Victims*,
Lawtech Publishing Company Ltd.

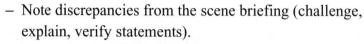
Article 10.2 A Special Investigation

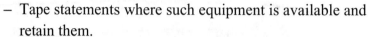

A LONG TIME COMING

Thirty years earlier, LAPD had worked the case 24/7 for over a year. Yet it went unsolved, the seemingly random murder; the teenage daughter of a prominent Judge, killed in her own bed in the middle of the day, in a "safe" neighborhood. The news media had a field day with the story. All leads were dead ends; all evidence went nowhere. The only remaining possibility was a single fingerprint. They spent 30 years trying to identify the owner of the print. All family members, neighbors, gardeners had been eliminated.

Finally, a "hit" on the print. The suspect was traced to my city, where he had lived, quietly, for many years. The plan was to do a "knock and talk" at the suspect's home. Approach him in a low-key manner and hope that he'll make some admission to the crime, or perhaps better yet, deny ever being at the scene. If he didn't want to talk, a search warrant had already been signed and he would be arrested. A division commander was on scene with a press release in hand, ready to honor the tenacity of his department.

The day had come; the surveillance teams followed his wife away from the home and for the 20 miles to her work. Another team followed the stepson to school. Now the detective, wired for sound to record any spontaneous statement, went to the door. The plan was set into motion; he opened the door and invited everyone inside. The conversation went as follows.

"We're investigating a case from a long time ago; the murder of a young girl." The detective said.

"Do you mean the judge's daughter?"

"Yes", was the detective's reply.

"Did you ever solve it?" "Ya' know, I was visiting the girl's neighbor when the older sister came running over, yelling and screaming that something was wrong at her house. So, I ran over there and found her on top of the bed, blood everywhere. I wanted to help, but I'm a plumber, not a doctor, so I called the police. When they arrived they kicked everyone out of the house, so I went home. No one ever called to talk to me about it, so I figured they didn't need me. Strange, you getting a hold of me so many years later."

His story checked out. He wasn't a suspect. How many thousands of hours of work would have been saved if someone would have written his name down, before "kicking him out".

DOCUMENTING AND EVALUATING THE BODY

- Photograph the Body. The photographic documentation of the body at the scene provides for documentation of the body position, identity, and appearance. The details of the body at the scene provide investigators with pertinent information of the terminal events.
  - Photograph the body and immediate scene (including the decedent as initially found).
  - Photograph the decedent's face.
  - Take additional photographs after removal of objects/items that interfere with photographic documentation of the decedent (e.g., body removed from car).
  - Photograph the decedent with and without measurements (as appropriate).
  - Photograph the surface beneath the body (after the body has been removed, as appropriate).

Note: Never clean a face, do not change a condition. Take multiple shots if possible.

- Conduct External Body Examination (Superficial). Depending on the agency in charge, investigators and crime scene techs may not be allowed to touch the body. Certain jurisdictions provide the coroner or medical examiners office with authority over the body. Conducting the external body examination provides the investigator with objective data regarding the single most important piece of evidence at the scene, the body. This documentation provides detailed information regarding the decedent's physical attributes, his/her relationship to the scene, and possible cause, manner, and circumstances of death. Thorough evaluation and documentation (photographic and written) of the deceased at the scene is essential to determine the depth and direction the investigation will take.
- If necessary, take additional photographs after removal of objects/items that interfere with photographic documentation of the decedent.
  - Photograph the decedent with and without measurements (as appropriate), including a photograph of the decedent's face.
  - Document the decedent's position with and without measurements (as appropriate).
  - Document the decedent's physical characteristics.

- Document the presence or absence of clothing and personal effects.
- Document the presence or absence of any items/objects that may be relevant.
- Document the presence or absence of marks, scars, and tattoos.
- Document the presence or absence of injury/trauma, petechiae, etc.
- Document the presence of treatment or resuscitative efforts.

- Preserve Evidence (on Body). The photographic and written documentation of evidence on the body allows the investigator to obtain a permanent historical record of that evidence. To maintain chain of custody, evidence must be collected, preserved, and transported properly. In addition to all of the physical evidence visible on the body, blood and other body fluids present must be photographed and documented prior to collection and transport. Fragile evidence (that which can be easily contaminated, lost, or altered) must also be collected and/or preserved to maintain chain of custody and to assist in determination of cause, manner, and circumstances of death. It is essential that evidence be collected, preserved, transported, and documented in an orderly and proper fashion to ensure the chain of custody and admissibility in a legal action. The preservation and documentation of the evidence on the body must be initiated by the investigator at the scene to prevent alterations or contamination.

  - Document blood/body fluid on the body (froth/purge, substances from orifices), location, and pattern before transporting.

- Establish Decedent Identification. The establishment or confirmation of the decedent's identity is paramount to the death investigation. Proper identification allows notification of next of kin, settlement of estates, resolution of criminal and civil litigation, and the proper completion of the death certificate. To establish identity, the investigator should document use of:

  - Direct visual or photographic identification of the decedent if visually recognizable.

- Document Post Mortem Changes. The documenting of post mortem changes to the body assists the investigator in explaining body appearance in the interval following death. Inconsistencies between post mortem changes and body location may indicate movement of body and validate or invalidate witness statements. In addition, post mortem changes to the body, when correlated with circumstantial information, can assist the investigators in estimating the approximate time of death. The investigator shall document all post mortem changes relative to the decedent and the environment. Documentation of post mortem changes in every report is essential to determine an accurate cause and manner of death, provide information as to the time of death, corroborate witness statements, and indicate that the body may have been moved after death. Upon arrival at the scene and prior to moving the body, the investigator should note the presence of each of the following in his/her report:

– Liver (color, location, blanchability, Tardieu spots) consistent/inconsistent with position of the body.

– Rigor (stage/intensity, location on the body, broken, inconsistent with the scene).

– Degree of decomposition (putrefaction, adipocere, mummification, skeletonization, as appropriate).

– Insect and animal activity.

– Scene temperature (document method used and time estimated).

– Description of body temperature (e.g., warm, cold, frozen) or measurement of body temperature (document method used and time of measurement).

• Determine Notification Procedures (Next of Kin). The investigator is responsible for ensuring that the next of kin is identified, located, and notified in a timely manner. The time and method of notification should be documented. Failure to locate next of kin and efforts to do so should be a matter of record. This ensures that every reasonable effort has been made to contact the family.

• Ensure Security of Remains. Ensuring security of the body requires the investigator to supervise the labeling, packaging, and removal of the remains. An appropriate identification tag is placed on the body to preclude misidentification upon receipt at the examining agency. This function also includes safeguarding all potential physical evidence and/or property and clothing that remain on the body. Prior to leaving the scene, the investigator should:

- Ensure that the body is protected from further trauma or contamination (if not, document) and unauthorized removal of therapeutic and resuscitative equipment.
- Inventory and secure property, clothing, and personal effects that are on the body (remove in a controlled environment with witness present).
- Identify property and clothing to be retained as evidence (in a controlled environment).
- Place identification on the body and body bag.

ESTABLISHING AND RECORDING DECEDENT PROFILE INFORMATION

- Document the Discovery History. Establishing a decedent profile includes documenting a discovery history and circumstances surrounding the discovery. The basic profile will dictate subsequent levels of investigation, jurisdiction, and authority. The focus (breadth/depth) of further investigation is dependent on this information. The investigator shall document the discovery history, available witnesses, and apparent circumstances leading to death. The investigator must produce clear, concise, documented information concerning who discovered the body, what are the circumstances of discovery, where the discovery occurred, when the discovery was made, and how the discovery was made. For an investigator to correctly document the discovery history, he/she should:

- Establish and record person(s) who discovered the body and when.

- Document the circumstances surrounding the discovery (who, what, where, when, how).

- Determine Terminal Episode History. Pre-terminal circumstances play a significant role in determining cause and manner of death. Obtaining records of pre-terminal circumstances and medical history distinguishes medical treatment from trauma. Documentation of medical intervention and/or procurement of ante mortem specimens help to establish the decedent's condition prior to death. The investigator shall document known circumstances and medical intervention preceding death. In order for the investigator to determine terminal episode history, he/she should:

- Document when, where, how, and by whom decedent was last known to be alive.
- Document the incidents prior to the death.
- Document complaints/symptoms prior to the death.
- Document and review complete EMS records (including the initial electrocardiogram).
- Obtain relevant medical records (copies).
- Obtain relevant ante mortem specimens.

• Document Decedent Medical History. The majority of deaths referred to the medical examiner/coroner are natural deaths. Establishing the decedent's medical history helps to focus the investigation. Documenting the decedent's medical signs or symptoms prior to death determines the need for subsequent examinations. The relationship between disease and injury may play a role in the cause, manner, and circumstances of death. Through interviews and review of the written records, the investigator should:

• Document medical history, including medications taken, alcohol and drug use, and family medical history from family members and witnesses.

• Document information from treating physicians and/or hospitals to confirm history and treatment.

• Document physical characteristics and traits (e.g., left-/right-handedness, missing appendages, tattoos, etc.).

• Document Decedent Mental Health History. The decedent's mental health history can provide insight into the behavior/state of mind of the individual. That insight may produce clues that will aid in establishing the cause, manner, and circumstances of the death. Knowledge of the mental health history allows the investigator to evaluate properly the decedent's state of mind and contributes to the determination of cause, manner, and circumstances of death

- Document the decedent's mental health history, including hospitalizations and medications.
- Document the history of suicidal ideations, gestures, and/or attempts.
- Document mental health professionals (e.g., psychiatrists, psychologists, counselors, etc.) who treated the decedent.

- Document Social History. Information from sources familiar with the decedent pertaining to the decedent's social history assists in determining cause, manner, and circumstances of death.
  - Document marital/domestic history.
  - Document family history (similar deaths, significant dates).
  - Document sexual history.
  - Document employment history.
  - Document financial history.
  - Document daily routines, habits, and activities.
  - Document relationships, friends, and associates.
  - Document religious, ethnic, or other pertinent information (e.g., religious objection to autopsy).
  - Document educational background.
  - Document criminal history.

COMPLETING THE SCENE INVESTIGATION

- Maintain Jurisdiction Over the Body. By providing documented secure transportation of the body from the scene to an authorized receiving facility, the investigator maintains jurisdiction and protects chain of custody of the body.
  - Arrange for, and document, secure transportation of the body to a medical or autopsy facility for further examination or storage.
  - Coordinate and document procedures to be performed when the body is received at the facility.
- Release Jurisdiction of the Body. The investigator releases jurisdiction only after determining who will sign the death certificate; documenting the date, time, and location of death; collecting appropriate specimens; and releasing the body to the funeral director or other authorized receiving agent.
- Perform Exit Procedures. Conducting a scene "walk through" upon exit ensures that all evidence has been collected, that materials are not inadvertently left behind, and that any dangerous materials or conditions have been reported to the proper entities.
  - Identify, inventory, and remove all evidence collected at the scene.
  - Report and document any dangerous materials or conditions.

SUMMARY

It should be noted that all crimes are different and this material is only a guide. When determining how to handle and document a death scene, it is important to use good judgment and work in conjunction with other scene members. The materials and information you collect at the scene and during follow up investigations should all be noted in formal reports and included in the case file.

DISCUSSION QUESTIONS

1. If evidence has been moved prior to photography what should you do?
2. Why is it essential that evidence be collected, preserved, transported, and documented in an orderly and proper fashion?

ADDITIONAL READING

Death Investigation: A Guide for the Scene Investigator
http://www.ncjrs.org/pdffiles/167568.pdf

Figure 10.1 Death Investigation: A Guide for the Scene Investigator

The following is a commentary by Bruce H. Hanley, Esq., Partner, Hanley & Dejoras, P.A., Minneapolis, Minnesota:

The development of Death Investigation: A Guide for the Scene Investigator will be of great benefit to all citizens. The guidelines will help to promote consistency, accuracy, predictability, and reliability in death-scene investigations. As a criminal defense lawyer, it is a chief concern that a person is not wrongfully accused of having participated in a homicide. Complete, thorough, and careful death-scene investigations can lead to greater faith in the system by family and friends of those whose deaths may have been caused by homicide, suicide, accident, or natural causes. Elimination of unanswered questions, confusion, sloppiness, and the lack of attention to detail all can contribute to the genuine acceptance that the cause of death has been properly determined. Moreover, in the case of homicide, all can have a strong belief in the accuracy of the identification of the perpetrator. The guidelines will assist the actual investigators in following the proper protocol and consistently obtaining all available evidence to show that the death was the result of either unlawful or lawful activity. Proper adherence to the guidelines, coupled with proper training to implement the guidelines, will serve to satisfy finders of fact in criminal cases that the State has presented accurate, reliable, and trustworthy evidence. Additionally, it will serve to defuse attacks by defense counsel on the investigative methods and techniques, chain of custody, and the reliability of any testing that may have been conducted during the course of the investigation. It may also serve to prevent innocent people from being accused of criminal activity when, in fact, a crime was not committed, or the person suspected was not involved. The truth is the outcome sought, and the guidelines will assist the system in obtaining the truth. In a criminal investigation, when the government follows the rules and properly conducts its investigation, it will win most of the time. When it does not follow the rules or properly conduct its investigation, it should lose.

Chapter 11

Computer Crime

CHAPTER OVERVIEW

Electronic data can include any record, file, source code, program, and computer manufacturer specifications. Electronic evidence will include such things as word processing documents, personnel records, financial information, email, computer operation logs and voice mail transcriptions, whether or not they are ever printed.

Did you know that in many cases "deleted" evidence that is needed to make or break a case is still on the hard drive of suspect computers? This information cannot be ignored and can be retrieved even if it has been tampered with, deleted or damaged. Magnetic recordings (audiotape, videotape, or computer disks) can be examined for authentication, enhancement, voice identification, etc.).

There are many types of computer crimes. Embezzlement, theft of computer programs, telecommunications fraud, computer hacking, sabotage, and terrorism are only a few of types of crime which can be, and are daily being, committed using computers.

OBJECTIVES

At the end of this chapter, you will be able to:

1. Explain the use of computers in the commission of crimes.
2. Understand the proper procedures and methods for preserving computer information as evidence.

AUTHORITY TO USE COMPUTER FILES AS EVIDENCE

Courts have long recognized that deleted computer files are discoverable. New methods of investigation are allowing investigators to look deep into hard drives to obtain valuable information. Much of the important and vital information that can be obtained by investigators is invisible and unknown to the computer owner or operator.

Much of this hidden information is generated by the computer's operating system during normal use. Because the computer generates this information and not the user, experts generally refer to this data as "OS artifacts".

Obviously, "OS artifacts" have significant evidentiary value and clearly qualify as "writings" or "recordings" under Federal Rule of Evidence 1001. When presenting evidence in court, an "original" of a record is the record itself, which can pose a problem regarding computer printouts in the face of the "best evidence rule." The ***best evidence rule*** simply precludes admissibility of anything but an original document. Recognizing the impracticality of this rule when applied to computer files, many states and the Federal government have adopted rules that define computer printouts as original, provided that they have been shown to accurately reflect the information in the computer files. At least one court has taken the view that printouts of records stored in computer files are admissible because they are "unavailable and useless except by means of the printout sheets." ***Kind v. State ex. rel. Murdock Acceptance Corp.***, 222 So.2d 393, 398 (Miss. 1969).

However, agents and prosecutors occasionally continue to express concern that a mere printout of a computer-stored electronic file may not be an "original" for the purpose of the best evidence rule. After all, the original file is merely a collection of 0's and 1's. In contrast, the printout is the result of manipulating the file through a complicated series of electronic and mechanical processes.

Fortunately, the Federal Rules of Evidence have expressly addressed this concern. The Federal Rules state:

> *[i]f data are stored in a computer or similar device, any printout or other output readable by sight, shown to reflect the data accurately, is an "original". Federal Rule of Evidence 1001(3)*

Thus, an accurate printout of computer data always satisfies the best evidence rule. ***Doe v. United States***, 805 F. Supp. 1513, 1517 (D. Hawaii. 1992).

WHERE COMPUTER EVIDENCE HIDES

Several litigation matters have been significantly impacted by the recovery of OS artifacts by computer investigators. For example, in the case of the **United States v. Tucker**, 150 F. Supp.2d 11263 (D. Utah 2001) the conviction was largely supported by the evidence found in the form of a deleted computer file. Litigators have become familiar with the concept of OS artifacts and their important potential as key evidence. It has been discovered that computer evidence can be retrieved from many different areas of the computer system. The cache file, the swap file, the spooler files are just a few of the locations where evidence may reside. Additionally, email attachments, folder entries and link files, and recycle bin files are areas where vast amounts of information or evidence can be found. An examination of each of these areas reveals important information.

Swap Files

The swap file is typically a large collector of data and one of the major areas reviewed by investigators. Swap files are located on the computer's hard disk and used as the virtual memory extension of the computer's RAM (random access memory). Swap files are used to manage memory and improve performance by "swapping out" less active open files to a hard disk until they are needed, thereby creating more space for active files.

Spooler Files

When documents are printed in Windows, the OS creates a "temporary" copy of the file being printed. This file is called an EMF (enhanced metafile). This temporary file is then sent to the printer allowing the printing to occur in the background while the user continues to work. Windows then deletes the EMF file. However, computer investigators routinely search for these files and can retrieve the "spooled" information as a deleted file.

Email Attachments

When files are transmitted over the Internet as e-mail attachments, a process similar to the printing process occurs. Windows creates a temporary encoded copy of the file being transmitted and stores it as a MIME (Multi-Purpose Internet Mail Extensions) file. MIME files can be recovered and any encryption present can be circumvented.

Folder Entries/File Links

Some computer operating systems will create a folder entry whenever the user moves or renames a file. These files contain information that the investigator can use to identify the user's activities, such as determining when a file was created, modified, moved or renamed.

Likewise, when a user accesses a particular file the operating system will create a "link file" which can give investigators information regarding which files have been accessed or changed. Any time a file is opened it is registered by the operating system and maintained by default until deleted. Oftentimes investigators are able to recover hundreds of these types of files easily from a hard drive.

For example, in the case United States v. Dean 138 F. Supp. 2d 207 (2001 D. Me) a defendant accused of possessing child pornography on various floppy disks denied ever accessing the illegal images. However, investigators were able to reveal several link files pointing to the exact floppy disk image files. The defendant was convicted by the use of this evidence.

Recycle Bin Info Files

The Windows operating system tracks files deleted by users by generating temporary INFO files that, when recovered by investigators tell a complete history of the user's file deletion activity. This info can be scattered throughout a computer's hard drive and is normally hidden. Even though files have been deleted from the Recycle Bin, investigation can reveal such things as when files were deleted and the sequence of the deletion.

INFO files are only created when files are deleted by the user and not automatically by the operating system The presence of an INFO file indicates that the user knowingly and voluntarily deleted a file.

These are only a few of the ways in which investigators can retrieve information. Other files, such as log files, event files, index buffers, registry entries, Internet history files, and bitmap files are other common areas for evidence searching.

COMPUTER EVIDENCE PROCESSING GUIDELINES

Computer evidence is fragile. The potential to destroy programs and data is high. Even the normal use of a computer can destroy evidence that might be hiding in unallocated spaces. Every case is different and flexibility on the part of the investigator is important. While there may be no "strict" rules that must be followed regarding the processing of computer evidence, consistency is essential and documenting the process is critical. The computer evidence must be preserved and protected. Therefore, it is important that things are done correctly as soon as a computer incident is identified. Following are some guidelines to assist with the proper collection and preservation of the computer and its evidentiary content.

Don't Turn On or Operate the Computer If It is Off

Computers should not be turned on until it is backed up using bit stream backup software. If the computer is turned on, the swap files can be overwritten or deleted files can be destroyed.

Be Careful To Use Only Computer Experts

Preserving computer evidence is tricky at best. Seek the assistance of a computer specialist who has been trained in computer evidence processing procedures. Do this BEFORE you turn on the computer.

Shut Down The Computer If It is On

Shutting down the computer usually involves pulling the plug or using relevant commands required by the system. Generally, time is very important and computers should be shut down as quickly as possible. Prior to shutdown, pictures should be taken of the screen image if possible. Always consider that possible destructive processes may be operating in the background that can erase memory. Passwords can kick in at any time and complicate the shutdown of the computer. Use caution when disconnecting the system.

Document the Hardware Configuration of the System

Assuming that the computer will be moved to a secure location where a proper chain of custody can be maintained and evidence processing can begin, pictures should be taken of the computer from all angles to document what components may be connected to the computer and how those components are connected. Wiring to the wall should also be photographed. Labeling each wire is as important as photographing it. Once at a location, labeling will allow the system to easily be restored to its original condition.

Transport the Computer Safely and Securely

Do not leave the seized computer unattended unless it is locked in a secure location. It is imperative that the computer be treated and preserved with the same professionalism and caution that any other evidence would be. Using the seized computer can cause critical evidence to be destroyed and the chain of custody voided.

Make Bit Stream Backups of Hard Disks and Floppy Disks

The seized computer should not be operated and computer evidence should not be processed until bit stream backups have been made of all hard drives and floppy disks. Because computer data is vitally important and can be fragile and easily altered or destroyed, once the backups are complete, the evidence processing tasks should be performed on the backup copies and never on the original computer. The original evidence should be left untouched unless there is some compelling reason not to do so.

Mathematically Authenticate Data on All Storage Drives

Because it may be necessary for an investigator to prove that evidence was not altered after the computer was seized, military and law enforcement agencies use a 32-bit mathematical process to do the authentication process. This 32-bit process has been in place since 1989 and can validate accuracy to approximately one in 4.3 billion. However, as progress moves forward and computers become more powerful these processes will be strengthened to run at a 128-bit level.

Document The System Date and Time

Manually documenting the date and time that a system is seized and taken into evidence is extremely important because dates and times associated with computer files can be critically important from an evidence standpoint. If the computer's system clock is incorrect or has not changed with daylight saving time, then file time stamps will also reflect the wrong time.

Make a List of Key Search Words

Because computer hard drives are usually voluminous, it becomes a very difficult task for an investigator to manually view and evaluate every file. The investigator should therefore, enlist the help of others involved in the case in order to compile a list of common words pertaining to the case. These key words can then be used to search the hard drives for relevant information or evidence.

Document File Names, Dates, Times

It is important to document file names, creation dates, and last modified dates and times. All "erased" files should be cataloged as well. Documenting this type of evidence can establish a pattern for simply allowing investigators to follow the day-to-day activities of the user.

Identify File, Program and Storage Anomalies

Encrypted, compressed and graphic files store data in binary format. Because of this, manual evaluation of these files is often required. The contents of these files should always be viewed and evaluated for potential evidence.

Reviewing the partitioning on a seized hard disk is also important. The potential for hidden partitions exists and these hidden partitions may contain the evidence that concludes the case.

Evaluate Program Functionality

Running programs on the computer to learn their purpose can be a useful tool for collecting evidence. However, caution should be taken that destructive processes have not been set using "hot keys". If this happens and destructive processes can be tied to relevant evidence, this information can be used to prove willfulness on the part of the criminal.

Retain Copies of Software

Because computer software is routinely updated, and can change the look and feel of documents, copies of software used on the seized computer should also be copied and retained with any extracted evidence. This will eliminate future confusion and questions regarding the software, or versions of software. Documenting all of the software used, including the version numbers of the programs is important. Screen prints of the operating software will help document the version of the software and how it is used.

Make sure that the software used for evidence processing is licensed. Investigators do not want to have to answer in court as to why "unlicensed" copies of software, which is against the law, were used.

Document Findings

As always, it is critically important to document your findings as issues are identified and evidence is found. Document information about the relevant system and/or network. Include written log records made by any person who has had access to the seized computer, any other auditing information produced by tools, full backups, partial backups, screen shots, videotapes and photographs.

Documentation should include responses to the entire standard, who, what, where, when, why and how questions. This information can be recorded on a specific log or data sheet for ready reviewing. Form 11.1 below is an example of a data sheet, which could be used each time the computer is accessed.

Form 11.1 Computer Access Data Sheet

Case Number: _____

Person Accessing Item: _____

Date/Time of Access: _____

Purpose for Access: _____

_____

Action Taken: _____

_____

Data collected:_____

_____

_____

_____

Date/Time Access Terminated: _____

SURROUNDING EQUIPMENT

Seizing a computer is not enough. Investigators must be aware of the surrounding equipment as well. This includes, peripherals, modems, the external components, the mouse pad and even the "sticky notes" which may be attached to the computer screen or laying on the desk. All of these items may contain significant information or evidence.

Care should be taken to protect the computer and its components from outside interference and possible destruction. These outside interferences can include, but are not limited to, radios of cars in the area, microwaves, high-pitched frequency sounds, etc.

TRACKING HACKERS

"The modern thief can steal more with a computer than with a gun. Tomorrow's terrorist may be able to do more damage with a keyboard than with a bomb." 1 Computer hackers receive notoriety for breaking into computer sites and doing damage. Other hackers, however, cause even greater damage and try to avoid notice.

Computer websites are set up that teach users to be hackers and provide the potential hackers with advice. Hackers advise system administrators to download and install patches so that the systems will no longer be vulnerable, but then use these systems to launch their attacks.

Most computer operators do not share information or contact authorities when hackers victimize them. Users instead prefer to fix the damage and take action to try to prevent the hackers from gaining future access.

In an effort to minimize or stop computer hacking, an investigator can use subpoenas to obtain subscriber information from an Internet Service Provider, including the name, address, local and long distance telephone records. [18 U.S.C § 2703 (c)(1)(C)] This information can then be used to track the activities of the hacker.

FIGHTING CYBERCRIME

Authorities and experts have profiled computer criminals as having some or all of the following characteristics:
- 15-45 years of age
- Male
- Wide range of computer expertise
- No criminal record
- Bright, motivated and loves a technical challenge
- Deviates little from accepted norms of society
- Holds a position of trust within a company with easy access to computers
- Almost always targets his activities toward government or business
- Fears exposure
- Works alone
- Has an "always on guard" personality

- Justifies his actions as "just a game"

Legislation is being considered and/or recommended for fighting computer offenses. Many governments are looking at serious penalties for the following crimes:

- Unauthorized access to information
- Illegal interception of information
- Interference/destruction/modification or concealment of data
- Computer counterfeiting
- Computer swindle
- Distribution of child pornography
- Copyright infringements
- Spamming or distributing unwanted information

Proper control of these issues, and others, has become a matter of local, federal and national security.

SUMMARY

Preserving electronic data is not merely a "surface" issue. Investigators must look deep into computer hard drives to obtain valuable information. Important and vital information can be obtained by investigators even though it is invisible and/or unknown to the computer owner or operator. Much of what we know today is not found in the pages of books but in the memories of computers. More and more of what we do today is not stored on paper, but in computers. New technologies will invariably replace older ones, and therefore methods of preservation and documentation of those objects of technology cannot be minimized. Investigation in these areas must be exact to preserve issues such as legal admissibility.

DISCUSSION QUESTIONS

1. What penalties would you establish for someone convicted of computer crime?

2. List and discuss the proper manner of preserving computer evidence.

Chapter 12

Identity Theft

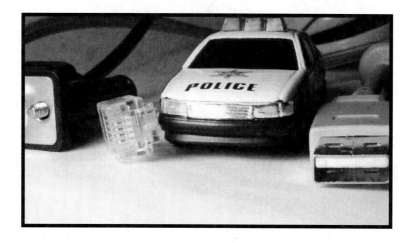

CHAPTER OVERVIEW

"But he that filches from me my good name/robs me of that which not enriches him/ and makes me poor indeed."

Shakespeare, Othello, act iii. Sc. 3

Little did Shakespeare know that his words would have so much meaning in the 21st century. Thieves steal personal information – social security numbers, driver's license numbers, credit card numbers. They open accounts, run up charges, travel, work, and in some cases even get arrested using the stolen information.

OBJECTIVES

At the end of this chapter, you will be able to:
1. Understand the concepts of identity theft and identity fraud.
2. Explain the types of identity theft and fraud.

In an effort to curb the activity of those who would steal and use the identity of another, Congress passed the Identity Theft and Assumption Deterrence Act in 1998 declaring identity theft a federal crime. This offense, in most circumstances, is punishable by a maximum of 15 years imprisonment, a fine, and criminal forfeiture of any personal property used or intended to be used to commit the offense.

In addition, these offenses may also involve violations of many state and Federal statutes that can result in penalties of up to 30 years imprisonment, additional fines and criminal forfeiture.

So then, given these deterrents, why are identity theft and fraud increasing?

CRIME

According to the FBI, identity theft is the fastest-growing white-collar crime in America.

According to the Federal Trade Commission, 42% of all identity thefts come from credit card fraud. Phone and utility fraud is the second most common at 22%, followed closely by bank fraud.

According to the FBI, there are 900,000 new victims of identity theft and/or fraud each year.

According to U. S. Postal Inspectors, more than 1,000 people a week nationwide have their identities stolen.

Depending upon whom you ask, these statistics can very greatly; however, all will agree that ***identity theft***, or more appropriately titled ***identity fraud*** is increasing at alarming rates. But, exactly what is identity theft/fraud.

Identity theft is a crime. Identity theft/identity fraud are synonymous terms used to refer to all types of crime in which someone wrongfully obtains and uses another person's personal data in a way that involves fraud or deception, typically for economic gain.

Many people do not realize how easy it is for criminals to obtain personal data, and once obtained, the information can and will be used to commit any number of types of fraud.

TYPES

Financial Fraud

This type of identity theft includes, but is in no way limited to, the stealing of bank account information, credit card information, mail fraud, computer theft, telephone information and numbers, and home and vehicle information.

Bank Fraud

Thieves can obtain copies of your bank statements simply by rummaging through trash left at the side of the curb. Using that information, they can obtain checks, and wipe out checking and savings accounts. They can get loans, buy cars, obtain insurance and, essentially, do all the things you wish you could afford to do.

Credit Card Fraud

Credit card theft is the most simple and most common use of identity theft. Your credit card information can be obtained in a variety of ways. Have you ever eaten at a restaurant and paid for your dinner with a credit card. Many receipts have your credit card number and expiration date printed right on the receipt for anyone to see. Once you sign it, your signature is also available to the "would-be-thief." With this information, the thief can begin making purchases either by phone or on the Internet using your card number.

Mail Fraud

Thieves are experts at obtaining information from your mailbox. Simply paying your credit card bill by writing the check and putting it into an "open" or unlocked mailbox for your mail carrier to pick up can give the "would-be-thief" information regarding your bank account, credit card account number, address, and telephone number. Thieves will obtain valuable information from trashcans and dumpsters. Shred documents before discarding them. Think about what you throw away.

Criminal Activities

This type of fraud will include taking your identity in order to commit a crime, enter a foreign country, get special licenses or permits, and commit acts of terrorism. The person whose identity has been stolen could even be arrested, charged with a crime and imprisoned instead of the thief.

VICTIM

Anyone can become a victim of identity theft. Your personal information can be found in many different places. For example, it can be:

- Retrieved from trash cans and dumpsters, also known as "dumpster diving"
- Memorized or copied by sales clerks and waiters/waitresses
- Removed from your mailbox
- Stolen from your employer's files
- Copied from medical records
- Taken from financial lender's files
- Purchased (or obtained for free) from online companies and databases
- Collected from websites
- Stolen by computer hackers
- Gathered from computer "chat" rooms
- Obtained from public records such as real estate transactions, vehicle information and licensing agencies
- Found by reading newspapers and telephone books

The scariest of all is that, according to the Federal Trade Commission, in 2000, 19% of all victims who reported identity theft had a personal relationship with the thief and 10% of those were family members.

The Department of Justice recommends some basic steps that can be taken to reduce or minimize the risk of becoming a victim of identity theft or fraud. For example, the most basic of the steps is to simply remember the work "**SCAM**".

"**S**" Be *stingy* about giving out your personal information to others unless you have a reason to trust them completely. Take a "need to know" approach to your personal data and don't give information over the telephone to anyone you have not called.

"**C**" *Check* your financial information regularly, and look for what should be there and what shouldn't. If you have bank or credit card accounts, make sure you are receiving monthly statements. If anything is there that shouldn't be or if something is missing that should be there, contact the financial institution immediately.

"**A**" *Ask* periodically for a copy of your credit report. Your credit report should list all bank and financial accounts under your name, and will provide other indications of whether someone has wrongfully opened or used any accounts in your name.

"**M**" *Maintain* careful records of your banking and financial transactions. Even though financial institutions may be required to keep copies of transactions for five years, you should retain your own.

REPORTING AND DOCUMENTING

Documenting identity theft is more importantly done by the victim than by law enforcement agencies and must be done quickly, with complete accuracy and must record even the smallest items. Victims of identity theft have found themselves involved in one or more of the following situations related to the reporting and documenting of the crime.

One of the biggest complaints from victims of identity theft is that law enforcement will not take a report. The bank, credit card company or business against which the fraud was committed is considered to be the "victim" instead of the individual whose identity was stolen and used to commit the fraud.

Many identity theft cross state lines. The credit card may have been stolen in Denver but the purchases were made in Utah. Who has jurisdiction to handle the crime?

With no police report to document the crime, victims have found it difficult to convince credit card companies and banks that they are not the person making the purchases or writing the checks.

The burden of proving innocence lies with the victim. Obtaining and disseminating the truth can be lengthy, complicated and expensive, although laws are changing to help establish and report the theft of one's identity, especially in those jurisdictions where "identity theft" has been declared to be a separate crime from the fraud.

Anyone who finds themselves a victim should use the following checklist to help minimize damage to their personal and financial reputations. When completing the steps of the checklist, care should be taken to record all conversations, including, but not limited to, dates, names, and phone numbers. A record should also be kept recording any and all time spent and expenses incurred as a result of the theft.

Form 12.1   Checklist For Identity Fraud Victims

CHECKLIST FOR IDENTITY FRAUD VICTIMS

- ❑ Complete the sample Identity Theft Complaint forms below if your complaint is about a company and the Identity Theft Affidavit for personal use.

- ❑ Contact the local office of the FBI and U.S. Secret Service to report the crime.

- ❑ Contact the Postal Inspection Service if you suspect that mail fraud is involved.

- ❑ Contact the Social Security Administration (1-800-269-0271) to report the theft.

- ❑ Contact the Internal Revenue Service (IRS) (1-800-829-9433) if you suspect that someone will use your tax identification information.

- ❑ Call the fraud units of the three principal credit-reporting agencies.

Form 12.1 Checklist For Identity Fraud Victims (Cont.)

Equifax

To Report Fraud or dispute information: (1-800-425-6285) or P.O. Box 740250, Atlanta, GA 30374

To order a copy of a credit report: (1-800-685-1111) or P.O. 740241, Atlanta, GA 30374

To opt out of pre-approved offers of credit and marketing lists: (1-800-353-0809) or P.O. Box 919, Allen, TX 75013

Experian (Formerly TRW)

To Report Fraud or dispute information: (1-888-397-3742) or P.O. Box 1017, Allen, TX 75013

To order a copy of a credit report: (1-888-397-3742) or P.O. 2104, Allen, TX. 75013

To opt out of pre-approved offers of credit and marketing lists: (1-800-353-0809) or P.O. Box 919, Allen, TX 75013

Trans Union

To Report Fraud or dispute information: (1-800-680-7289) or P.O. Box 6790, Allen, TX 92734

To order a copy of a credit report: (1-800-888-4213) or P.O. 390, Springfield, PA 19064

To opt out of pre-approved offers of credit and marketing lists: (1-800-680-7293) or P.O. Box 97328, Jackson, MS 39238

- ❏ Contact all telephone companies
- ❏ Contact all cellular phone companies
- ❏ Contact all financial institutions
  - Change ATM numbers and PIN numbers
- ❏ Contact all credit card companies
- ❏ Contact all check verification companies. For example:
  - CheckRite - 1-800-766-2748
  - ChexSystems - 1-800-428-9623
  - CrossCheck - 1-800-552-1900
  - Equifax - 1-800-437-5120
  - National Processing Co. (NPC) - 1-800-526-5380
  - SCAN - 1-800-262-7771
  - TeleCheck - 1-800-710-9898

Form 12.1 Checklist For Identity Fraud Victims (Cont.)

❏ Report the crime to all local law enforcement agencies, and make sure to obtain a copy of the report. Write to the passport office to alert them. This can be done online at www.travel.state.gov/passport_services.html

❏ Report the theft to the Driver's License Bureau

❏ Contact legal help if needed

❏ Contact a victim's support group if needed

❏ Don't give in – do not pay any bill or portion of any bill that is a result of fraud. Do not let anyone coerce you into paying these with any type of threats.

❏ Contact anyone else who may be able to help or may need to know about the theft.

❏ Complete the Complaint Form 12.2 below and file it with the Federal Trade Commission if your complaint involves a company. The FTC maintains a database of identity theft cases used by law enforcement agencies for investigations.

Form 12.2 Complaint Form

Top of Form

HOW DO WE REACH YOU?

First Name: _____

Last Name:_____

Age Range: _____

Street Address:_____

City: _____

State or Canadian Province:_____

Country:_____

Zip Code or Postal Code:_____

E-Mail Address:_____

Home Phone:( ) _____ - _____

Work Phone:( ) _____ - _____

Form 12.1 Complaint Form (Cont.)

TELL US YOUR COMPLAINT ABOUT A COMPANY...

Subject of Your Complaint:_____

_____

Name of Company You Are Complaining About: _____

_____

Street Address: _____

City: _____

State or Canadian Province: _____

Country: _____

Zip Code or Postal Code: _____

Company Web Site: _____

Company E-Mail Address: _____

Phone Number:( ) _____ - _____

How Did the Company Initially Contact You?:_____

_____

How Much Did the Company Ask You to Pay?:_____

HOW DO WE REACH YOU?

First Name: _____

Last Name:_____

Age Range: _____

Street Address:_____

City:_____

State or Canadian Province:_____

Country:_____

Zip Code or Postal Code:_____

E-Mail Address:_____

Home Phone:( ) _____ - _____

Work Phone:( ) _____ - _____

Form 12.1 Complaint Form (Cont.)

TELL US YOUR COMPLAINT ABOUT A COMPANY...

Subject of Your Complaint: _____

_____

Name of Company You Are Complaining About: _____

_____

Street Address: _____

City: _____

State or Canadian Province: _____

Country: _____

Zip Code or Postal Code: _____

Company Web Site: _____

Company E-Mail Address: _____

Phone Number:( ) _____ - _____

How Did the Company Initially Contact You?: _____

_____

How Much Did the Company Ask You to Pay?: _____

How Much Did You Actually Pay the Company?: _____

How Did You Pay the Company?: _____

REPRESENTATIVE OR SALESPERSON

First Name _____

Last Name: _____

Date Company Contacted You: _____

Explain Your Problem: _____

_____

_____

_____

_____

How Much Did You Actually Pay the Company?: _____

How Did You Pay the Company?: _____

REPRESENTATIVE OR SALESPERSON

First Name _____

Last Name: _____

Form 12.1 Complaint Form (Cont.)

Date Company Contacted You: _____

Explain Your Problem: _____

_____

_____

_____

_____

Source: https://rn.ftc.gov/pls/dod/wsolcq$.startup?Z_ORG_CODE=PU01

When completing this affidavit, use a separate affidavit for each company you're notifying and only send it to that company. List only the account(s) you're disputing with the company receiving this form. If a collection agency sends you a statement, letter or notice about the fraudulent account, send them a COPY of this document (NOT the original).

FUTURE

Future efforts for preventing identity theft will likely come from technological advancements that incorporate some physical aspect of a person's body in order to verify identity. Known as **biometrics** this type of authentication uses such things as eyes, fingerprints, facial structure, speech, hand geometry and digital signatures. These things can be used to authenticate both your identity, as well identify any person who may be trying to use your identity.

Form 12.3 ID Theft Affidavit

Complete the following:

(1) My full legal name is:

_____

　　　(First)　　　　　　　(Middle)　　　　　(Last)(Jr., Sr., III)

(2) (If different from above) When the events described in this affidavit took place, I was known as

_____

　　　(First)　　　　　　　(Middle)　　　　　(Last)(Jr., Sr., III)

(3) My date of birth is _____ (day/month/year)

(4) My Social Security number is _____

(5) My driver's license or identification card state and number is

_____

(6) My current address is:

_____

City _____ State _____ Zip Code _____

(7) I have lived at this address since _____/_____ (month/year)

(8) (If different from above) When the events described in this affidavit took place, my address was:

_____

City　_____　State　_____　Zip　Code

_____

(9) I lived at the address in Item 8 from _____ until _____ (month/year)

(10) My daytime telephone number is: (____)_____

My evening telephone number is: (____)_____

How the Fraud Occurred - Check all that apply for items 11 - 17:

(11) [   ] I did not authorize anyone to use my name or personal information to seek the money, credit, loans, goods or services described in this report.

(12) [   ] I did not receive any benefit, money, goods or services as a result of the events described in this report.

(13) [   ] My identification documents (for example, credit cards; birth certificate; driver's license; Social Security card; etc.) were
[ ] stolen [ ] lost on or about ___/_____/_____(day/month/year).

Form 12.3 ID Theft Affidavit (Cont.)

(14) [ ] To the best of my knowledge and belief, the following person(s) used my information (for example, my name, address, date of birth, existing account numbers, Social Security number, mother's maiden name, etc.) or identification documents to get money, credit, loans, goods or services without my knowledge or authorization:

Name (if known): _____

Address (if known): _____

_____

_____

Phone number(s) (if known): _____

_____

Additional information (if known): _____

_____

_____

_____

(15) [ ] I do NOT know who used my information or identification documents to get money, credit, loans, goods or services without my knowledge or authorization.

(16) [ ] Additional comments: (For example, description of the fraud, which documents or information were used or how the identity thief gained access to your information.)

_____

_____

_____

_____

(Attach additional pages as necessary.)

Law Enforcement Actions

(17) (check one) I [ ] am [ ] am not willing to assist in the prosecution of the person(s) who committed this fraud.

(18) (check one) I [ ] am [ ] am not authorizing the release of this information to law enforcement for the purpose of assisting them in the investigation and prosecution of the person(s) who committed this fraud.

(19) (check all that apply) I [ ] have [ ] have not reported the events described in this affidavit to the police or other law enforcement agency. The police [ ] did [ ] did not write a report. *In the event you have contacted the police or other law enforcement agency, please complete the following:*

Form 12.3 ID Theft Affidavit (Cont.)

(Agency #1) _____

(Officer/Agency personnel taking report) _____

_____

(Date of report) _____

(Report number, if any) _____

(Phone number) _____

(email address, if any) _____

- - - - - - - - - -

(Agency #2) _____

(Officer/Agency personnel taking report) _____

_____

(Date of report) _____

(Report number, if any) _____

(Phone number) _____

(email address, if any) _____

Documentation Checklist

Please indicate the supporting documentation you are able to provide to the companies you plan to notify. Attach copies (NOT originals) to the affidavit before sending it to the companies.

(20) [ ] A copy of a valid government-issued photo-identification card (for example, your driver's license, state-issued ID card or your passport). If you are under 16 and don't have a photo-ID, you may submit a copy of your birth certificate or a copy of your official school records showing your enrollment and place of residence.

(21) [ ] Proof of residency during the time the disputed bill occurred, the loan was made or the other event took place (for example, a rental/lease agreement in your name, a copy of a utility bill or a copy of an insurance bill).

(22) [ ] A copy of the report you filed with the police or sheriff's department. If you are unable to obtain a report or report number from the police, please indicate that in Item 19. Some companies only need the report number, not a copy of the report. You may want to check with each company.

Signature

I declare under penalty of perjury that the information I have provided in this affidavit is true and correct to the best of my knowledge.

_____

Form 12.3 ID Theft Affidavit (Cont.)

(signature)

_____

(date signed)

Knowingly submitting false information on this form could subject you to criminal prosecution for perjury.

_____

(Notary)

Witness:

_____

(signature)

_____

(printed name)

(date) _____ (telephone number) (   ) _____ - _____

I declare (check all that apply):

[ ] As a result of the event(s) described in the ID Theft Affidavit, the following account(s) was/were opened at your company in my name without my knowledge, permission or authorization using my personal information or identifying documents:

Fraudulent Account Statement

Creditor Name/Address (the company that opened the account or
   provided the goods or services)

Account _____

Number _____

Type of unauthorized credit/goods/services provided by creditor (if known)

_____

Date issued or opened (if known) _____

Amount/Value provided (the amount charged or the cost of the goods/services)

_____

[ ] During the time of the accounts described above, I had the following account open with your company:

Billing name: _____

```
┌─────────────────────────────────────────────────────────────┐
│ Form 12.3  ID Theft Affidavit  (Cont.)                        │
├─────────────────────────────────────────────────────────────┤
│                                                               │
│   Billing address:_____    │
│                                                               │
│   _____    │
│                                                               │
│   Account number: _____   │
│   [Check with each company. Creditors sometimes require       │
│      notarization. If they do not, please have one witness    │
│      (non-relative) sign below that you completed and signed  │
│      this affidavit.]                                         │
│                                                               │
│   Source: https://rn.ftc.gov                                  │
│                                                               │
└─────────────────────────────────────────────────────────────┘
```

SUMMARY

Identity theft is a serious crime. People whose identities have been stolen can spend months or years – and their hard-earned money – cleaning up the mess thieves have made. In the meantime, victims may lose job opportunities, be refused loans, education, housing or cars, or even get arrested for crimes they didn't commit.

DISCUSSION QUESTIONS

1. Why is it more important for the victim to document incidents of identity theft than it is for law enforcement to do it?

2. Indicate several ways in which citizens can protect themselves from identity theft.

3. What can be done if someone is a victim of identity theft?

ADDITIONAL READINGS

*National and State Trends in Fraud and Identity Theft, January – December 2003.*Consumer Sentinel, Identity Theft Data Clearinghouse.
http://www.consumer.gov/sentinel/pubs/Top10Fraud2003.pdf

Federal Identity Theft Assumption and Deterrence Act of 1998 – 18 USC 1028

Federal Privacy Act of 1974 – 5 USC Code 552a

Financial Services Modernization Act, Gramm-Leach-Bliley (GLB), Privacy Rule – 15 USC 6801-6827

Health Information Portability and Accountability Act of 1996 (HIPAA, Standard for Privacy of Individually Identifiable Health Information, Final Rule – 45 CFR Part 160)
www.ftc.gov/privacy/glbact/index.html

Chapter 13

Drugs

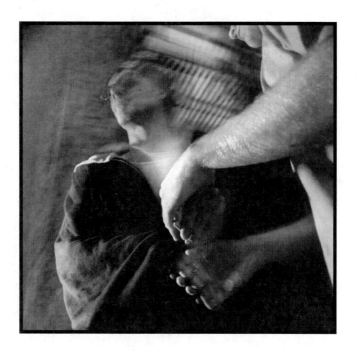

CHAPTER OVERVIEW

Drugs today have no boundaries - they cut across all classes of social and economic backgrounds. In the 1970s, then President Richard Nixon established a policy known as the "War on Drugs." Since that time, the U.S. government's aggressive efforts to curtail drug use have seen many challenges, failures and changes.

OBJECTIVES

At the end of this chapter, you will be able to:
1. Describe several types and uses of drugs
2. Recognize commonly used drugs.
3. Understand drug evidence processing

Basic Facts About The War On Drugs, written by Clifford A. Schaffer, tells us that in 1875 a San Francisco ordinance was passed outlawing the smoking of opium. The belief was that the drug was used to lure women. In 1937 Marijuana was outlawed under the guise that the drug had a violent effect on workers who crossed the borders seeking jobs during the Depression. The law was put into place to curtail its violent effect on people. Newspapers quickly joined the bandwagon writing excessive stories about the horrors of drugs. It was not entirely the damage or impact that drugs were having on society or individuals that caused it to be outlawed, but rather the movement to outlaw drugs arose because of fear. If we fast forward to the 21st century, the atmosphere and concerns are much wider spread.

WAR ON DRUGS

The term "War on Drugs" encompasses a wide array of public policies and programs designed to address the problem of illegal drug use, drug abuse, and drug dependency by residents of the United States and its outlying areas. While drug addiction used to be considered a personal failure, its redefinition as a public problem began to take hold in the United States around the turn of the 20th century, coincident with the peak of a cocaine epidemic that revealed the harmfulness to society of drug addiction.[1] Many believe that the War on Drugs has failed miserably and cannot be won. Statistical information has been gathered, analyzed and redirected by many public and private agencies. Listed below are some examples of the latest statistics that support those who believe we are not winning the war on drugs.

In February 2003, President George Bush transmitted to Congress the 2003 National Drug Control Strategy outlining three core priorities; 1) stopping drug use before it starts, 2) healing America's drug users, and 3) disrupting the drug market.[2]

This strategy proposed $2.1 billion in FY2004 for border drug interdiction, an increase of 7.3% from FY2003, and $731 million for the Andean Counterdrug Initiative. Internationally, the strategy intends to continue to target the supply of illegal drugs in the source countries, and domestically to promote the use by law enforcement agencies of a single list identifying high-level drug trafficking targets – the Consolidated Priority Organization Targeting (CPOT) list. The 28 High Intensity Drug Trafficking Areas (HIDTAs) around the country, according to the strategy, are now using the CPOT list to coordinate their activities against organizations at the top of the trafficking pyramid.[3]

Statistics

Money Spent

According to the Drug War Clock$_4$ as of, January 29, 2004 at 9:30:30 A.M. money spent on drugs during the first 29 day of 2004 total is:

Federal:	$1,547,474,243
State:	$1,610,741,375
Total:	$3,158,215,618

The U.S. Federal government spent $19.179 billion dollars in 2003 on the war on drugs, a rate of about $600 per second.[5] In addition, at least another 20 billion was spent by State and Local governments during 2003.[6]

People Arrested

Arrests for drug related offenses in the first 29 days of 2004 total 127,218. The year 2000 saw 1,579,566 arrests and it is estimated that the year 2004 will far exceed this number. Approximately every 20 seconds someone is arrested. Of the 127,218 arrested for drug law offenses, 46.5% were for Cannabis.[7] Incarcerations during the first 29 days of 2004 already stands at 19,073. It is expected that at least 236,800 people will be incarcerated for drug offenses in 2004.[8]

Disease

Preventable HIV Infections in the first 29 days of January, 2004 total 304. Nearly 4000 new HIV infections can be prevented before the year 2005 if the federal ban on needle exchange funding is lifted this year. About 10 new cases preventable every day.[9]

CATEGORIES

In 1970, the Federal Controlled Substances Act grouped drugs into categories or schedules and established the following criteria for drugs being placed into each of the schedules.

Schedule I

- Includes heroin, LSD and marijuana. The drug or other substance has a high potential for abuse
    - The drug or other substance has no currently accepted medical use in treatment in the U.S.

– There is a lack of accepted safety for use of the drug or other substance under medical supervision.

Schedule II

- Includes morphine, used as a pain-killer, and cocaine, used as a topical anesthetic.
  – The drug or other substance has a high potential for abuse.
  – The drug or other substance has a currently accepted medical use in treatment in the U.S. or a currently accepted medical use with severe restrictions.
  – Abuse of the drug or other substance may lead to severe psychological or physical dependence.

Schedule III

- Includes anabolic steroids and Marinol.
  – The drug or other substance has a potential for abuse less than the drugs or other substances in Schedules I and II.
  – The drug or other substance has a currently accepted medical use in treatment in the U.S.
  – Abuse of the drug or other substance may lead to moderate or low physical dependence or high psychological dependence.

Schedule IV

- Includes Valium or other tranquilizers.
  – The drug or other substance has a low potential for abuse relative to the drugs or other substances in Schedule III.
  – The drug or other substance has a currently accepted medical use in treatment in the U.S.
  – Abuse of the drug or other substance may lead to limited physical dependence or psychological dependence relative to the drugs or other substances in Schedule III.

Schedule V

- Includes codeine-containing analgesics.
  – The drug or other substance has a low potential for abuse relative to the drugs or other substances in Schedule IV.
  – The drug or other substance has a currently accepted medical use in treatment in the U.S.
  – Abuse of the drug or other substance may lead to limited physical dependence or psychological dependence relative to the drugs or other substances in Schedule IV.

CLASSES

The Misuse of Drugs Act 1971 also not only classified drugs by categories, it put them into type "classes", Class A, Class B, and Class C. Listed below are examples of the types of drugs in each class.

Class A

- alfentanil
- cocaine
- dextromoramide
- dipipanone
- heroin
- lofentamil
- LSD
- methadone
- morphine
- opium
- pethidine
- phencyclidine
- injectable Class B drugs

Class B

- oral preparations of amphetamine
- barbiturates
- cannabis
- codeine
- gluthethamide
- pentazocine
- phenmetrazine
- pholcodine

Class C

- phentamine
- diethylpropion
- mazindol
- meprobamate
- most benzodiazepines

TYPES

In addition to being placed into categories and classes, there are laws prescribing penalties for the use of different types of drugs. There are countless types of drugs making it impossible to discuss them all. However, listed below are a few of the more common types and the basic laws pertaining to each type of drug.[10]

Alcohol

- it is basically illegal to sell alcohol to minors
- Police have the legal power to confiscate alcohol from anyone they know or reasonably believe to be under age and drinking in a public place.
- Corporate Bylaws sometimes prohibit the consumption of alcohol in designated places.
- The following alcohol related issues can all be offences under the law:
  - driving or riding vehicles and animals, including motor vehicles, horses and bicycles, while under the influence of alcohol.
  - anti-social and irresponsible behavior, including being drunk and disorderly, and placing the health and safety of others at risk while under the influence alcohol.
- Licensing laws currently prohibit the sale or consumption of alcohol at unlicensed premises, or at licensed premises outside certain hours.
- Consumption of alcohol by workers in certain occupations or situations is also regulated under the law.

Amphetamines (Speed)

- Amphetamines are Class B drugs, but carry Class A penalties if prepared for injection.

Anabolic Steroids (Roids)

- Anabolic steroids are prescription only medicines. It is not illegal to possess them for your own use, or to import them for own use, but it is illegal to supply them without a license, or to import them for supply to somebody else: Class C penalties apply. The use of anabolic steroids in sports is prohibited. A positive test can end a sporting career.

- The steroids used to treat eczema and asthma are generally of a different type, although some countries treat asthma using Clenbuterol, which is also used for its anabolic effects.

Cannabis/Marijuana

- Cannabis is currently a Class B drug.
- There are currently proposals to reclassify cannabis as a Class C drug-however:
  - there are no plans to decriminalize the possession or supply of cannabis; these will remain an offense.
  - whatever the current classification of a drug is, the law will be enforced and the penalties relating to the classification may be applied.

Cocaine (Cocaine Hydrochloride)

- Cocaine Hydrochloride is a Class A drug
- Crack cocaine, also a Class A drug, is given a separate entry here, as it is used differently and has different effects.

Ecstasy

- Ecstasy (MDMA) is a Class A drug.

GHB (Date Rape Drug)

- GHB is now a Class C drug, having been reclassified in July 2003.
- There have been reports of GHB being used in sexual assaults and rapes. The Sexual Offenses Act of 1956 states:
  … (it is an offence for a person to apply or administer to, or cause to be taken by, a woman any drug, matter or thing with intent to stupefy or overpower her as so thereby to enable any man to have unlawful sexual intercourse with her.}
- The offense is committed if the drug is administered with this intent, even if no intercourse takes place, and can result in up to two years imprisonment. It is worth noting that the definition of a (drug, matter or thing(can also include alcohol.

Heroin (Diacetylmorphine Hydrochloride)

- Heroin is a Class A drug.

- There are several other drugs with similar properties to heroin. Illegal possession and supply of Methadone carries Class A penalties. Remifentanil and Dihydroetrophine became Class A drugs in July 2003.

Ketamine

- Ketamine is a prescription-only medicine. Possession without a prescription is not illegal, but supply/possession with intent to supply without a license is against the law under the Medicines Act.

LSD (Acid)

- Lysergic Acid Diethlamide or Lysergide (LSD) is a Class A drug.

Magic Mushrooms (Psilocybe Semilanceata)

- While it is not illegal to possess magic mushrooms, it is an offense to possess any preparation of the plant (e.g. when dried or stewed)
- When prepared, magic mushrooms are a Class A drug.

Methadone

- Methadone is a prescription-only drug used to treat people who have become dependent on opiates such as heroin. It is now also used by the medical field to treat intense chronic pain.
- When possessed without a prescription, or supplied illegally, methadone is treated as a Class A drug.

Solvents

- It is illegal to sell anything containing solvents to anyone under 18, or anyone acting for them, if they suspect the product is intended for abuse.

Tobacco

- Supplying tobacco to underage persons is illegal
- It is an offense to resell duty-free tobacco.

Tranquilizers (Benzodiazepines)

- The family of drugs called benzodiazepines include:

- diazepam (valium), temazepa, (mazzies), nitrazepam (mogadon, or moggies) and lorazepam (ativan), and flunitrazepam (trade name Rohypnol,) Zolpidem, a prescription medicine that acts in the same way as benzodiazepines, has recently been reclassified to have the same legal status as these drugs.

- Tranquilizers can only be supplied lawfully by a pharmacist to someone with a doctor's prescription.

- All Tranquilizers listed above carry Class C penalties for unauthorized possession and supply/possession with intent to supply.[11]

Federal and State penalties relating to drugs vary with the quantity of the drug. Additionally, if death or serious injury is associated with the sale and/or if it is a second offense, penalties are more severe.

In Table 13-1 you will find the most commonly abused drugs, street names, any medical use the drug may have, how the drug is taken, and category schedule of the drug.

Table 13.1 Commonly Abused Drugs				
SUBSTANCE	Example Of Proprietary Or Street Names	Medical Uses	How Taken	Drug Sched
STIMULANTS				
AMPHETAMINE	Biphetamine; Dexedrine; Black- Beauties; Crosses; Hearts	Attention Deficit Hyperactivity Disorder (ADAH), Obesity, Narcolepsy	Injected, Oral, Smoked, Sniffed	II
COCAINE	Cock, Crack, Flake, Rocks, Snow	Local Anesthetic, Vasoconstrictor	Injected, Smoked, Sniffed	II
METHAMPHETAMINE	Desoxyn, Crank, Crystal, Glass, Ice, Speed	ADHD, Obesity, Narcolepsy	Injected, Oral, Smoked, Sniffed	II
NICOTINE	Habitrol Patch, Nicorette Gum, Nicotrol Spray Prostep Patch, Cigars, Cigarettes, Smokeless Tobacco, Snuff, Spit Tobacco	Treatment For Nicotine Dependence	Smoked, Sniffed, Oral, Transdermal	Not Scheduled
HALLUCINOGENS AND OTHER COMPOUNDS				

Table 13.1	Commonly Abused Drugs			
SUBSTANCE	Example Of Proprietary Or Street Names	Medical Uses	How Taken	Drug Sched
LSD	Acid, Microdot	None	Oral	I
MESCALINE	Buttons, Cactus, Mesc, Peyote	None	Oral	I
PHENCYCLIDINE & ANALOGS	Pcp, Angel Dust, Boat, Hog, Love Boat	Anesthetic (Veterinary)	Injected, Oral, Smoked	I, II
PSILOCYBIN	Magic Mushroom, Purple Passion, Shrooms	None	Oral	I
AMPHETAMINE VARIANTS	DOB, DOM, MDA, MDMA; Adam, Ecstasy, STP, XTC	None	Oral	I
MARIJUANA	Blunt, Grass, Herb, Pot, Reefer, Sinsemilla, Smoke, Weed	Cancer, Aids, Glaucoma	Oral, Smoked	I
HASHISH	Hash	None	Oral, Smoked	I
TETRAHYDRO CANNABINOL	Marinol, THC	Antiemetic	Oral, Smoked	I, II
ANABOLIC STEROIDS	Testosterone (T/E Ratio), Stanazolol, Nandrolene	Hormone Replacement Therapy	Oral, Injected	III
OPIOIDS AND MORPHINE DERIVATIVES				
CODEINE	Tylenol W/Codeine, Robitussin A-C, Empirin W/ Codeine, Fiorinal W/Codeine	Analgesic, Antitussive	Injected, Oral	II, III, IV

Table 13.1	Commonly Abused Drugs			
SUBSTANCE	Example Of Proprietary Or Street Names	Medical Uses	How Taken	Drug Sched
HEROIN	Diacetylmorphne, Horse, Smake	None	Injected, Smoked, Sniffed	I
METHODONE	Amidone, Dolophine, Methadose	Analgesic, Treatment For Opiate Dependence, Severe Chronic Pain	Injected, Oral	II
MORPHINE	Roxanol, Duramorph	Analgesic	Injected, Oral, Smoked	II, III
OPIUM	Laudanum, Paregoric, Dover's Powder	Analgesic, Antidiarrheal	Oral, Smoked	II, III, V
DEPRESSANTS				
ALCOHOL	Beer, Wine, Liquor	Antidote For Methanol Poisoning	Oral	Not Scheduled
BARBITURATES	Amytal, Nembutal, Seconal, Phenobarbital; Barbs	Anesthetic, Anticonvulsant, Hypnotic, Sedative	Injected, Oral	II, III, IV
BENZODIAZEPINES	Activan, Halcion, Librium, Rohypnol, Valium; Roofies, Tranks, Xanax	Antianxiety, Anticonvulsant, Hypnotic, Sedative	Injected, Oral	IV
METHAQUOLONE	Quaalude, Ludes	None	Oral	1
Source: National Institute on Drug Abuse. www.drugstv.com/commonlyabuseddrugs.htm				

Schedule I and II drugs have a high potential for abuse. They require greater security and have a quota on manufacture among other restrictions. Schedule I drugs are available for research and have no approved medical use. Schedule II drugs are available only through prescription, cannot have refills and require a form for ordering. Schedule III and IV drugs are available with prescription, may have 5 refills in 6 months and may be ordered orally. Most Schedule V drugs are available over the counter.[12]

USERS

Drug users now encompass every ethnic, social, economic and age group across the entire nation. There are many reasons individuals become drug users. It could just as easily be you as it could be your child, your grandmother, grandfather, mother, father, sister, brother, nephew, niece, the person sitting next to you right now, your instructor, your best friend, your co-worker, your neighbor, your car mechanic, the builder building your new home or the contractor replacing your furnace, the person driving next to you, the little sixth grader down the street from you. It could be the president of the corporation where you are employed, or your doctor or the nurse taking care of you in the hospital. It could be the surgeon scheduled to perform life-threatening surgery. It could be the pilot flying the aircraft you're about to board. It could be your pharmacist that is about to fill your medical prescription. It could be the daycare provider that takes care of your child. It could be the quarterback of your favorite ball team. It could be your attorney. It could be the principal or teacher at your child's school. But why do all of these types of people depend upon drugs?

Personal Satisfactions

Although there have always been drug abusers, it has been suggested that real abuse of such drugs as hallucinogens, amphetamines, marijuana, cocaine, alcohol and barbiturates began in the 1960's. It was a time to buck authority and live FREE.

What determines the difference between those who experiment with drugs by using it as a recreational past time and those who are seriously addicted and can no longer function without prescribed or illegal drugs.

Popular ways to separate the differences and define addiction are 1) how an individual interacts with the drug, and 2) how the drug impacts society. One can also look at two very different aspects of human behavior. 1) psychological (pertaining to the mind or to mental phenomena) dependence, or 2) physical (pertaining to the body) dependence.

When considering the psychological factor, the reason individuals started using drugs in the first place must be examined. It may be trying to escape a personal problem, to get a handle on daily stress or a needed sense of well-being that most drugs supply. Addicts don't realize they have become dependent and that dependence leads to addiction.

Physical dependence encourages the continued use of drugs. Most drugs, while increasing irritability and depression, also give the user more energy in the beginning. The user needs less sleep giving a false confidence that more can be accomplished.

Below is a listing of some of the signs that may be present in individuals addicted to drugs.

1. Red or bloodshot eyes
2. Change in eating habits
3. Change in sleeping habits
4. A change in behavior (withdrawn, spending more time alone)
5. Changes in school grades
6. Acting depressed, lack of energy
7. Careless about personal hygiene and appearance
8. Lost interest in school, family, or activities they used to enjoy
9. Frequently needing money[13]

Medical Purposes

Although there is extreme controversy regarding the prescribing of drugs for medical purposes, many drugs are frequently prescribed. Before drugs are prescribed, physicians should counsel the patient on the dangers and benefits of the drug. Once prescribed, the physician must monitor the use and any reactions the patient may incur. It is often difficult for physicians to know when abuse takes place. Medical drug abusers will often (doctor shop," going from one doctor to another receiving prescriptions from each.

Table 13.2 below catalogs some of the drugs that are or can be prescribed and their medical uses.

Table 13.2 Prescribed Drugs	
DRUG	**MEDICAL USE**
Amphetamine	ADD (Attention Deficit Disorder)
Cocaine	Local Anesthetic
Methamphetamine	Vasoconstrictor
Nicotine (Patch)	ADHD, Obesity, Narcolepsy, Nicotine Dependence
Phencyclidine (PCP)	Anesthetic (Veterinary)
Marijuana	Cancer, Aids Pain, Glaucoma
Anabolic Steroids	Hormone Replacement
Methadone	Antidote For Heroin Treatment, Severe Chronic Pain
Alcohol	Antidote For Methanol Poisoning
Barbiturates	Anesthetic, Anticonvulsant, Hypnotic, Sedative
Codeine	Analgesic, Antitussive

Source: www.drugstv.com/CommonlyAbusedDrugs.htm

ASSOCIATED CRIMES

Drug users do not believe they are doing damage and therefore adopt an attitude of so what's the big deal. However, that damage soon involves all of society. Addicts begin to commit crimes to support drug habits. Statistics have proven that the following variety of crimes are related to drug use. The following listing identifies some, but not all, of the more common crimes committed as a result of drug use.

CRIMES RELATED TO DRUG USE

- Terrorism
- Burglary
- Homicide
- Armed Robbery
- Home Robberies
- Graffiti
- Crimes Against the Elderly
- Domestic Violence
- Child Abuse
- Check Fraud
- Contributing to the Delinquency of a Minor
- Prostitution
- DUI - DWI
- Rape
- Sexual Assault
- Auto Theft
- Possession of a Controlled Substance With Intent To Sell
- Assault And Battery
- Embezzlement
- Criminal Mischief
- Criminal Trespass
- Under Age Possession of Drugs and Alcohol

These criminal acts not only victimize individuals and groups, they also have a much larger impact. Costs related to these types of drug offenses have skyrocketed. Arrests and convictions have out paced the number of prisons available.

TRANSPORTATION

Drug trafficking or the transportation of drugs has become a very lucrative business. It has been reported that 8% of all global exports are drugs. These drugs are imported into the United States through a variety of locations and ports. Border agencies have unified into a single border agency, Central Border Patrol (CBP), to achieve "one face at the border." The officers and agents use advance information, risk management, and technology to make our borders more secure and ensure the efficient flow of legitimate trade and travel.[14]

The creativity drug traffickers use to transport the drugs and currency is remarkable. One such example of this creativity appeared in an article written by Sharron Cohen of the Associated Press. The article stated:

> *"... a roving U.S. Customs Inspector in Atlanta, stopped a woman suspected of smuggling drugs in infant formula cans. One of the children was identified. An address for the parents was located and a U.S. Custom Agent knocked on a door in Chicago looking for the young couple identified as the parents. Their eight month old baby girl was with a woman who was arrested at Heathrow International Airport in London, England. This was the fifth time this eight month old baby girl had traveled to Panama and London, usually in the arms of a stranger and often exposed to danger. The parents were extremely calm as the Agent advised them that their eight month old baby girl was with a woman caught with drugs in London."* [15]

Meanwhile the U.S. Custom Agents in Atlanta were already suspicious. In recent weeks they had encountered several women with small children who had claimed to have visited their husbands or boyfriends in the military in Panama. However, these agents had been in the military in Panama and the information supplied by the women as to where they went and stayed was never anywhere near a military base. Some of them could not even supply the agents with the name of the airbase or the name of their husband, son or boyfriend that they had supposedly just visited.

What was actually happening was someone would "recruit" drug users/addicts with small children. They would pay them with a small amount of money or drugs for the "use/rental" of their infant child. (The going rate was $200-$300). The "MULE" (paid up to $4000.00 or supplied with drugs) would then travel aboard with the small child. The drugs, liquid cocaine and heron were injected into cans of baby formula, thus being undetectable by drug sniffing dogs. The "MULE" would then pack the formula into suitcases and travel back into the United States, or some other country where it would be distributed throughout the general population. The smugglers, (woman with small child) flew from Panama City and Montego Bay and Kingston, Jamaica to Chicago, New York, London and Birmingham before being detected.

In the end it took over 22 years to make arrests. During that period of time, 48 defendants pleaded guilty. The "MULES" were sentenced to 5-10 years in prison. The parents who rented their children received 10 months to 8 years in prison. The only person who stood trial received a sentence of life in prison. The leader who obtained drugs and organized several of the Jamaican trips has yet to be sentenced. The scheme that was used is unthinkable by most, but for the drug trafficker's and users it was simply a means to an end. The stopping of this woman and the investigation conducted by the CBP, unraveled an international drug ring.[16]

There are no countries that do not export some quantity of illegal or prescription drugs. This example was just one of the more creative methods used in drug trafficking. Drugs are imported and exported using elaborate methods. The following methods are the most commonly used:

- Air — commercial or private airplanes, military air equipment(helicopter, fighter planes etc)
- Water — boats-sea worthy or non-sea worthy, private yachts, small personal sea craft, commercial liners, cruise vessels
- Land — personal vehicles-trucks, cars, motorcycles, hearses, rental trucks and trailers — -Leased vehicles, public transportation, borrowed or stolen vehicles

There is little doubt that drug trafficking not only threatens our country's economic future but also has become a serious threat to Homeland Security. It has been said that each time someone makes a purchase of an illegal drug or a black market prescription the funds reach the hands of terrorists who in turn use those funds for intelligence gathering and more sophisticated weapons. Educate is the key. Never pass up an opportunity to enlighten the young, the old, the drug users and drug "Mules" that they are financing those who flew the planes into the World Trade Center , the Pentagon and crashed the airplane into a Pennsylvania field on September 11, 2001.

DISTRIBUTION

The drugs somehow survived all attempts of seizure. They have gotten past the border patrol, they have gotten by the drug sniffing dog, they have gotten past Highway Patrols, State Patrols, and local law enforcement. They are now at the destination - the distribution center.

That center can be the local drug dealer on a corner, a clandestine lab, a warehouse, an apartment/residence, a movie theater, a bar, a garage, a laundry mat, a grocery store, an elementary, middle or high school yard or classroom. It can be a vehicle, a park, a church, a prison yard, a juvenile detention center or rehabilitation center. It can be a hospital or doctor(s office, the bathroom at work. Anywhere can be classified or considered a distribution center.

It can be distributed in several ways. A large drug ring or an independent dealer can break it down into small amounts for distribution and/or sale or for individual use. It can be packaged as an ounce, a kilo, a gram, a single rock, a single reefer, a single injection, a single pipe full, a single snort, a single tablet, a single hit on a postage stamp or blotter paper. The larger amounts will more than likely be (stomped(on and broken down even further for more money. Each person who receives an illegal/prescription drug and then either sells it or gives it to another individual is considered a distributor/dealer and if busted will be charged under the law as such. Penalties can range from simple probation to a prison sentence.

EVIDENCE COLLECTION

"Actions taken at the outset of an investigation at a crime scene can play a pivotal role in the resolution of a case. Careful, thorough investigation is key to ensure that potential physical evidence is not tainted or destroyed or potential witnesses overlooked."

Janet Reno
U.S. Attorney General

Before evidence collecting can commence, the first responder will assess the situation to see if there are any individuals that require medical care and, if so, call for medical assistance. The first responder will then secure the boundaries of the crime scene. This is done by roping or taping off all areas that could fall within the crime scene. This could encompass a driveway, an alley, a dirt road leading away from the crime scene, an entrance or exit from the scene. When establishing and securing the boundaries, it is always easier to go back and shorten those boundaries than it is to extend them - error on the side of caution. The establishment of all boundaries is critical to preserving the integrity of the evidence. The first responder will also secure all individuals, including but not limited to, the victim, the offender, eye witnesses, and neighbors.

Once the scene is completely secured the evidence collection can begin. Someone will be identified as the 'person in charge'. That individual will assign specific responsibilities, share preliminary information, and develop investigative plans in accordance with departmental policy and local, state and federal laws. Procedures can vary from one agency to another but will generally include:

- Conversation with the first responder regarding observations / activities
- Evaluation of safety issues that will affect all personnel entering the scene
- Evaluation of search/seizure issues to determine necessity of obtaining consent to search and/or obtain search warrants
- Evaluation and establishment of a path of entry / exit to the scene to be used by authorized personnel
- Evaluation of initial scene boundaries
- determination of number / size of scene(s) and prioritization
- Establishing a secure area within close proximity to the scene(s) for the purpose of consulting and equipment staging
- Establishing / maintaining communication with personnel at all locations if multiple scenes exist
- Establishing a secure area for temporary evidence storage in accordance with the rules of evidence or chain of custody
- Determining and requesting additional investigative resources as required
- Ensuring continued scene integrity
- Ensuring that witnesses to the incident are identified and separated.
- avoiding contamination of the scene by using the establishing path or entry
- Preparing documentation of the scene as observed
- Identifying / protect fragile and /or perishable evidence
- Ensuring that all evidence that may be compromised is immediately documented, photographed and placed in the appropriate container[17]

Essential items needed to collect evidence should be a permanent part the of the investigator's vehicle. Optional items can be brought to the scene by another officer. Some of the essential and optional items appear in the list below. The list is in no way intended to include everything that will be needed to collect evidence at the scene. Each drug scene is unique; therefore, the items needed to collect evidence will vary.

- Consent and search forms
- Crime scene barricade tape

- First aid kit
- Flashlight and extra batteries
- Personal protective equipment
- Paper/plastic bags
- Bio-hazard bags
- Chemical enhancement supplies
- Pocket knife/tool kit
- Tarps (protection against weather)
- Evidence collection containers
- Direction marker/compass
- Disinfectant
- Evidence identifiers
- Measuring devices
- Sketch paper
- Latex gloves
- Tweezers/forceps
- Templates (scene & human)
- List of frequently called numbers (crime lab, fire dept, chemical experts)
- Boxes
- Air tight containers
- Permanent markers
- Measurement scales
- Glass vials[18]

When collecting drug evidence, it is imperative though that the integrity of the collection container be maintained. It must be properly marked as to date, time, location, amount, and description of the drug. It must also be logged on to the "Chain of Custody" form.

DOCUMENTING

Most law enforcement agencies have specific methods or rules for documentation. The crime scene investigator or evidence technician should be aware of the department's requirements and follow those guidelines. Remember, numerous people will rely on the accuracy of this documentation. The evidence must tell the story so that the scene can be reconstructed.

The checklist, Form 13.1, below may be helpful in ensuring that proper documentation will become part of the (case file.)

Form 13.1 Drug Documentation Checklist

- Review what type of documentation will be needed.
- Coordinate photographs, video, sketches, measurements and notes.
- Photograph:
  - Scene utilizing overall, medium and close-up coverage.
  - Evidence collected with/without measurement scale and/or evidence identifiers.
  - Victims, suspects, witnesses, crowds and vehicles.
  - Additional perspectives (aerial photos, witness view, area under body/bodies before and after moved.
- Videotape as optional supplement to photos.
- Preliminary sketch(s) and measure:
  - Immediate area of scene, noting case identifiers/and indicating north on the sketch.
  - Relative location of items or evidence and correlate evidence items with evidence records.
  - Evidence prior to movement
  - Rooms, furniture or other objects.
  - Distance to adjacent buildings or other landmarks
- Generate notes at scene:
  - Documenting location of the scene, time of arrival/departure.
  - Describing the scene as it appears.
  - Recording transient evidence(e.g. smells, sounds, sights) conditions(temperature/weather)
  - Documenting circumstances that require departures from usual procedures.

  With proper and methodical documentation, the integrity of the investigation will provide a permanent record for later use.

PROCESSING

Processing drug evidence is accomplished the same as for other evidentiary material. Take special care to ensure that there is no skin contact with the substance and that the substance is not inhaled. Maintaining the legal chain of custody is extremely vital to introducing drugs into evidence at the time of trial. The number of individuals who come into possession of drug evidence should be kept to an absolute minimum.

Drug evidence is usually found in minute quantities and often in small containers. The drug evidence and the container should be placed in a suitable outer container as soon as possible and both containers marked with the initials of the investigator, the date and the time the evidence was obtained.

Without chemical analysis by a competent chemist, pills, capsules, powders and vegetable matter cannot be positively identified. When referring to substances suspected of being drugs, law enforcement must refer to the evidence by its physical appearance, such as "a white crystalline powder suspected as being cocaine," or "a vegetable matter suspected to be marijuana." Exact weight statement should be avoided. The amount may be referred to as approximately 1 cup of vegetable matter, or approximately ¼ teaspoon of powder, or 24 tablets (or capsules).

Drugs and drug evidence should be stored in a safe or security container inside the evidence room for proper security and should be kept there at all times except when required during the course of investigation or trial.[19]

Field Testing

Field tests may be used to screen many of the commonly used drugs offered for sale by illegal sources. There are several drug identification kits used in the field. These kits' capabilities are constantly being improved. The kits provide all the necessary elements to perform color tests for major narcotics and dangerous drug classifications.

Field tests are extremely reliable as negative tests (no drug present). Their reliability as positive tests varies in degree between the different tests and changes from time to time as cutting agents that interfere with the tests are sometimes added or sold in the illicit drug traffic. There are no valid field tests at present for tranquilizers, many hallucinogens, and several other less commonly found controlled substances. Field testing of a tablet or capsule should always be preceded by an attempt to identify it.

Any drug that will be used as evidence must be identified by a qualified chemist using approved procedures in an adequately equipped laboratory. If the suspected material is minute, field tests should not be attempted and all of the substance should be forwarded to a laboratory for analysis.

In many cases, the color reactions produced by field tests are only indicative that the suspected sample is a drug product. Many non-controlled substances give color reactions similar to those given by controlled substances. In addition, there are numerous controlled drugs that give no color reactions at all, or give color reactions other than those usually described by field test kits.

Finally, the testing of a suspected material through sampling should never be permitted. There is great danger that poisons might be introduced in a drug or that the material may be a poison.[20]

Laboratory Processing

All drug testing laboratories are staffed with qualified chemists and excellent equipment to identify suspected material. The chemists are prepared to testify in court, if required, as to the chemical analysis of the suspected material. Most laboratories use advanced techniques and sophisticated chemical compounds and equipment to analyze chemicals.

Field tests are preliminary and only indicative that a drug may be present. Laboratory examinations are precise, expert, and in most cases, positive proof of drug existence. When suspected drugs are to be shipped to the laboratory for analysis, take care to ensure the packaging container is complete sealed and packed so spillage or breaking will not occur in transit. Tablets and capsules should be packed in sterile cotton and placed in a suitable container. A single package of evidence should never contain evidence from more than one investigation.

Finally, once narcotics or abuse-type drugs have served their purpose as trial evidence, the evidence custodian should make every effort to obtain disposition instructions as quickly as possible. Destruction of drugs should be by fire and witnessed by a disinterested person.[21]

SUMMARY

The use and abuse of illegal/prescription drugs is having a profound effect on societies everywhere. The (War on Drugs(is not one with victory in sight. For more than a decade, state and federal officials have invoked the language of war in an effort to eradicate the use of those drugs the government has decreed illicit. Since then state and federal governments have spent billions of dollars on drug courts, law enforcement, foreign aid, and treatment and prevention programs. Prisons are full of drug offenders, and asset forfeiture laws have enabled police to confiscate millions of dollars in property from citizens merely suspected of involvement in drug. trafficking. The U.S. prohibition on certain drugs has affected direct repercussions on domestic and foreign policy, criminal justice, public safety, personal liberty, health care and countless other spheres of society.[22]

DISCUSSION QUESTIONS

1. Why is the proper collection of evidence and documentation so vital to the "case file?"

2. How does one become a drug user or abuser?

3. What are the functions of the CBP?

4. Would crime rates/drug use/abuse be lowered by the legalization of certain drugs?

SUGGESTED READINGS

Mark Eddy, War on Drugs: Legislation in the 108th Congress and Related Developments. April 14, 2003. Domestic Social Policy Division, Congressional Research Service-The Library of Congress

U.S. Congress, Senate Committee on Appropriations, Effectiveness of the National Youth Anti-Drug Media Campaign, special hearing, 107th Cong. 2nd sess. June 19, 2002 (Washington: GOP 2002).

Belenko, Steven R. Drugs and drug Policy in America: A Documentaty History. Westport, CT, Greenwood Press [2000] 380 pp.

Keliman, Mark A. R. Against Excess: Drug Policy for Results. New York, Basic Books [992] 474 pp.

Musto, David F., M.D. The American Disease: Origins of Narcotic Control. New York,

Oxford University Press [1987]384 pp.

United States. Office of National Drug Control Policy. National Drug Control Strategy. Washington, D.C. Office of National Drug Control Policy, Executive Office of the President [February 2003] 54 pp Available at [http://www.whitehousedrugpolicy.gov/policy/inds.html]

National Drug Control Strategy. FY 2004 Budget Summary. 118 pp. Available at [http://www.whitehousedrugpolicy.gov/policy/budget.html]

Endnotes

1. Eddy Mark, War on Drugs: Legislation in the 108th Congress and Related Developments. April 14, 2003. Domestic Social Policy Division, Congressional Research Service-The Library of Congress. CRS-2

2. Eddy Mark, War on Drugs: CRS10

3. Eddy Mark, War on Drugs: CRS11

4. Drug War Clock established and maintained by DrugSense at www.drugsense.org/wodclock.htm

5. Office of National Drug Control Policy

6. Drucker, Dr. Ernest, (1998, Jan/Feb.) Public Health Reports, "Drug Prohibition and Public Health." U.S. Public health Service, Vol. 114.

7. Uniform Crime Reports, Federal Bureau of Investigation

8. U.S. Department of Justice, Bureau of Justice Statistics

9. Center for AIDS Prevention Studies, University of California, San Francisco

10. Thames Valley Police Department. www.thamesvalley.police.uk/about/drugs

11. Thames Valley Police Department.

12. National Institute on Drug Abuse

13. Government Publications. www.health.org/govpubs/phd640i

14. Daily Washington File, Embassy of the United States of America, Department of Homeland security January 14, 2004.
http://www.usembassy.ro/WF/500/04-01-16/eur510.htm

15. Sharron Cohen - Associated Press. Published in The Pueblo Chieftain, Pueblo, Colorado, Sunday January 25, 2004.

16. Sharron Cohen - Associated Press. p.10F

17. Crime Scene Investigation: A Guide for Law Enforcement, National Institute of Justice.
http://www.ncjrs.org/pdffiles1/nij/178290.pdf

18. Crime Scene Investigation, NIJ

19. Processing Drug Evidence. Integrated Publishing. www.tpub.com/maa/83.htm

20. Processing Drug Evidence. Integrated Publishing

21. Processing Drug Evidence. Integrated Publishing

22. CATO Institute. www.cato.org/current/drug-war/index.html

Chapter 14

Documenting an Arson Scene

CHAPTER OVERVIEW

Basically all serious crime scenes require the same tools for documentation; notes, photos, sketches, logs, reports etc. Although the tools are the same how they are applied can vary. The elements that need to be documented differ with each scene. The chapter pertaining to sexual assault demonstrated the nuances of obtaining and recording the victim's statements and the need for timeliness. Fire, bombing, explosion, arson scenes have unique properties that one must be aware of in order to properly document them.

OBJECTIVES

1. Summarize the history and cause for investigating fires.
2. Explain the various factors that impede fire investigations.
3. Outline the recommended practices for the collection, preservation and documentation of evidence at fire/arson scenes.
4. Identify the different agencies involved in arson and bombing scene investigations.

The National Institute of Justice published a research report written by the Technical Working Group on Fire/Arson Scene Investigation. It is entitled "Fire and Arson Scene Evidence: A Guide for Public Safety Personnel". This guide outlines the unique attributes of documenting the fire and arson scene. (To obtain an electronic version of this document, access the NIJ Web site:

http://www.ojp.usdoj.gov/nij/pubs-sum/181584.htm)

The following information is from the above mentioned NIJ report.

INTRODUCTION

It is a capital mistake to theorize before one has data. Insensibly, one begins to twist facts to suit theories instead of theories to suit facts.

*Sherlock Holmes, A Study in Scarlet, by Sir Arthur Conan Doyle.

As Sherlock Holmes pointed out, many types of investigations are susceptible to prejudgment, but few as often as fire scene investigations. Fires, by their destructive nature, consume the evidence of their initiation and progress as they grow. Investigations are compromised, and often scenes are further destroyed by the activities of the fire service, whose primary responsibilities are to save lives and protect property against further damage. Fire scenes often involve all manner of public entities: emergency medical, law enforcement, and fire services. Public utilities such as gas and electric companies may be involved.

Passers-by, owners, tenants, customers, delivery agents all may have relevant information. The press and curious individuals attracted to large fire scenes can complicate investigations, as they make security a necessity. As has frequently been said, "A fire investigation is like a picture puzzle. Everyone involved with it has some of the pieces, but no one has the whole picture. It is up to the investigator to gather enough of these pieces together to solve the puzzle."

WHY INVESTIGATE FIRES?

Since Roman times, civil authorities have recognized the threat that fire represents, not only to the well-being of individuals, but also, and perhaps more importantly, to the welfare and security of the community as a whole. In the days of wooden walls and roofs and straw-covered floors, any fire could ravage an entire city. So, it was in the interest of all concerned to investigate fires and establish how they began. Civil authorities attempted to control the fire risk by assessing penalties if an accidental fire was allowed to get out of control.

Dangerous practices, such as leaving cooking fires unguarded, were identified and controlled. William the Conqueror issued an edict that cooking fires be damped or covered after a particular time of evening so that unattended fires could not flare up. This policy of couvre feu (cover the fire) gave rise to the "curfew" of today. If authorities could determine the fire was deliberately set, the perpetrator could be identified and punished. Some of the oldest English common laws regarded arson to be the crime of burning the house or dwelling of another. The crime of arson was considered to be such a danger that it was punishable by death.

The same rationale applies today. Fires of accidental cause need to be identified, so that dangerous practices, such as filling kerosene room heaters with gasoline, can be eliminated by public education, or so that defective or dangerous products, such as instant-on televisions or room heaters with no overheating or tip-over protection, can be taken off the market or modified so they no longer pose a significant fire risk. Fires of incendiary (i.e., deliberate) cause must be detected, so that the arsonist can be intercepted before doing more harm and punished as necessary.

THE FIRE PROBLEM IN THE UNITED STATES

According to the National Fire Incident Reporting System (NFIRS) of the U.S. Fire Administration (USFA), Federal Emergency Management Agency, the United States has one of the highest per capita fire death rates among industrialized nations. In 1997, the U.S. fire death rate was 15.2 deaths per million. This was reflected in approximately 4,050 deaths and more than 23,000 injuries for that year alone. Nearly 2 million fires occurred in 1997, with a total estimated dollar loss of $8.5 billion.

Thirty-one percent of these fires were in structures. Residential fires comprised 23 percent of all fires and 74 percent of all structure fires. Eighty-four percent of all fatalities occurred in homes. In addition to structure fires, each year hundreds of thousands of vehicle and outside fires occur. In 1997, vehicle fires accounted for nearly 400,000 incidents, resulting in approximately 450 civilian deaths and 1,700 civilian injuries. Outside fires were estimated at more than 700,000 occurrences, accounting for 40 percent of the total number of reported fires.

Arson fires (defined as incendiary/suspicious in NFIRS) comprised almost 16 percent of all reported fires in 1997 and accounted for more than $554 million, or 15 percent, of the total estimated dollar loss. Since all fires are considered accidental until they can be proven to be intentionally set, the reported numbers are probably very conservative. There is also reluctance to report arson fires, as it is feared that it may cause a negative impact on the community or its economy.

While the general trend in numbers of fires and fire deaths has shown a steady gradual decline over the past decade, the overall costs are still significant. A continuing effort must be made to accurately identify the exact origin (where the fire started) and cause (the factors that brought the ignition source and first material ignited together) of all fires. This will assist in learning more about how to prevent fires in the future. Perhaps more important are preventive measures such as installing working smoke detectors and residential sprinklers in every home and using public education programs to effect behavior change.

THE PROBLEM OF FIRE INVESTIGATIONS

The advantages of accurate and thorough fire investigations are obvious. The United States is one of the few countries where public authorities have statutory responsibility to investigate all fires and determine their origins and causes.

While this may appear to be a solution to the problem of fires and arsons, a number of major complications in fire investigations exist in the United States:

- A fire can be a complex event whose origin and cause are not obvious.
  - Investigators may have to expend considerable time and effort before the cause can be identified. This is the area where Holmes' dictum is especially applicable.

– Without gathering data, the investigator can only guess at what might have caused the fire, based on circumstances alone. The training and preparation of qualified investigators are often costly and time-consuming, requiring dedication to the profession over many years.

• The destructive power of the fire itself compromises evidence from the outset. The larger a fire becomes and the longer it burns, the less evidence of causation will remain. In some fires, sufficient data to establish the origin and cause (i.e., evidence) do not survive no matter how diligent the search or well prepared the searcher. This destruction may be exacerbated by the normal and necessary duties of fire personnel carrying out rescue, suppression, overhaul, and salvage tasks.

• The complexity of the threat a major fire presents to the health and welfare of the community means that representatives from law enforcement, fire, rescue, and emergency medical services; hazardous materials teams; utility company personnel; health and safety officers; and other public agency personnel may be on hand and may conduct some obligatory official duties. The presence of so many people, in addition to members of the press and the public who were attracted by the sights and sounds of a major fire, offers yet more chances for scene security to be compromised and critical evidence to be contaminated, moved, or destroyed.

• Responsibility for the investigation of fires is split. While the fire service has the primary civil responsibility to establish a fire's cause, if the cause is determined to be accidental, the scene is released to the owner or the owner's insurance company for further examination. If the conclusion is that the fire was purposely set, a crime has been committed and law enforcement authority is needed to investigate the crime. This often means releasing the scene and evidence to a local law enforcement agency. Where local law enforcement has inadequate resources or personnel, an outside agency such as a State fire marshal, or even a Federal agency (e.g., the Bureau of Alcohol, Tobacco and Firearms (ATF) may be asked to investigate. Any such transfer may cause complications in establishing lines of authority.

- In some agencies, investigative teams are composed of individuals from both law enforcement agencies and fire departments so that the continuity of the investigation can be maintained through both civil and criminal phases. In a few cases, individuals have both law enforcement and fire authority, thanks to extensive cross-training, so cases are handled from start to finish by a minimal number of trained, motivated investigators.

- A lack of commitment to conduct fire investigations exists on the part of some law enforcement and fire agencies. Because of the demand for rescue, hazardous materials, and emergency medical assistance, in addition to their traditional duties of fire suppression, fire departments often find themselves with fewer resources to stretch to cover all obligations. As a result, the less visible responsibilities of fire investigation and fire prevention are often scaled back.

These cutbacks occur despite the advantages that aggressive programs in both areas could provide to the individual department and to the community it serves: Preventing a fire means there is no loss of life or property, no risk to personnel, and no equipment costs; investigating a fire means that potential accidental or criminal threats to the community may be averted in the future. Law enforcement agencies, facing similar overwhelming demands for their time, might prefer not to become involved in cases where the scene is destroyed or at the very least compromised, time-consuming scene examination and interviews are required, and the resulting evidence is often complex and circumstantial (meaning prosecutors may not want to use it even if it is properly and completely collected).

Then Who Investigates Fires?

As might be gathered from the preceding points, who actually will investigate a fire is not an easy question to answer. In addition to law enforcement and fire authorities, there may be prosecuting attorney investigators, forensic laboratory experts, engineering specialists (fire, chemical, mechanical, or electrical), and private investigators representing insurance companies, owners, tenants, and manufacturers of the myriad ignition sources found in a modern home or business.

Figure 14.1 Excerpt from the NIJ Fire and Arson Scene Evidence: A Guide for Public Safety Personnel

This handbook is intended as a guide to recommended practices for the collection and preservation of evidence at fire/arson scenes. Jurisdictional, logistical, or legal conditions may preclude the use of particular procedures contained herein.

Actions taken pursuant to this Guide shall be performed in accordance with department policies and procedures and Federal and State laws.

Not every portion of this document may be applicable to all fires. It is at the discretion of responding personnel (depending on their responsibilities, as well as the purpose and scope of their duties) to apply the procedures recommended in this Guide to a particular incident. Some of the procedures described in this Guide may not be performed in the sequence described or may be performed simultaneously.

Figure 14.1 Excerpt from the NIJ Fire and Arson Scene Evidence: A Guide for Public Safety Personnel (Cont.)

Section A. Establishing the Role of First Responders

Note: The actions of public safety personnel providing emergency services at a fire scene are critical not only to lifesaving and fire suppression efforts but also to any subsequent investigation of the incident.

1. Observe the Fire and Scene Conditions

Principle: Public safety personnel responding to a fire should observe conditions and activities at or near the scene so they can give investigators arriving later an accurate and complete description. First responders can gain information valuable to the fire investigation during their approach to and arrival at the scene.

Procedure: While approaching a fire scene, first responders should observe and mentally note the following conditions and activities and, as soon as conditions permit, initiate permanent documentation of the information (e.g., written notes, voice recordings, videotapes):

  A. The presence, location, and condition of victims and witnesses.

  B. Vehicles leaving the scene, bystanders, or unusual activities near the scene.

  C. Flame and smoke conditions (e.g., the volume of flames and smoke; the color, height, and location of the flames; the direction in which the flames and smoke are moving).

  D. The type of occupancy and use of the structure (e.g., a residential occupancy being used as a business).

  E. Conditions of the structure (e.g., lights turned on; fire through the roof; walls standing; open, closed, or broken windows and doors).

  F. Conditions surrounding the scene (e.g., blocked driveways, debris, damage to other structures).

  G. Weather conditions.

  H. Unusual characteristics of the scene (e.g., the presence of containers, exterior burning or charring on the building, the absence of normal contents, unusual odors, fire trailers. (Physical trails of fuel and the burn patterns caused by those trails).

Figure 14.1 Excerpt from the NIJ Fire and Arson Scene Evidence: A Guide for Public Safety Personnel (Cont.)

I.   The fire suppression techniques used, including ventilation, forcible entry, and utility shutoff measures.

J.   The status of fire alarms, security alarms, and sprinklers.

Summary: First responders' initial observations provide investigators with information pertinent to the investigation. As the investigation unfolds, these observations may provide the starting point for evidence collection and preservation efforts.

2. Exercise Scene Safety

Principle: Safety overrides all other concerns: Ensuring the safety of victims, bystanders, and public safety personnel is the first responders' foremost concern at a fire scene. First responders must take steps to identify and remove or mitigate safety hazards that may further threaten victims, bystanders, and public safety personnel. They must exercise due caution to avoid injuries to themselves and others.

Procedure: Upon arrival at the scene, first responders should:

A.   Evaluate the scene for safety hazards (e.g., structural collapse of the building; smoke; electrical, chemical, or biological hazards; other health risks).

B.   Establish safety/hazard zones.

C.   Communicate hazards to other personnel arriving at the scene.

D.   Use tools and personal protective equipment appropriate to the task during all operations.

Danger: Beware of incendiary or explosive devices!

The scene may contain devices specifically designed to kill or maim public safety responders. Do not touch any suspected incendiary or explosive device. Evacuate the area, and request the services of personnel trained in the removal of such items.

Summary: Safety is the overriding concern during emergency operations and the subsequent investigation. To ensure the safety of civilians and public safety personnel, first responders should take steps to identify, evaluate, and mitigate scene hazards, and they should communicate those hazards to other public safety personnel

Figure 14.1 Excerpt from the NIJ Fire and Arson Scene Evidence: A Guide for Public Safety Personnel (Cont.)

arriving at the scene. Necessary safety zones should be established to receive victims as they are evacuated. Personal protective equipment and other measures should be used to ensure the safety of all persons at the scene. The scene should continually be reassessed to evaluate safety hazards that may change due to fire conditions or suppression efforts.

3. Preserve the Fire Scene

Principle: Evidence at a fire scene takes many different forms, some of which are transient (i.e., they are not permanent and may disappear quickly, such as impressions in snow or evaporating liquids). First responders must understand how rescue, medical, fire suppression, overhaul, (the process of opening concealed spaces to find pockets of fire and removing smoldering materials) and salvage (the process of protecting, moving, or removing items) efforts can adversely affect different forms of evidence and take steps to preserve evidence accordingly. First responders should assess the fire scene to identify potential evidence, take preliminary steps to preserve it, and notify appropriate authorities about its existence.

Procedure: To preserve evidence, first responders should:

    A.   Observe and mentally note evidence that may be present at the scene, such as:
- Fire patterns (including multiple fire locations).
- Burn injuries to victims and fire patterns on clothing.
- Trailers, ignitable liquids, or other unusual fuel distribution (e.g., piles of newspapers, furniture pushed together).
- Incendiary/ignition/explosive devices (e.g., lighters, matches, timing devices).
- Shoe prints and tire impressions.
- Broken windows and doors.
- Distribution of broken glass and debris.
- Indications of forced entry (tools and tool marks).
- Containers.
- Discarded clothing.
- Trace evidence (e.g., hairs, fibers, fingerprints, blood, other body fluids).

Figure 14.1 Excerpt from the NIJ Fire and Arson Scene Evidence: A Guide for Public Safety Personnel (Cont.)

- Evidence of crimes in addition to the possible arson (e.g., weapons, bodies, drugs, clandestine drug laboratory equipment).
- Witnesses, bystanders, and victims.
- Any other unusual items or the absence of normal contents or structural components.

B. Recognize threats to evidence (i.e., its movement, removal, contamination, or destruction) from any of the following sources:
  - Fire suppression activities, such as a straight stream applied at the point of origin or deluge applications that may wash away or dilute potential evidence.
  - Overhaul activities that destroy fire patterns.
  - Salvage activities that involve moving or removing potential physical evidence.
  - Use of a tool in any manner that causes destruction of evidence.
  - Movement of knobs, switches, and controls on appliances and utilities.
  - Weather conditions that affect transient evidence (i.e., wind, precipitation, or temperature changes).
  - Personnel walking through the scene.
  - Witnesses and victims leaving the scene.
  - Medical intervention and treatment of victims (e.g., by damaging evidence at the scene or destroying victims' clothing).
  - Premature removal or movement of bodies.
  - Vehicles at the scene (e.g., that introduce fluid to the scene through vehicle leaks or destroy other evidence, including shoe prints and tire impressions).
  - Contamination from external sources, such as fuel-powered tools or equipment.

C. Protect evidence by:
  - Limiting excessive fire suppression, overhaul, and salvage.
  - Avoiding needless destruction of property.
  - Leaving bodies undisturbed.
  - Flagging items of evidence with cones or markers.
  - Recording observations through written notes or voice recordings.

Figure 14.1 Excerpt from the NIJ Fire and Arson Scene Evidence: A Guide for Public Safety Personnel (Cont.)

- Covering items or areas containing evidence with objects that will not contaminate the evidence (e.g., clean boxes or tarpaulins).
- Isolating items or areas containing evidence with rope, barrier tape, barricades, or sentries.
- Retaining and securing clothing items removed from victims and suspects.
- Obtaining information about victims and witnesses (i.e., their names, addresses, and telephone numbers).
- Preserving transient evidence (e.g., trace evidence, shoe prints, tire impressions).
- Removing evidence at risk of imminent destruction by the fire or the structural collapse of the damaged building.
- Ensuring that later arriving investigators are fully apprised of the evidence discovered.

Summary: First responders should recognize items that may have evidentiary value in a subsequent investigation and take steps to protect them from damage that could result from the fire, fire suppression, or rescue efforts.

4. Establish Security and Control

Principle: Fire suppression and rescue efforts can be performed more efficiently and effectively if only essential authorized personnel are permitted access to the area. Restricting access also ensures the safety of civilians and helps to preserve the scene for subsequent investigation. First responders should immediately establish control of the scene. Then, as soon as conditions permit, first responders should initiate documentation of the scene to aid in the investigation.

Procedure: To establish security and control, first responders should:

A. Set up a security perimeter (e.g., using barrier tape, fire line, sentry).

B. Control access into the scene through the security perimeter.

C. Initiate documentation of the scene. (See "Section C: Documenting the Scene.")

Figure 14.1 Excerpt from the NIJ Fire and Arson Scene Evidence: A Guide for Public Safety Personnel (Cont.)

Summary: The actions of first responders at a fire scene are not only critical to saving lives and suppressing fires; they also set the stage for the investigators arriving to process the scene by establishing a controlled security perimeter and initiating documentation of the scene.

5. Coordinate Activities

Principle: Emergency operations at the fire scene may involve many different agencies and organizations, each having a different focus and performing different activities. These activities must be well coordinated to accomplish emergency operations efficiently and to preserve the integrity of the scene.

Upon arrival at the scene, first responders must establish an incident command system, which allows for a systematic flow and transfer of critical scene information.

Procedure: To coordinate activities at the scene, first responders should:

    A.   Establish a command post and implement an incident command system (i.e., a point of contact and line of communication and authority for public safety personnel).

    B.   Establish staging areas to ensure that emergency and support vehicles have access into the area.

    C.   Request additional personnel resources, such as firefighters, EMS personnel, law enforcement officers, investigators, and representatives of utility companies.

    D.   Inform authorities about the status of the incident, hazards, injuries, witnesses, the location of evidence, and other pertinent facts.

5. Coordinate Activities

Principle: Emergency operations at the fire scene may involve many different agencies and organizations, each having a different focus and performing different activities. These activities must be well coordinated to accomplish emergency operations efficiently and to preserve the integrity of the scene.

Figure 14.1 Excerpt from the NIJ Fire and Arson Scene Evidence: A Guide for Public Safety Personnel (Cont.)

Upon arrival at the scene, first responders must establish an incident command system, which allows for a systematic flow and transfer of critical scene information.

Procedure: To coordinate activities at the scene, first responders should:

A. Establish a command post and implement an incident command system (i.e., a point of contact and line of communication and authority for public safety personnel).

B. Establish staging areas to ensure that emergency and support vehicles have access into the area.

C. Request additional personnel resources, such as firefighters, EMS personnel, law enforcement officers, investigators, and representatives of utility companies.

D. Inform authorities about the status of the incident, hazards, injuries, witnesses, the location of evidence, and other pertinent facts.

Summary: First responders must establish an incident command system to coordinate activities at the scene and communicate information to responsible authorities.

Section B. Evaluating the Scene

Note: This and subsequent sections of this Guide are intended for the individual responsible for the investigation of a fire incident. At the time the scene is determined to involve arson or other crime, the investigator must address legal requirements for scene access, search, and evidence seizure.

1. Introduce Yourself and Your Role as the Investigator

Principle: Introductions at the scene allow the investigator to establish formal contact with other official agency representatives. The investigator should meet with the incident commander and first responders to assess previous events and the current status of the fire scene, introduce himself or herself, identify essential personnel, and determine what the scene safety and integrity issues are.

Procedure: Upon arrival at the scene, and prior to entering the scene, the investigator should:

Figure 14.1 Excerpt from the NIJ Fire and Arson Scene Evidence: A Guide for Public Safety Personnel (Cont.)

A. Identify and contact the current incident commander and present identification.

B. Conduct a briefing with the incident commander to determine who has jurisdiction and authorization (legal right of entry) and to identify other personnel at the scene (e.g., law enforcement, firefighting, EMS, hazardous materials, and utility services personnel).

C. Determine the level of assistance required and whether additional personnel are needed.

D. Determine initial scene safety prior to entry through observations and discussions with first responders. Consider environmental as well as personnel safety concerns. Assess changes in safety conditions resulting from suppression efforts.

Summary: On scene introductions establish formal contact with the incident commander and other official agency representatives and promote a collaborative investigative effort. Preliminary scene safety concerns are addressed and continually reevaluated due to the effects of changing fire conditions, suppression efforts, and scene reconstruction.

2. Define the Extent of the Scene

Principle: To provide for the safety and security of personnel and to protect the evidence, the investigator should perform a preliminary scene assessment. The investigator should determine the area in which the site examination will be conducted and establish or adjust the scene perimeter.

Procedure: To determine the boundaries of the scene, the investigator should:

A. Make a preliminary scene assessment (an overall tour of the fire scene to determine the extent of the damage, proceeding from areas of least damage to areas of greater damage) to identify areas that warrant further examination, being careful not to disturb evidence.

Authors' Note:

Photographs are going to be the major source of evidence used in the court room in an arson case. This is because the physical evidence from scene would be difficult at best to bring to the courtroom, i.e. ashes, burnt trusses, broken windows. The photos are going to tell the story to the judge and jury. The story the photos should tell are:

- The cause of the fire (eliminating other causes).
- The overall view of the damage to the building.

A panoramic view can be achieved by a wide angle lens or taking a series of photographs and joining them together.

An overhead view or aerial shot from airplane, helicopter, cherry picker or neighboring building.

Noting the burn patterns or vent openings the fire caused.

Noting the type of construction and materials of the building (brick, stucco, etc.)

Noting the locations of chimneys, windows, doors, etc.

- Where the building is in reference to adjoining to neighboring buildings.
- Where the firefighters were located when working the scene.
- The location of relevant items to the fire, such as; power lines, fuse boxes, fire hydrants, fuel tanks or any suspect item that could be a source of the fire.
- The damage to the interior showing the least amount of damage to the greatest.

Use a quality flash to provide detail in the black dark soot and ash.

- Tell what the room was, i.e. kitchen, living room, bedroom.
- Where the fire started and where it didn't start (elimination of other causes to rebut defense accusations or another or different cause).
- The damage to the floor, walls doors, windows and ceilings.
- How the area looked after the fire and how it looked after technicians processing.
- How things looked after clean up and excavation, i.e. damage to flooring, ceiling etc.
- The trail or direction the fire spread between rooms.
- The fire and rescue efforts and effects on the building, i.e. tool marks on entryway, doors or windows open or kicked in.
- Should tell position of windows doors at the time of the fire.

Figure 14.1 Excerpt from the NIJ Fire and Arson Scene Evidence: A Guide for Public Safety Personnel (Cont.)

B. Inspect and protect adjacent areas, even areas with little or no damage, that may include nonfire evidence (e.g., bodies, blood stains, latent prints, tool marks) or additional fire-related evidence (e.g., unsuccessful ignition sources, fuel containers, ignitable liquids).

C. Mark or reevaluate the perimeter and establish or reassess the procedures for controlling access.

Summary: Procedures focusing on the perimeter and on control of access to the fire scene protect the integrity of the scene.

3. Identify and Interview Witnesses at the Scene

Principle: Persons with information about the scene, activities prior to the fire, the fire, and its suppression are valuable witnesses. The investigator should determine the identities and locations of witnesses and make arrangements to conduct interviews.

Procedure: To develop a witness list, the investigator should:

A. Contact the incident commander, identify first responders and first-in firefighters, and arrange to document their observations either in writing or through recorded interviews.

B. Determine who reported the fire. (Secure a tape or transcript of the report if available.)

C. Identify the owner of the building/scene, any occupants, and the person responsible for property management.

D. Identify who was last to leave the building/scene and what occurred immediately before they left.

E. Identify and interview other witnesses (e.g., neighbors, bystanders, people injured during the fire, later arriving public agency personnel) and record their statements.

Summary: Developing a list of persons who have information about the scene, activities prior to the fire, the fire, and its suppression assists investigators with the subsequent investigation.

4. Assess Scene Security at the Time of the Fire

Principle: The investigator should determine whether the building or vehicle was intact and secure and if intrusion alarms or fire detection and suppression systems were operational at the time of the fire. This

Figure 14.1 Excerpt from the NIJ Fire and Arson Scene Evidence: A Guide for Public Safety Personnel (Cont.)

information helps to establish factors such as ventilation conditions, possible fire development timelines and scenarios, and whether vandalism of the property or systems occurred prior to the fire.

Procedure: To determine the status of security at the time of the fire, the investigator should:

   A.   Ask first responders where entry was made, what steps were taken to gain entry, and whether any systems had been activated when they arrived at the scene.

   B.   Observe and document the condition of doors, windows, other openings, and fire separations (e.g., fire doors). Attempt to determine whether they were open, closed, or compromised at the time of the fire.

   C.   Observe and document the position of timers, switches, valves, and control units for utilities, detection systems, and suppression systems, as well as any alterations to those positions by first responders.

   D.   Contact security and suppression system monitoring agencies to obtain information and available documentation about the design and functioning of the systems.

Summary: Determining and documenting system operations and scene security at the time of the fire establishes existing conditions of the scene. Data from detection and suppression systems can provide information about the fire's origin and spread.

5. Identify Resources Required to Process the Scene

Principle: The investigator should recognize limitations of his or her own expertise and knowledge and determine what personnel may be required to process the scene according to NFPA 921 and other recognized national guidelines. Except in the most obvious cases, the determination of a fire's origin and cause may be a complex and difficult undertaking that requires specialized training and experience as well as knowledge of generally accepted scientific methods of fire investigation. The investigator must either have appropriate expertise or call upon the assistance of someone with that knowledge. This is especially true in cases involving deaths, major injuries, or large property losses.

Figure 14.1 Excerpt from the NIJ Fire and Arson Scene Evidence: A Guide for Public Safety Personnel (Cont.)

Procedure: Based on the preliminary scene assessment and analysis of fire patterns and damage at the scene, the investigator should:

A. Identify a distinct origin (location where the fire started) and an obvious fire cause (ignition source, first fuel ignited, and circumstances of the event that brought the two together). If neither the origin nor the cause is immediately obvious, or if there is clear evidence of an incendiary cause, the investigator should conduct a scene examination in accordance with NFPA 921 and other recognized national guidelines or seek someone with the expertise required.

Note: At the time the scene is determined to involve an arson or other crime, the investigator must address legal requirements for scene access, search, and evidence seizure.

B. Know when to contact or request the assistance of specialized personnel and to obtain specialized equipment as required to assist with the investigation.

Standard equipment should include the following:
- Barrier tape.
- Clean, unused evidence containers (e.g., cans, glass jars, nylon or polyester bags).
- Compass.
- Decontamination equipment (e.g., buckets, pans, detergent).
- Evidence tags, labels, and tape.
- Gloves (disposable gloves and work gloves).
- Hand tools (e.g., hammers, screwdrivers, knives, crowbars).
- Lights (e.g., flashlights, spotlights).
- Marker cones or flags.
- Personal protective equipment.
- Photographic equipment.
- Rakes, brooms, spades, etc.
- Tape measures.
- Writing equipment (e.g., notebooks, pens, pencils, permanent markers).

Figure 14.1 Excerpt from the NIJ Fire and Arson Scene Evidence: A Guide for Public Safety Personnel (Cont.)

C.   Recognize and consider the interests of parties that may be affected by the outcome of the investigation and, to the extent possible, avoid jeopardizing those interests by taking steps to protect evidence. These issues include spoliation (damage or loss of evidence that would compromise a legal case), subrogation (recovering damages by a finding of fault; finding that the cause of the fire was the failure of some product or system), and third-party claims.

Summary: Identifying the required resources ensures that the scene is processed by qualified individuals and that evidence necessary for both criminal and civil litigation will be preserved.

Section C. Documenting the Scene

1. Photograph/Videotape the Scene

Principle: Photographic documentation creates a permanent record of the scene and supplements the written incident report(s), witness statements, or reports on the position of evidence. The investigator should create and preserve an accurate visual record of the scene and the evidence prior to disturbing the scene. Additional photography or videography should occur as the investigation progresses.

Procedure: The scene should be photographed prior to the disturbance or removal of any evidence and throughout the scene investigation. The investigator (or other individual responsible for evidence) should:

A.   Photograph and/or videotape the assembled crowd and the fire in progress.

B.   Remove all nonessential personnel from the background when photographing the scene and evidence.

C.   Photograph the exterior and interior of the fire scene (consider walls, doors, windows, ceilings, floors) in a systematic and consistent manner. (Videotaping may serve as an additional record but not as a replacement for still photography.)

D.   Photograph any points or areas of origin, ignition sources, and first material ignited.

Figure 14.1 Excerpt from the NIJ Fire and Arson Scene Evidence: A Guide for Public Safety Personnel (Cont.)

> E. Photograph any physical reconstruction of the scene.
>
> F. Maintain photo and video logs. Record the date, the name of the photographer, and the subject.
>
> G. Determine whether additional photographic resources are necessary (e.g., aerial photography, infrared photography, stereo photography, photogrammetry). [Photogrammetry is considered a science or an art for obtaining reliable measurements or physical dimensions from photographs.]
>
> Summary: Photographic documentation provides a permanent record of the scene.
>
> 2. Describe and Document the Scene
>
> Principle: Written documentation of the scene provides a permanent record of the investigator's observations that may be used to refresh recollections, support the investigator's opinions and conclusions, and support photographic documentation.
>
> Procedure: The investigator should:
>
> A. Prepare narrative, written descriptions and observations, including assessments of possible fire causes.
>
> B. Sketch an accurate representation of the scene and its dimensions, including significant features such as the ceiling height, fuel packages (e.g., combustible contents of the room), doors, windows, and any areas of origin.
>
> C. Prepare a detailed diagram using the scene sketch(es), preexisting diagrams, drawings, floor plans, or architectural or engineering drawings of the scene. This may be done at a later date.
>
> D. Determine whether additional documentation resources are necessary.
>
> Summary: Written descriptions of the scene, along with accurate sketches and measurements, are invaluable for focusing the investigation. Written scene documentation recreates the scene for investigative, scientific analysis, and judicial purposes and correlates with photographic evidence.

Figure 14.1 Excerpt from the NIJ Fire and Arson Scene Evidence: A Guide for Public Safety Personnel (Cont.)

Tip on Note-taking, From Retired Police Lieutenant Daniel Byram
"My field notes helped me more than once on the street as a beat officer. Once I investigated several suspicious fires in my beat. I had the foresight to document the names of the people in the area of the crime scene while I was conducting my investigation. On one case I recognized that several juvenile males appeared at a previous scene according to my notes. I went to their house and found piles of burned matches outside the door in their carport, and the rest was history."

Section D. Processing Evidence at the Scene

Note: At the time the scene is determined to involve an arson or other crime, the investigator must address legal requirements for scene access, search, and evidence seizure.

1. Identify, Collect, and Preserve Evidence

Principle: Collecting evidence at a fire scene requires attention to documenting and maintaining the integrity of the evidence. The investigator should ensure that evidence collectors identify and properly document, collect, and preserve evidence for laboratory analyses, further investigations, and court proceedings, in accordance with NFPA 921 and other recognized national guidelines, including American Society for Testing and Materials standards E860, E1188, and E1459. This will ensure that critical evidence is not contaminated or lost prior to analysis and that the chain of custody is maintained.

Procedure: To optimize the recovery and evaluation of physical evidence, evidence collectors should:

    A.   Take precautions to prevent contamination.

    B.   Document the location of evidence using written notes, sketches, photographs, photo and video logs, the evidence recovery log, evidence tags, and container labels. When evidence is excavated, additional photographs may be of value.

    C.   Take special care to collect evidence in any areas of origin (such as the first fuel ignited and ignition source) in cases where the fire is not accidental.

Figure 14.1 Excerpt from the NIJ Fire and Arson Scene Evidence: A Guide for Public Safety Personnel (Cont.)

Note: In cases where the fire appears to be accidental, evidence should not be needlessly disturbed, but the property owner or insurer should be notified to avoid issues of spoliation.

D.   Place evidence in labeled containers for transportation and preservation.

Evidence collected for laboratory identification of ignitable liquids must be immediately placed in clean, unused, vapor tight containers (e.g., clean, unused paint cans; glass jars; laboratory-approved nylon or polyester bags) and then sealed.

E.   Label each container so that it is uniquely identified. Labeling may include the name of the investigator, date and time of collection, case number, sample number, description, and location of recovery.

F.   Collect and preserve suitable comparison samples but recognize that such samples may be unavailable.

G.   Package evidence in accordance with their laboratories' policies and procedures.

H.   Recognize the presence of other physical evidence, such as blood stains, shoe prints, latent prints, and trace evidence, and use proper preservation and collection methods or seek qualified assistance.

Summary: Proper collection and packaging preserve the value of physical evidence.

2. Prevent Contamination

Principle: Preventing contamination during evidence collection protects the integrity of the fire scene and evidence. The investigator should ensure that access to the fire scene after fire suppression is controlled and that evidence is collected, stored, and transported in such a manner that it will not be contaminated.

Figure 14.1 Excerpt from the NIJ Fire and Arson Scene Evidence: A Guide for Public Safety Personnel (Cont.)

Procedure: To prevent contamination, personnel (e.g., evidence collectors) should:

A.   Establish and maintain strict control of access to the scene.

B.   Recognize that fuel-powered tools and equipment present potential contamination sources and should be avoided. When it is necessary to use these tools and equipment, the investigator should document their use.

C.   Wear clean, protective outer garments, including footwear.

D.   Use clean disposable gloves for collecting items of evidence. (To avoid cross-contamination, gloves should be changed between collection of unrelated items of evidence or when visibly soiled.)

E.   Use clean tools for collecting items of evidence from different locations within a scene. (Disposable tools also can be used.)

F.   Place evidence in clean, unused containers and seal immediately.

G.   Store and ship fire debris evidence containers of evidence collected from different scenes in separate packages.

H.   Package liquid samples to prevent leakage and ship them separately from other evidence.

I.   Store and ship fire debris evidence separately from other evidence.

J.   Follow any specific laboratory requests, such as submitting an unused sample container or absorbent medium for detection of any contaminants.

Summary: Attention to scene control and evidence collection and packaging helps to prevent contamination and ensures the integrity of the evidence.

3. Package and Transport Evidence

Principle: Preventing changes in the condition of a sample after it has been collected ensures the integrity of the evidence and requires controlled packaging and transportation. The investigator should ensure that packaging, transportation, and storage procedures are followed to prevent any destructive changes in the condition of samples.

Figure 14.1 Excerpt from the NIJ Fire and Arson Scene Evidence: A Guide for Public Safety Personnel (Cont.)

Procedure: To minimize changes in the condition of samples, the personnel responsible for packaging and transport should:

    A.   Take precautions to prevent contamination.

    B.   Package fragile items carefully.

    C.   Freeze or immediately transport items containing soil to the laboratory.

    D.   Transport all volatile samples to the laboratory in a timely manner.

    E.   Comply with shipping regulations.

Summary: Adherence to approved packaging and transportation procedures safeguards the condition of the evidence and ensures its continued integrity.

4. Establish and Maintain the Chain of Custody

Principle: Establishing and maintaining a chain of custody verifies the integrity of the evidence. The investigator should ensure that the chain of custody is maintained.

Procedure: Personnel responsible for the chain of custody should:

    A.   Maintain written records documenting the sample number, description of the evidence, date and location where it was found, collector's name, and miscellaneous comments.

    B.   Document all transfers of custody, including the name of the recipient and the date and manner of transfer.

    C.   Document the final disposition of the evidence.

Summary: Maintaining the chain of custody for evidence, from collection through final disposition, ensures its integrity.

Section E. Completing the Scene Investigation

1. Release the Scene

Principle: The investigator should ensure that the scene is not released until reasonable efforts have been made to identify, collect, and remove all evidence from the scene for further examination and that all physical characteristics of the scene have been documented. In addition, prior to releasing the scene, associated legal, health, and

Figure 14.1 Excerpt from the NIJ Fire and Arson Scene Evidence: A Guide for Public Safety Personnel (Cont.)

safety issues must be articulated to the party receiving the scene and reported to public safety agencies if necessary. Doing so minimizes the risk of a further incident or injury and the potential liability of the authority releasing the scene.

Procedure: The investigator should ensure that the following tasks are completed before releasing the scene:

A. Perform a final critical review:
- Ensure that all evidence is inventoried and in custody.
- Discuss preliminary scene findings with team members.
- Discuss post scene issues, including forensic testing, insurance inquiries, interview results, and criminal histories.
- Assign post scene responsibilities to law enforcement personnel and other investigators (Remember that this Guide focuses on the documentation and collection of physical evidence at fire/arson scenes. Other issues of investigation, such as insurance inquiries, background information, fire deaths, the interpretation of physical evidence, and case analysis and profiling, are not addressed in this document).
- Address legal considerations.

B. Verify that all scene documentation has been completed. (This can be accomplished using an incident documentation checklist or closure form)

C. Address structural, environmental, health, and safety issues.

D. Remove all investigative equipment and materials.
- Recover and inventory equipment.
- Decontaminate equipment and personnel.

E. Record the following information:
- Time and date of release.
- Receiving party.
- Authority releasing the scene.

Figure 14.1 Excerpt from the NIJ Fire and Arson Scene Evidence: A Guide for Public Safety Personnel (Cont.)

- Condition of the scene at the time of release (e.g., structural, environmental, health, and safety issues). Consider photographing and/or videotaping the final condition of the scene.
- Cautions given to the receiving party upon release (e.g., safety concerns, conditions, evidence, legal issues).

Summary: Responsibility for the scene should be transferred to an authority having jurisdiction or to the party with the legal right to the scene, after the scene examination, the condition of the scene, and any cautions supplied have been documented.

2. Submit Reports to the Appropriate Databases

Principle: Detailed fire information is collected, integrated, and disseminated through national and State databases. These data help authorities identify fire trends and develop innovative procedures and equipment. The responsible agencies must file incident reports with the appropriate databases.

Procedure: The investigator should collect sufficient information to facilitate reporting to the following databases as appropriate:

    A.   Arson and Explosives National Repository (Bureau of Alcohol, Tobacco and Firearms).

    B.   Bomb Data Center (Federal Bureau of Investigation).

    C.   National Fire Incident Reporting System (U.S. Fire Administration).

    D.   National Incident-Based Reporting System (Federal Bureau of Investigation).

    E.   State and local fire incident reporting systems.

Summary: The responsible agencies should contribute to databases that compile information for purposes of identifying fire trends and developing suspect profiles.

Why This Guide?

Considering the wide spectrum of people involved in the investigation of fires, perhaps it is understandable why uniform guidelines for fire scene documentation and evidence collection have not been previously crafted for those public safety personnel who may not be trained in the specialized aspects of fire scene investigation but may be in the position of having to respond to a fire/arson scene. Whether from law enforcement or fire agencies, the public-sector individuals responsible for investigations have had access to specialized training programs through USFA's National Fire Academy, ATF, the Federal Bureau of Investigation (FBI), State fire marshal offices, professional organizations such as the International Association of Arson Investigators, and various private-sector groups. In 1992, the National Fire Protection Association (NFPA) issued NFPA 921: Guide for Fire and Explosion Investigations, a consensus document reflecting the knowledge and experience of fire, engineering, legal, and investigative experts across the United States. This document is continuously reviewed, public proposals and comments are solicited, and a revised edition is produced every 3 to 5 years. It has become a benchmark for the training and expertise of everyone who purports to be an expert in the origin and cause determination of fires.

Unfortunately, not everyone involved in the process of scene examination and evidence documentation and collection will have the opportunity to master the entire contents of comprehensive manuals, such as NFPA 921. As previously discussed, fires are common occurrences that threaten lives and communities, so many people are involved in fire investigations, and many people hold pieces of the puzzle, often without knowing it.

CAR FIRES

As with structure fires; the cause is not always known at the time. When photographing a car fire it's preferable to take photos at the scene. That way the surrounding areas can be included.
  • Photograph the VIN number.

- Photograph all four sides.
  - With the doors, hood and trunk open (take photos of trunk contents).
  - With the doors, hood and trunk closed.
- Photograph the under carriage.
  - Noting fuel line, brake line, hoses, wiring, carburetor (if there is one) exhaust pipe, battery etc.
- Photograph the engine from above.
  - Noting fuel line, brake line, hoses, wiring, carburetor (if there is one) exhaust pipe, battery etc.
  - Having the photos of the same model car (un-burnt) are good for comparison.
- Photograph interior.
  - Dashboard (glove compartments and contents).
  - Front and back seats.
  - Doors and windows.

EXPLOSIVE DEVICES

The National Institute of Justice has published a guide for investigating bomb scenes titled "A Guide for Explosion and Bombing Scene Investigation". The guide covers the investigation of bombings, explosions, evidence identification and analysis, evidence collection, chain of custody, and public safety coordination. The basic steps to documenting are the same; notes, photos, sketches and final reports. However, it points out subtle differences in the practice of processing the scene. Since the basic steps are same we will spare you the re-run but we have provided a segment from the guide that provides a useful background into bombing and explosion related incidents.

Figure 14.2 Excerpt From: A Guide for Explosion & Bombing Scene Investigation

The principal Federal partners in the collection of data related to explosives incidents in the United States are the Bureau of Alcohol, Tobacco and Firearms (ATF), the Federal Bureau of Investigation (FBI), the U.S. Postal Inspection Service (USPIS), and the U.S. Fire Administration (USFA). These Federal partners collect and compile information supplied by State and local fire service and law enforcement agencies throughout the United States and many foreign countries.

According to ATF and FBI databases, there were approximately 38,362 explosives incidents from 1988 through 1997 (the latest year for which complete data were available) in the United States, including Guam, Puerto Rico, and the U.S. Virgin Islands. Incident reports received by ATF and the FBI indicate that the States with the most criminal bombing incidents are traditionally California, Florida, Illinois, Texas, and Washington. Criminal bombings and other explosives incidents have occurred in all States, however, and the problem is not limited to one geographic or demographic area of the country.

The number of criminal bombing incidents (bombings, attempted bombings, incendiary bombings, and attempted incendiary bombings) reported to ATF, the FBI, and USPIS fluctuated in the years 1993-97, ranging between 2,217 in 1997 and 3,163 in 1994. Incendiary incidents reached a high of 725 in both 1993 and 1994. Explosives incidents reached a high of 2,438 in 1994 and a low of 1,685 in 1997. It is important to note that these numbers reflect only the incidents reported to Federal databases and do not fully reflect the magnitude of the problem in the United States.

Of the criminal bombing incidents reported during 1993-97, the top three targets—collectively representing approximately 60 percent of the incidents— were residential properties, mailboxes, and vehicles. Motives are known for about 8,000 of these incidents, with vandalism and revenge by far cited most frequently.

The most common types of explosive/incendiary devices encountered by fire service and law enforcement personnel in the United States are traditionally pipe bombs, Molotov cocktails, and other improvised explosive/incendiary devices. The most common explosive materials used in these devices are flammable liquids and black and smokeless powder.

To view the entire document go to A Guide for Explosion and Bombing Scene Investigation: http://www.ncjrs.org/pdffiles1/nij/181869.pdf

Intentional fires or explosions will be the interest of the criminal justice community; but private and civil entities will be as well.

Intentional fires could be set by those trying to claim insurance money, cover up another crime, or psychological dysfunction. Accidental fires could be caused by faulting manufacturing or maintenance; causing civil interest in a liability suit.

SUMMARY

Documentation of the fire scene is obviously important to help establish the cause of the fire. As with all crime scene documentation and processing; safety is important. In the case of arson, bombing or explosions the issue of safety becomes even more paramount. So do the issues of contamination. The natures of fire scenes are messy at best and following proper procedures will help eliminate contamination.

DISCUSSION QUESTIONS

1. Explain the importance of investigating fires and their causes.
2. Among industrialized nations, what country has one of the highest per capita fire death rates?
3. What happens the larger a fire becomes and the longer it burns?

ADDITIONAL READING

The documents listed below are for informational purposes and should not necessarily be considered authoritative in their entirety.

American Society for Testing and Materials. E860-97 Standard Practice for Examining and Testing Items That Are or May Become Involved in Products Liability Litigation. West Conshohocken, Pennsylvania: American Society for Testing and Materials, 1999.

American Society for Testing and Materials. E1188-95 Standard Practice for Collection and Preservation of Information and Physical Items by a Technical Investigator. West Conshohocken, Pennsylvania: American Society for Testing and Materials, 1999.

American Society for Testing and Materials. E1459-92 Standard Guide for Physical Evidence Labeling and Related Documentation. West Conshohocken, Pennsylvania: American Society for Testing and Materials, 1998.

Bureau of Alcohol, Tobacco and Firearms. ATF Arson Investigative Guide. Washington, D.C.: U.S. Department of the Treasury, Bureau of Alcohol, Tobacco and Firearms, 1997.

Cole, Lee S. The Investigation of Motor Vehicle Fires. 3d ed. Novato, California: Lee Books, 1992.

DeHaan, John D. Kirk's Fire Investigation. 4th ed. Upper Saddle River, New Jersey: Brady Publishing/Prentice Hall, 1997.

DiNenno, Philip J., ed. The SFPE Handbook of Fire Protection Engineering. Quincy, Massachusetts: National Fire Protection Association and Society of Fire Protection Engineering, 1999.

"Glossary of Terms." Fire and Arson Investigator 40 (2): 25-34. International Fire Service Training Association. Introduction to Fire Origin and Cause. 2d ed. Stillwater, Oklahoma: Fire Protection Publications, 1997.

Munday, J.W. Safety at Scenes of Fire and Related Incidents. London: Fire Protection Association, 1995.

National Fire Protection Association. Fire Protection Handbook. 18th ed. Quincy, Massachusetts: National Fire Protection Association, 1997.

National Fire Protection Association. NFPA 472: Standard for Professional Competence of Responders to Hazardous Materials Incidents. Quincy, Massachusetts, 1999.

National Fire Protection Association. NFPA 906: Guide for Fire Incident Field Notes. Quincy, Massachusetts: National Fire Protection Association.

National Fire Protection Association. NFPA 921: Guide for Fire and Explosion Investigations. Quincy, Massachusetts: National Fire Protection Association.

A Pocket Guide to Accellerant Evidence Collection. 2d ed. Saugus, Massachusetts: Massachusetts Chapter, International Association of Arson Investigators, 2000.

Quintiere, James G. Principles of Fire Behavior. Albany, New York: Delmar Publishers, 1997.

National Resources

interfire 877-INTERFIRE
URL: http://www.interfire.com

International Association of Arson Investigators
314-739-4224
URL: http://www.fire-investigators.orgNational Resources

International Fire Service Training Association
405-744-5723
URL: http://www.ifsta.org

National Association of Fire Investigators
312-427-6320
URL: http://www.nafi.org

National Center for Forensic Science
407-823-6469
URL: http://ncfs.ucf.edu

National Fire Protection Association
617-770-3000
URL: http://www.nfpa.org

Points of Contact

Bureau of Alcohol, Tobacco and Firearms
Headquarters Enforcement Operations Center
888-ATF-FIRE
URL: http://www.atf.treas.gov

Arson and Explosives National Repository
800-461-8841
202-927-4590

Arson and Explosives Programs Division
202-927-7930

National Laboratory
301-762-9800

Chemical Transportation Emergency Center (CHEMTREC")
800-262-8200
URL: http://www.chemtrec.org

Federal Bureau of Investigation
Chemistry Division
202-324-4318
URL: http://www.fbi.gov

Federal Emergency Management Agency
U.S. Fire Administration
301-447-1000
URL: http://www.usfa.fema.gov

National Institute of Standards and Technology
Building and Fire Research Laboratory
301-975-6850
URL: http://www.bfrl.nist.gov

U.S. Consumer Product Safety Commission
800-638-2772
URL: http://www.cpsc.gov

U.S. Environmental Protection Agency
National Response Center
800-424-8802
URL: http://www.epa.gov

Chapter 15

Accident Investigation & Reconstruction

CHAPTER OVERVIEW

Traffic accidents happen, it's inevitable, and people unfortunately get injured or killed. Once an accident has occurred, investigating that accident must take into account many areas including, but not limited to, location, weather, vehicle dynamics, speed analysis, braking analysis, visibility, road conditions, human factors, and driver ability and experience. There are times when the reason why an accident occurred is obvious, other times the reason is not clear.

All of the information obtained during the investigation is evidence for a court hearing, and can be given to appropriate officials such as a coroner, a reconstructionist, road safety engineers, insurance adjusters, litigators or law enforcement personnel.

OBJECTIVES

At the end of this chapter, you will be able to:
1. Explain the reasons why accident investigation and reconstruction are important.
2. Evaluate the methods of accident investigation and reconstruction.

ACCIDENT DEFINED

According to Black's Law Dictionary, 6th ed, 1990 at p.15, an accident *"... in its most commonly accepted meaning, or in its ordinary or popular sense, the word may be defined as meaning: a fortuitous circumstance, event, or happening; an event happening without any human agency, or if happening wholly or partly through human agency, an event which under the circumstances is unusual and unexpected by the person to whom it happens; an unusual, fortuitous, unexpected, unforeseen or unlooked for event, happening or occurrence. An event that takes place without one's foresight or expectation, an undersigned, sudden and unexpected event..."*

When applied to traffic, the word "accident" is generally considered to be synonymous with such terms as collision, crash or incident and simply means "an unforeseen occurrence, or sequence of events, in the operation of an automobile which results in injury to a person(s) or damage to property."

OBJECTIVES OF TRAFFIC INVESTIGATION AND RECONSTRUCTION

The objectives of traffic investigation and reconstruction are simple. They must determine:

- WHAT happened
- WHERE the accident happened
- WHEN the accident happened
- WHY the incident occurred
- WHO was involved

ACCIDENT INVESTIGATION

For anyone investigating a traffic accident, the minutes immediately following a motor vehicle accident are of the utmost importance. Work must be done quickly and confidently to preserve physical evidence of the accident before it disappears or becomes contaminated. Investigators need to be trained in the skills needed to systematically investigate the traffic accident to be able to recognize critical evidence at the accident scene, and to preserve and record it appropriately. Proper techniques for recognizing and accurately recording accident results are a must. Techniques including measurements, sketches, after-accident diagrams, and photographs are used.

Information must be gathered to aid in reconstruction of the accident if needed for prosecution or litigation of the accident. Properly documenting this data is critical because once the scene is cleared, the data may be lost forever.

The duties of investigators at an accident scene generally involve two phases: 1) the collecting of data at the scene; and 2) analyzing the data once it is collected. However, before the process of collecting the data can begin, law enforcement personnel must ensure that both the scene and the traffic are controlled.

Scene Control

As with any crime or accident scene, the evidence must be obtained and preserved. No one should be allowed to enter the scene of an accident without property authority to do so. Those who do enter must be cautious to insure that evidence is not moved or contaminated.

Traffic Control

Maintaining orderly and safe movement of traffic is essential at the scene of an incident. It is normal for citizens to want to "rubberneck" or slow down to see what is happening. If at all possible, traffic should be diverted away from the scene and onto adjacent or connecting roadways. If diversion is not possible, then, at the very least, someone (preferably a law enforcement officer) should be placed between the incident scene and the flow of traffic to direct motorists past the location quickly and safely.

Data Collection

- Data collection will include such things as:
  - Statements of witnesses
  - Victims

Unfortunately, there may be times when the victims did not survive the accident and therefore their recollection of the events prior to and at the time of the accident will never be known. When this is the case, extreme care should be taken by the investigator to insure that all evidence is preserved so as to allow it to "speak for itself".

In addition, many times the victims, or injured persons, involved in the accident will not be able to verbalize to the investigator exactly what happened at the time of the accident. Initial statements taken from the parties involved may require follow-up questions.

Witnesses

All witnesses should be identified and statements taken as soon as possible. Should a witness reveal other aspects of the location, such as bad roads, non-working stoplights, etc., an independent investigation should be done into those areas as well.

Each witness may have a different recollection as to how the accident occurred. The investigator should allow each witness to verbalize what he or she saw. Each statement should be considered and evaluated as to whether it is credible given the circumstances and incident. All statements must be as detailed as accurately as possible and no statement should be totally discarded until all evidence and information is known.

Vehicle Information

All information concerning the vehicle's identification should be recorded. The vehicle may need to be preserved for further investigation and testing.

Road Conditions

Investigation of road conditions should document the overall condition of the road at the time of the accident and should include such things as traffic counts, traffic surveys, and any calls for repair to the portion of the road where the accident occurred. Also whether the roads were dry and clear, wet, icy or snow packed should be documented. Some of this information will likely be submitted as supplementary information once the investigator has cleared the scene.

Weather Conditions

Weather conditions should always be reported. Document whether it was sunny, cloudy, snowing, raining, or extremely hot. If the sun was shinning, did it blind the driver?

Headlight/Lamps

Filament *deformation* and *breakage* can occur when the filament of a headlight is hot or incandescent. This deformation or breakage will usually indicate that the lamp was on at the time the accident occurred. On the other hand, a cold *break* will result if the lights are off. Investigators should not jump to conclusions as to whether the headlights/lamps were on or off until a full investigation, including but not limited to, testing of the transition temperature of the filament is complete.

Air Bags/Seat Belts

Investigators are not always trained to understand how best to determine whether a safety restraint was being used or whether an air bag operated properly during an accident. Much evidence can be gathered at the scene and during follow-up investigations to allow for a correct interpretation.

Information such as the severity of the collision, the principal direction of the force involved, the size of the occupant and location and type of injuries suffered should be obtained. Once obtained, such tools as Newton's Law of Motion are available and can be applied to the information to assist in determining where the occupant(s) may have been seated in the vehicle as well as their subsequent movements inside the vehicle during a crash.

Date, Time and Location

Statistics regarding the date, time and location of the accident are critical and should be recorded accurately and with as much detail as possible.

Skid Marks

Any skid marks present should be recorded and properly inserted into a final sketch. Length of skid marks will be used to determine speed. The determining of speed based on skid marks takes into account many different factors. Two such factors are the skid marks left when all wheels of the vehicle lock up as opposed to a situation where all wheels do not lock up. Remember that vehicles with anti-lock brakes will not leave normal skid marks.

It is well know among investigators that when there is a weight shift to the front of the vehicle, such as when breaking quickly to stop, the vehicle will often leave what appears to be under-inflated tire marks.

These can extend for several miles and will have a *wavy* appearance. However, under-inflated tire marks should not be confused with flat tire marks that will usually show *flop* marks as opposed to wavy marks.

Tire Failure

A traffic accident investigator has a responsibility to ascertain whether or not a tire on a vehicle contributed in any way to the accident. The investigator must know what to look for and how to gather and preserve any available evidence.

Many times, the investigator must leave the tire analysis to someone with more expertise. While an investigator may understand that *tread* refers to a part of the tire that comes into contact with the road and that a *rip* or *tear* in a tire means that the edges are often frayed or worn, they may not understand such things as:

- Delamination: the splitting or separating of the layers of the tire
- Blemish: a flaw or defect in the tire
- Radial damage: damage radiating from a central core location
- Hysteresis: the failure of the tire to return to its original state following an accident
- Porosity: how porous the tire is
- Wicking: the cord, strand or braided fibers that make up the tire

Measuring/Sketching/Mapping

Measuring and sketching an accident scene must be carefully done so as to properly depict the visual description of the accident. Because an investigator may be called upon at a much later date, perhaps during a reconstruction effort or at the time of a trial, accurate and complete measurements taken during the on-scene investigation are critical. The measurements taken at the scene can help to refresh the investigator's memory, will enable the investigator to testify with accuracy and confidence, will assist in reconstructing the accident scene and will help in determining how and why the accident occurred.

Measurements and sketching of an accident scene must include:

- Grid
- Photogrammetry
- Measurement Techniques

- Diagrams/Sketches
- Systematic Methods of Organizing and Presenting Data
- Point of Impact (POI)
- Point of Rest (POR)

Once initial measurements are informally recorded, they should be used to complete a formal sketch. The sketch should be done to scale and should accurately reconstruct the location of vehicles, street markings/signs, road stripes, curves, and number of lanes. All lanes should be measured for width. Many things, such as coordinates, triangulation and grid measurements should be included at the time the initial sketch is being completed. While it is imperative that these things are included, the investigator must be extremely careful to include only those things that can be seen and measured and should not include things which cannot be explained.

Many companies have developed "reconstruction templates" to aid with the insertion of items into a sketch. These templates provide realistic depictions of such things as vehicles, motorcycles, boats, street sign shapes, road stripes and rulers for accurate visual completion of the information.

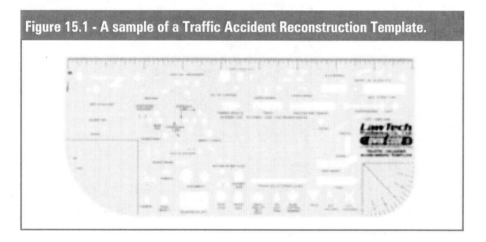

Figure 15.1 - A sample of a Traffic Accident Reconstruction Template.

PHOTOGRAPHY

Ground

Accident investigators will take photographs of the accident scene. Those photographs should include shots from all angles including close-up and wide angle shots of the approaches to the location of the accident. Photographs should be taken from as far away as a block or two to show a picture of what the driver may have seen when approaching the location.

Photographs of the scene should include stationary objects such as stop signs, trees, sidewalks, power poles and lines, and street signs. Close-up and wide angle shots should be taken of each object.

Pictures need to be taken of all sides of the vehicles involved. Be sure to photograph the seat position and seat belt.

Photograph and record the make and model of the tires, as well as the Vehicle Identification Number (VIN) and license plate number.

If need be, return to the scene on another day to observe the traffic flow. Be sure to return at the same time of day that the accident occurred.

Aerial

If available, photographs can be taken from the air, or an overhead location of the accident scene and the surrounding areas.

SPECIAL CIRCUMSTANCES

DUI / DWI / DWAI

The criminal charges commonly known as driving under the influence (DUI), driving while intoxicated (DWI), or driving while ability impaired (DWAI) are the most complicated and difficult types of cases with regard to legal issues.

It is essential that investigators in these types of cases work aggressively to further protect the scene of any accident involving these issues.

Form 15.1 below lists items which should be included in the investigation of any DUI/DWI/DWAI.

Form 15.1   DUI / DWI / DWAI - Investigation Checklist

IDENTIFICATION
- ❏ Name
- ❏ Address
- ❏ Phone Number
- ❏ Employment
- ❏ Gender
- ❏ Age
- ❏ Height
- ❏ Weight
- ❏ Eye Color

APPEARANCE
- ❏ Shoes
- ❏ Shirt
- ❏ Jacket
- ❏ Hat
- ❏ Scars
  - Visible
  - Non-Visible
- ❏ Injuries
  - Accident Related
  - Prior
  - Disabilities

BEHAVIOR
- ❏ Visibly Intoxicated
- ❏ Slurring Words
- ❏ Eye Contact
- ❏ Stumbling
- ❏ Attorney Requested

Form 15.1 - DUI/DWI/DWAI - Investigation Checklist (Cont.)

- When
- How

ROAD SIDE SOBRIETY

❑ Administered

❑ Not Administered

❑ Volunteered

❑ Proper Advisement Given

❑ Understood by Suspect

❑ Fresh Mouthpiece

❑ Number of Tries

❑ Final Reading Documented

❑ Transported for Further Testing

- Hospital
- Custody

SCENE ACTIONS

❑ Photographs

❑ Videotaping

❑ Statements

❑ Driver

❑ Passengers

❑ Witnesses

❑ Law Enforcement Officers at Scene

❑ Other Medical Personnel at Scene

❑ Complete Full Accident Scene Investigation

ACCIDENT

❑ Vehicle Information

❑ Lights On/Off

❑ Keys in Car

❑ Radio On/Off

❑ Heating/Air Conditioning On/Off

Form 15.1 DUI / DWI / DWAI - Investigation Checklist (Cont.)

- ❏ Driver In/Out of Car
- ❏ Passengers In/Out of Car
- ❏ Windows Rolled Up/Down
- ❏ Windows Broken
- ❏ Vehicle Damage
  - – Location
  - – Extent
  - – Suspect Transported
- ❏ Victims Transported
- ❏ Vehicle Secured
  - – Impound
  - – Further Testing
  - – Salvage

Form 15.2 below is an example of what a simple Accident Scene Investigation Checklist for regular passenger vehicles might include.

Form 15.2 Accident Scene Investigation Checklist

STATEMENTS
- ❏ Victims
- ❏ Witnesses

VEHICLE INFORMATION
- ❏ Year
- ❏ Make
- ❏ Model
- ❏ VIN No./License Plate No.
- ❏ Color
- ❏ Owner
- ❏ Insurance Company
- ❏ Manual/Automatic
- ❏ Seat Belt
- ❏ Air Bags
- ❏ Engine

Form 15.2 – Accident Scene Investigation Checklist (Cont.)

❏ Anti-Lock/Standard Brakes

❏ Were Lights On or Off?

❏ Was Radio On or Off?

❏ Does Speedometer Work Properly?

❏ Damage

- Extent

- Location

ROAD CONDITIONS

❏ Wet

❏ Dry

❏ Snow Packed

❏ Clear

❏ Traffic Count

❏ Repair Orders

WEATHER CONDITIONS

❏ Sunny

❏ Cloudy

❏ Raining

❏ Snowing

❏ Extremely Hot

DATE/TIME/LOCATION

❏ AM or PM

❏ Street/Intersecting Street

❏ Intersection

❏ City/County/State Street

SPECIAL CIRCUMSTANCES

❏ DUI

- Tests Administered

- Transported

- Towing Service

❏ Hit & Run

- Vehicle Description

- Witness Statements

- Location Search

Form 15.2 – Accident Scene Investigation Checklist (Cont.)

MEASUREMENTS/SKETCHING/MAPPING

- ❑ Vehicle Locations
- ❑ Body Locations
- ❑ Street Markings/Signs
- ❑ Road Stripes
- ❑ Curves
- ❑ Number of Lanes
  - – Width
  - – Length
- ❑ Skid Marks
  - – Number
  - – Length
  - – Width
  - – Type

PHOTOGRAPHY

- ❑ Close-up/Wide Angle
  - – Scene Location
  - – Vehicles
  - – Seat Position
  - – Bodies/Victims
  - – Tires
  - – VIN/License plate
  - – Stop Signs
  - – Trees
  - – Sidewalks
  - – Street Signs
  - – Seat Belts
- ❑ Need to Return on Another Day

SURROUNDING AREA

- ❑ Witnesses
- ❑ Conditions
- ❑ Distractions
- ❑ Obstructions

When an accident involves a commercial vehicle, additional checklist items must be obtained. Form 15.3 below lists items which should also be included in any checklist used for this type of accident.

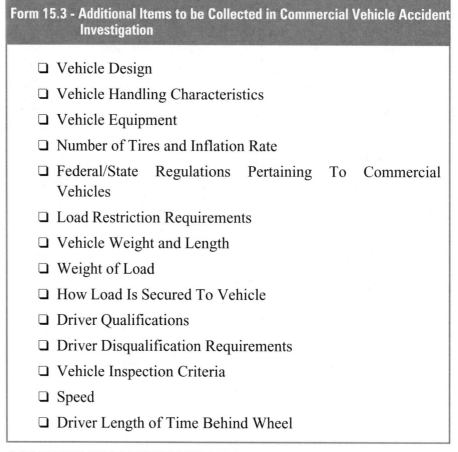

Form 15.3 - Additional Items to be Collected in Commercial Vehicle Accident Investigation

- ❑ Vehicle Design
- ❑ Vehicle Handling Characteristics
- ❑ Vehicle Equipment
- ❑ Number of Tires and Inflation Rate
- ❑ Federal/State Regulations Pertaining To Commercial Vehicles
- ❑ Load Restriction Requirements
- ❑ Vehicle Weight and Length
- ❑ Weight of Load
- ❑ How Load Is Secured To Vehicle
- ❑ Driver Qualifications
- ❑ Driver Disqualification Requirements
- ❑ Vehicle Inspection Criteria
- ❑ Speed
- ❑ Driver Length of Time Behind Wheel

ACCIDENT RECONSTRUCTION DEFINED

Traffic accident reconstruction is defined by R.W. Rivers, author of *Traffic Accident Investigation and Reconstruction*, as a process involving the application of principles of dynamics, perception and general physics to the movement of vehicles, bodies and other objects during and after a collision.

R.W. Rivers goes on to say that traffic accident reconstruction has been said to be an advanced level of investigation that starts with investigations and evidence gathering at the scene and continues until the objectives of traffic investigation and reconstruction have been satisfied. This simply means that reconstruction includes interpretation of evidence based on sound, scientific analysis of all available evidence.

J. Stannard Baker, a pioneer in accident reconstruction investigation, and former physics professor at Northwestern University, developed this subject into a science by applying the laws of physics and developing mathematical equations to assist law enforcement officers in their investigations. Mr. Baker once wrote, *"Reconstruction is not so much a matter of collecting information as it is of thinking about information which has been collected. Reconstructing an accident is like assembling a jigsaw puzzle to see what the picture or, at least part of it, looks like. The thinking required is essentially a disciplined and purposeful study of available data, always with two quite different ideas kept in mind: 1) the issues to be resolved, and 2) the principles of basic sciences to be applied."*

SUMMARY

Traffic Accident Reconstruction is simply an effort to determine, from whatever information is available, how an accident occurred. Data collected at the traffic accident is useful only if it is properly interpreted and analyzed. The chain of events must be reconstructed and must be able to tell the story of how the accident happened. Properly analyzing the collected evidence can answer questions regarding failure of vehicle components, such as steering, brakes, and tires. Driver responses, speed, and vehicle positions can also be determined. However, this can only happen after vehicle damage and behavior is analyzed, a thorough road analysis is completed, headlights and lamps are fully examined and documented, and tire failure is tested and analyzed.

DISCUSSION QUESTIONS

1. Define the objectives of accident reconstruction.
2. What issues for the accident reconstruction can you think of that may not have been discussed in this chapter?

Chapter 16

Rules of Evidence

OVERVIEW

In this chapter, we will address the rules of evidence and how the detailed preparation of documentation will preclude challenges in court. We will explore several cases involving the applications of technology, demonstrative evidence, and best evidence rulings.

OBJECTIVES

1. Compare and contrast the elements of the Kelly-Fry and Daubert decisions.
2. Illustrate how documentation procedures lead to evidence either being admissible or inadmissible.
3. Summarize how the "Best Evidence Rule" is applied.
4. Identify the Federal Rules of Evidence.

INTRODUCTION

Details, details, details. By now you may have realized that documenting a crime scene is more than showing up, snapping a few photos, jotting a few notes. To say the least it is a tedious job. Why should one be so detailed and tenacious in their documentation? Glad you asked!

Evidence can be defined as something legally submitted to a court of law as a means of determining the truth. That evidence (notes, photos, sketches, statements, etc) can tell the judge and jury just what happened at the crime scene. But what happens if the evidence you have been documenting and collecting doesn't meet the rules of evidence? It doesn't get into court. The murderer or arsonist, rapist, could go free!

Figure 16.1 National Conference on Science and the Law Proceedings

Title: National Conference on Science and the Law Proceedings.

Series: Research Forum

Author: National Institute of Justice

Published: NIJ, July 2000

Subject: Criminal justice system

Preface

The intersections of science and law occur from crime scene to crime lab to criminal prosecution and defense. Although detectives, forensic scientists, and attorneys may have different vocabularies and perspectives, from a cognitive perspective, they share a way of thinking that is essential to scientific knowledge. A good detective, a well-trained forensic analyst, and a seasoned attorney all exhibit "what-if" thinking. This kind of thinking in hypotheticals keeps a detective open-minded: it prevents a detective from ignoring or not collecting data that may result in exculpatory evidence. This kind of thinking in hypotheticals keeps a forensic analyst honest: it prevents an analyst from ignoring or downplaying analytical results that may be interpreted as ambiguous or exculpatory evidence. This kind of thinking in hypotheticals keeps attorneys thoroughly prepared: it prevents a prosecutor from ignoring alternative theories of the crime that will surely arise in the defense, and it keeps the defense open to

Figure 16.1 National Conference on Science and the Law Proceedings (Cont.)

raising alternative theories. Our adversarial system of justice relies on thinking in hypotheticals, examining each possibility, looking at all the angles because we expect proof beyond a reasonable doubt.

We have already seen too many times what happens when "what-if" thinking breaks down. Consider what happens when a detective refuses "what if" thinking. Exculpatory evidence is not collected at the crime scene; an innocent person may be convicted. Evidence is collected in such a sloppy manner that it cannot be processed by the crime lab; a guilty person may be set free. Consider what happens when a forensic analyst refuses "what if" thinking. A crime lab technique has been accepted for the last 50 years; no one has questioned its validity or reliability because everyone just believes that it works; people may be wrongfully convicted or exculpated by a scientifically unsound technique that is presented as scientific evidence. Or consider what happens when "what if" thinking breaks down in the courtroom. Judges naively accept whatever scientists with a particular set of credentials tell them, the scientist-witness is allowed to represent both the opinions of the entire scientific discipline as well as specific opinions with regard to the case, and the expert witness industry is thriving.

Currently, the criminal justice profession has several mechanisms for ensuring that "what-if" thinking does not break down. Daubert—and now Kumho—hearings can highlight serious deficiencies in traditionally accepted forensic sciences. Training for judges and lawyers can upgrade their ability to determine the value of scientific evidence and to distinguish between good investigative leads, which may result from pre- scientific techniques, and solid scientific evidence, which derives from the scientific method. Research by academics or scientific organizations such as the National Academy of Sciences can provide answers to methodological dilemmas which face any science moving from the laboratory to the crime scene. Law enforcement training can provide detectives and departments with best practices for investigation and evidence collection, such as the National Institute of Justice's recent

Figure 16.1 National Conference on Science and the Law Proceedings (Cont.)

publication on crime scene investigation. Technical working groups that are discipline based, such as the National Institute of Justice's Technical Working Group on Eyewitness Evidence, can provide checks on scientific and investigative procedures and interpretation of results.

But even with such homologous ways of thinking, judicial decisions, and educational safeguards in place, science and law continue to be uneasy partners. Questions about this partnership form the basis for the following papers, from scientists, attorneys, and judges, which all address, from differing aspects, the relationship between science and law. It is hoped that by facing these questions directly we shall find answers that enable us to use science and law in the service of truth and justice.

Carole E. Chaski, Ph.D.
Executive Director Institute for Linguistic Evidence, Inc.
Georgetown, Delaware
    The entire report can be viewed at: http://www.ncjrs.org/txtfiles1/nij/179630.txt

In a courtroom, the investigative case documents may face the scrutiny of the rules of evidence. Rules of evidence are proscribed rules the court uses for evaluating the admissibility of evidence. Our investigative documents may include sketches, photographs, charts, or graphs. These are known as demonstrative evidence or evidence that illustrates testimony.

The way evidence is collected, the quality of the evidence, and the documentation of the evidence can determine the prosecutor's success in getting the evidence admitted in trial and presented to a jury. Without quality documentation, important evidence, even if properly collected, may never get before a jury.

Check out the following case examples and consider the importance of proper documentation.

> "...In another case, involving roadside videotaping of a drunk driving suspect, the Court found that the slurred nature of the suspect's speech, as well as his answers to routine booking questions as to name, address, weight, height, eye color, date of birth, and current age, were not testimonial in nature. Pennsylvania v. Muniz, 496 U.S. 582 (1990)..." [1]

The officer involved used a video camera to document the "evidence" at the scene. Because the officer followed proper procedures the tape could be used in court.

> "...In other contexts, the Court has also elaborated the constitutional requirements affecting administrative inspections and searches. Thus, in Michigan v. Tyler...it subdivided the process by which an investigation of the cause of a fire may be conducted. Entry to fight the fire is, of course, an exception based on exigent circumstances, and no warrant or consent is needed; firemen on the scene may seize evidence relating to the cause under the plain view doctrine. Additional entries to investigate the cause of the fire must be made pursuant to warrant procedures governing administrative searches.
>
> Evidence of arson discovered in the course of such an administrative inspection is admissible at trial, but if the investigator finds probable cause to believe that arson has occurred and requires further access to gather evidence for a possible prosecution, he must obtain a criminal search warrant... 436 U.S. 499 (1978)...The Court also held that, after the fire was extinguished, if fire investigators were unable to proceed at the moment, because of dark, steam, and smoke, it was proper for them to leave and return at daylight without any necessity of complying with its mandate for administrative or criminal warrants. Id. at 510-11. But cf. Michigan v. Clifford, 464 U.S. 287 (1984) (no such justification for search of private residence begun at 1:30 p.m. when fire had been extinguished at 7 a.m.)"[2]

This relates to the chapter on Arson Documentation. Now would be a good time for you to go back and review Section B. Evaluating the Scene

Note: This and subsequent sections of this Guide are intended for the individual responsible for the investigation of a fire incident. At the time the scene is determined to involve arson or other crime, the investigator must address legal requirements for scene access, search, and evidence seizure. Conduct a briefing with the incident commander to determine who has jurisdiction and authorization (legal right of entry).

> "...in South Dakota v. Opperman... the Court sustained the admission of evidence found when police impounded an automobile from a public street for multiple parking violations and entered the car to secure and inventory valuables for safekeeping. Marijuana was discovered in the glove compartment"[3]

Recall the earlier chapters on records and evidence management. This evidence was admissible because the agency involved followed proper documentation procedures.

> "Emphasis upon the necessity of warrants places the judgment of an independent magistrate between law enforcement officers and the privacy of citizens, authorizes invasion of that privacy only upon a

showing that constitutes probable cause, and limits that invasion by specification of the person to be seized, the place to be searched, and the evidence to be sought... While a warrant is issued ex parte, its validity may be contested in a subsequent suppression hearing if incriminating evidence is found and a prosecution is brought...Most often, in the suppression hearings, the defendant will challenge the sufficiency of the evidence presented to the magistrate to constitute probable cause....A previously reliable, named informant reported to an officer that the defendant would arrive with narcotics on a particular train, and described the clothes he would be wearing and the bag he would be carrying; the informant, however, gave no basis for his information. FBI agents met the train, observed that the defendant fully answered the description, and arrested him. The Court held that the corroboration of part of the informer's tip established probable cause to support the arrest." [4]

Proper documentation and articulation of the informant's details by the investigators supported probable cause, thus allowing for the warrant to be issued and support the admittance of evidence in court.

"...In United States v. Cortez, 449 U.S. 411 (1981), a unanimous Court attempted to capture the "elusive concept'" of the basis for permitting a stop. Officers must have "articulable reasons'" or "founded suspicions,'" derived from the totality of the circumstances. "Based upon that whole picture the detaining officer must have a particularized and objective basis for suspecting the particular person stopped of criminal activity.'" Id. at 417-18. The inquiry is thus quite fact-specific" [5]

What if the officer had not recorded all the elements that founded their suspicions in their notes or final report? If something stands out at the time document it in your report, even if at the time you don't know its value. Documentation will support your actions; giving credibility to the evidence you collect.

Figure 16.2   Expert Witnesses: Is Justice Ruined by Expertism?

Title: Expert Witnesses: Is Justice Ruined by Expertism?

Series: Research Forum

Author: National Institute of Justice

Published: NIJ, July 2000

Subject: Criminal justice system

Panel VII. Expert Witnesses: Is Justice Ruined by Expertism?

—E. Michael McCann

Mr. E. Michael McCann: Good afternoon.

My work has been predominantly in criminal prosecution.

Obviously, justice ought be the object of what's happening in our courts and in our entire criminal justice system.

Any conviction that is secured in violation either of an ethical code or on the basis of incompetent or junk science, or because evidence was falsified, is not justice at all but injustice. Anyone who tolerates that whether a prosecutor, defense attorney, police officer, or agent for a laboratory is endangering his own or her own liberty. It seems to me that if we tolerate that type of conduct, no man or woman is safe from an unfounded prosecution, and those of us in the criminal justice system should know that better than anyone.

Bert has adverted to it in the Stifel case. There are many problems that flow from violations of the Brady v. Maryland requirement that evidence that tends to exculpate must be provided by the prosecutor to the defense. Every prosecutor ought to have an equivocal policy consistent with Brady and ought vigorously to ensure that all prosecutors on staff follow policy.

Destruction of evidence problems also occur in some cases. I chuckled in reading over Professor Giannelli's recounting of the Colorado case of People v. Morgan. In that case, police recovered a digit of the offender's finger. The police kept the digit in an inadequately refrigerated facility because, understandably, if they placed the digit in the refrigerator in the district station, it might pollute the officers' lunches. The finger decayed and the case was

Figure 16.2   Expert Witnesses: Is Justice Ruined by Expertism? (Cont.)

thrown out because the police were held responsible for the loss of the evidence.

Obviously, prosecutors can't fail to follow up on evidence. A beautiful quote emerged from a case arising in California involving a military Preparedness Day Parade in 1915. The best known of many appeals related to the case is styled Mooney v. Houlihan. The trial prosecutor in that case, one Brennan, described in almost poetic terms how a prosecutor caught up in the fevered chase of his quarry can overlook signals of potential innocence and thereby fail to follow avenues that might lead to exculpatory evidence. Such a danger always confronts police, prosecutors, and overzealous forensic analysts.

Partial understanding of evidence recovery limitations can also cause problems. Because of the public's partial knowledge about fingerprints, in stolen car cases where fingerprints are not discovered or the police have failed to search for the same in the recovered vehicle, the defense attorney often argues, "where are the fingerprints? The defendant must be innocent."

One must be alert to the possibility of errors even in dealing with very competent, scientific laboratories. In the Milwaukee County case of State v. Mendoza, the defendant was charged with slaying two off-duty police officers. The evidence showed the defendant had discharged a firearm and was then arrested by the two officers, who took the gun from the defendant. A struggle then ensued, and the defendant succeeded in getting one of the officers' firearms and shooting both officers to death. The defense indicated that at one point one of the officers was striking the defendant in his head, opening the door to a later argument that the defendant acted to prevent injury to himself. Evidence was submitted by the police to the FBI laboratory and, at the request of the defense, to the Wisconsin State Crime Laboratory as well. The FBI laboratory reported that with respect to one of the officers the killing shot entered the officer's front chest and exited his back, while the State crime lab reported that the bullet instead entered the back and exited the front. This was a

Figure 16.2 Expert Witnesses: Is Justice Ruined by Expertism? (Cont.)

case involving the death of two police officers, and one would anticipate that it would garner close and assiduous handling by every laboratory. I called the FBI expert, pointed out the conflict between the lab reports, and requested that he review his file. An hour later, the much chagrined FBI technician advised me that he had erred in recording his findings despite procedural protocols designed to prevent such errors, and that his findings in fact were consistent with the State crime lab report.

I'm sure many defense attorneys have had cases where the defendant says, "I didn't shoot him in the back, I shot him in the chest as he was attacking me." Where a killing bullet entered the body is often completely dispositive in any issue of self-defense. If the entry wound is in the back, self-defense is not going to fly. If the entry wound is in the front, at least there are some grounds to argue self-defense.

This wasn't a case of bad science. It wasn't a case of junk science. It was a case of human error.

The entire report can be viewed at: http://www.ncjrs.org/txtfiles1/nij/179630.txt

It doesn't matter whose case it was or who's fault it was, if you are the detective in charge of a case going to trial with problems, it's your responsibility to deal with it!

Figure 16.3 The Importance of Documentation

She answered the knock on the door at about 9 AM – it was a homeless man asking for recyclables. But she had recently moved to the USA from Japan, a country where "street crime" is unheard of. Her English was also very poor.

He conned his way into the kitchen and saw the knife set sitting on the counter. He pulled the largest knife from the wooden block, held it to her throat and walked her into the bedroom. At knife point she undressed, but refused to remove her underwear. Instead, she grabbed for the knife. There was a short struggle, some minor cuts on her hands and arms, but the suspect fled.

Figure 16.3 The Importance of Documentation (Cont.)

When the patrol officers arrived, they set up a perimeter and began the search for the suspect. While walking between the victim's home and her neighbor's, one officer lifted the lid on the neighbor's trash can. Laying in the bottom of the near empty can was the knife. He picked it up and returned to his car, placing the knife into an evidence bag. He also filled out an evidence tag and stapled it to the bag, then quickly returned to hunt for the suspect.

It was two years later that the suspect was actually caught. He had gone to a home in a neighboring city, knocked on the door and asked for aluminum cans. The woman, who was home alone, refused to open the door. The suspect left, but returned 15 minutes later. This time he kicked open the door and rushed through the empty living room, towards the bedroom. Unfortunately for him, all the condos in the complex looked alike and he had actually broken into the wrong place. The first hit from the metal softball bat stopped him in his tracks. We were never able to determine exactly how many times he was hit by the bat-swinging retired Marine Corp Master Sergeant, before he made it out the front door, but it slowed him down considerably. Patrol officers caught him limping down the street, a couple of blocks away.

The suspect, Michael, was in his thirties. He had first been arrested for rape when he was fourteen and living in the Midwest. A dozen more arrests for rape resulted in multiple life sentences in a Missouri mental hospital. It took him a year to escape, raping the night nurse along the way.

The argument between California and Missouri as to who would try him first dragged the case out for two more years. But finally we were in trial, so I went to the evidence room to get the knife and take it to court. "Surprised" doesn't really describe how I felt, when the Evidence Room Clerk told me that the knife had been thrown out a few months earlier. Since the evidence tag showed "attempted rape", it was thrown out per department policy, after the three-year statute of limitations had run out.

Having been a detective for a couple of decades, I knew that "weapons" were not tossed into the trash. Instead, they are thrown into a large wooden box in the back of the evidence room. When the box is full, they're taken to a county facility to be turned into manhole covers. So, I headed for the box. There were several hundred knives, but only one matching the written description by the patrol officer. But the knife itself had not been marked, nor had any photos been taken of it and the property tag had long since gone through the shredder.

Would the knife be excluded from evidence amidst cries from the defense about sloppy police work preventing his client from having a fair trial? A simple photograph, a scratch mark by the officer for identification – anything would have "saved the day".

Figure 16.3 The Importance of Documentation (Cont.)

When Michael was arrested, I asked to look at his hands. The victim described the attacker's fingers as being "shorter than normal". I had him place his hands on a legal pad and I traced both hands; his fingers where about an inch and a half shorter than normal. The judge would not force Michael to hold his hands up for the jury and he had been careful during the trial to keep them in his pockets. The tracing was entered into evidence, and along with the victim's identification, he was convicted.

> Don R. Howell, Retired Detective
> Huntington Beach, California
> B.S., California State University, Los Angeles
> 30 years Law Enforcement Experience
> Author of *Interviewing Sex Crime Victims*, Lawtech Publishing Co, Ltd.

Detective Howell illustrates an excellent example of the importance of documenting evidence, backing up the documentation, and preparing 'in advance' for the worst.

Defense teams will do their best to have evidence 'thrown out' by means of a suppression hearing during pretrial preceding. The better the documentation, the stronger the chances that the evidence can withstand an attack by a defense team in this hearing.

The rules of evidence are driven by court decisions, common law, and procedural rules of court. Some are older rules, like privileged communications, and others are more modern and scientific in nature like the Kelly–Frye and Daubert rules, which address the 'junk science' question of technical evidence.

KELLY / FRYE

Kelly / Frye precludes the use of evidence based on unproven science. DNA, Fingerprints, and breath and blood analysis are proven and accepted forms of scientific analysis, but some more exotic tests that have not stood extensive testing in the courts, like certain lie detection processes or unusual acoustic examinations that are seldom used in court may be subject to a Kelly / Frye test in a trial.

Figure 16.4 Kelly / Frye Daubert

In 1923, the D.C. Circuit announced its landmark decision regarding the admissibility of expert opinion testimony on novel scientific procedures in Frye v. United States. In Frye, the defendant attempted to show his innocence by proffering the results of a lie detector test that purportedly demonstrated that he was telling the truth when he denied killing the victim. The court ruled that the evidence was inadmissible because the scientific principles upon which the procedure was based were not, "sufficiently established to have gained general acceptance in the particular field in which it belongs." This so-called Frye general acceptance test remained the standard employed in both federal courts and state courts around the country for years to come.

Kelly / Frye: California's Dominant Standard

As early as the 1950's, California had adopted and was regularly using the Frye standard to assess the admissibility of scientific evidence. Specifically in People v. Kelly, the Supreme Court of California laid out what it felt were the main advantages of the Frye standard - uniformity and judicial restraint:

[A] beneficial consequence of the Frye test is that it may well promote a degree of uniformity of decision. Individual judges whose particular conclusions may differ regarding the reliability of particular scientific evidence, may discover substantial agreement and consensus in the scientific community. …The primary advantage, however, of the Frye test lies in its essentially conservative nature…. Frye was deliberately intended to interpose a substantial obstacle to the unrestrained admission of evidence based upon new scientific principles.

The Court found the Frye standard to be protective: it protects jurors from being unduly swayed by the impressive nature of testimony which is shrouded in science, it protects the rights of criminal defendants when new science is being used to connect them to the crimes, and it protects the common law in California from containing precedents which would allow the admission of evidence based on dubious scientific grounds.

Figure 16.4 Kelly / Frye Daubert (Cont.)

Logistically, Kelly / Frye requires "a preliminary showing of general acceptance of the new technique in the relevant scientific community." From there, California Evidence Code §§ 720 & 801 take over and require a two step process: "(1) the Reliability of the method must be established, usually by expert testimony, and (2) the witness furnishing such testimony must be properly Qualified as an expert to give an opinion on the subject." This system of admitting scientific evidence has remained virtually unchanged in California, and most notably, survived the United States Supreme Court Daubert decision.

In Frye v. United States, the Court of Appeals of the District of Columbia evaluated the admissibility of evidence resulting from a "systolic blood pressure deception test," a crude precursor to the modern polygraph machine.(3) The court held that:

> Just when a scientific principle or discovery crosses the line between the experimental and demonstrable stages is difficult to define. Somewhere in this twilight zone the evidential force of the principle must be recognized, and while courts will go a long way in admitting expert testimony deducted from a well-recognized scientific principle or discovery, the thing from which the deduction is made must be sufficiently established to have gained general acceptance in the particular field in which it belongs.

Until 1993, the Frye "general acceptance" test was the governing law in federal courts regarding admissibility of scientific evidence.

Frye involved a novel technique that was introduced as evidence of an individual's guilt or innocence. But as scientific technology improved and experts used mainstream techniques in unfamiliar territory or to achieve unusual results, the distinction between proven methodology and novel experimentation blurred. In large-scale tort cases, for example, expert testimony was used to prove subtle issues, such as increased probability and causal links between exposure to an agent and incidence of a disease.

THE DAUBERT DECISION

With the adoption of the Federal Rules of Evidence in 1975, courts, scholars and practitioners alike began to question whether Frye would survive as the sole admissibility standard for expert

Figure 16.4 Kelly / Frye Daubert (Cont.)

testimony. Under the Federal Rules, judges were seemingly afforded more discretion in making admissibility determinations. Rule 104(a) assigns judges the responsibility of making a preliminary determination on whether to allow a given expert to testify. Rule 702 goes on to guide this decision by requiring the judge to determine whether the admission of such testimony will assist the trier of fact to understand evidence or determine a fact at issue. Finally, Rule 403 suggests that the judge may exclude evidence if its likely prejudicial effect outweighs its probative value. The question was then to what degree would the arguably conservative Frye general acceptance standard survive in the wake of the presumably more liberal admissibility framework embodied in the new Federal Rules of Evidence.

The U.S. Supreme Court endeavored to answer the question of Frye's continued viability in Daubert v. Merrell Dow Pharmaceuticals, Inc. In Daubert the Court held that Rule 702 did in fact supersede the Frye standard and enumerated a new standard to instruct judges on how to act as judicial gatekeepers. This new approach consisted of a two-pronged analysis of the testimony centering on the testimony's reliability and relevance. In determining reliability the court must engage in a, "preliminary assessment of whether the reasoning or methodology underlying the testimony is scientifically valid and of whether that reasoning or methodology properly can be applied to the facts at issue." In addition, when determining scientific reliability the trial judge should consider:

(1) whether the proffered knowledge can be or has been tested, (2) whether the theory or technique has been subjected to peer review and publication, the known or potential rate of error, and whether the theory or technique has gained general acceptance in the relevant scientific discipline.(5)

This nonexhaustive list of indicia of reliability relegated the Frye standard to one of a handful of guidelines that may be employed in ruling on admissibility. In conjunction with the newly ordained relevancy prong, the reliability criteria form a substantially more robust framework with which to analyze given scientific testimony.

Figure 16.4 Kelly / Frye Daubert (Cont.)

Where the Courts Are Now

Courts adopting Daubert interpreted the Supreme Court decision as a reaction to the increasing use of expert scientific testimony in a wide variety of both civil and criminal cases. Regardless of whether the Supreme Court was reacting to this trend, many of the lower courts have used Daubert to restrict the admission of testimony. For example, the District Court of Oregon applied Daubert to eliminate the plaintiffs' use of expert testimony in a case that consolidated several breast implant suits. In this case, the judge rejected expert testimony offered to prove that silicone breast implants cause auto-immune disease and other illnesses. The court viewed Daubert as imposing a significantly higher level of scrutiny than Frye, especially for evidence attempting to prove causation.

California

Some states did not adopt the Daubert test for fear that it was too liberalizing. For example, in 1994 the Supreme Court of California rejected the Daubert test. Instead, the court reaffirmed its allegiance to Frye by using the test to evaluate the admissibility of a horizontal gaze nystagmus field sobriety test. The court observed that Frye has several advantages:

(1) assuring that those persons most qualified to asses the validity of a scientific technique would have the determinative voice, (2) providing a "minimal reserve of experts" to critically examine each technique in a particular case, promoting uniformity of decision based on finding a consensus in the scientific community, and protecting the parties by its "essentially conservative nature."

Therefore, in California, Daubert is considered a liberalizing test and thus judges prefer the more "conservative" Frye analysis set forth in their Kelly decision.

Kentucky - Forty Years of "General Acceptance"

In 1940 Kentucky began to follow the "general acceptance" test as described in Frye. Interestingly, although Kentucky was indeed applying the Frye principles of "general acceptance," these early opinions did not claim to have adopted the Frye decision, and in fact, made no mention of Frye's existence at all. It was not until 1983 in

Figure 16.4 Kelly / Frye Daubert (Cont.)

Perry v. Commonwealth that the Kentucky Supreme Court finally specifically cited Frye to support its use of the "general acceptance" test.

Notably, the year before the Perry decision's first mention of Frye, Kentucky all but rejected the Frye standard in favor of a Daubert-like relevancy test in Brown v. Commonwealth. In Brown, the Kentucky Supreme Court admitted identification evidence based on a novel blood testing technique more rudimentary than modern DNA testing despite the fact that this procedure had not gained "general acceptance." Moreover, the opinion failed to contain any reference to Frye or prior Kentucky case law. Quoting a major critic of Frye, the court stated that "[a]ny relevant conclusions which are supported by a qualified expert witness should be received unless there are other reasons for exclusion." This abrupt departure from prior case law has been characterized as an "aberration" by some scholars because it failed to mention Frye and had little impact on the law in this area. It seems likely, however, that as a result of this extraordinary departure from precedent in Brown the Perry court felt compelled to mention Frye by name for the first time.

In 1992, the Kentucky Supreme Court expressly embraced Frye in Harris v. Commonwealth. In Harris, the Court concluded that, "[i]n deciding whether to allow the admission of new, scientific evidence, this Court has required trial courts to follow the dictates of Frye v. United States. But 1992 also promised to make this clear statement of Kentucky's adoption of Frye quite short-lived. With the adoption of the Kentucky Rules of Evidence in 1992, the continued validity of the "general acceptance" standard seemed in question. Kentucky Rule of Evidence 702 governing the admissibility of expert testimony mirrors its Federal counterpart and makes no mention of "general acceptance" or the Frye standard. Although the Commentary to Kentucky Rule of Evidence 702 indicates that the Rule is identical to the law which had existed in Kentucky to date (i.e. "general acceptance"), the Rule's silence seems to have set the stage for a repudiation of the Frye standard..

Figure 16.4 Kelly / Frye Daubert (Cont.)

DNA and Daubert in Massachusetts

Gatekeeping in Massachusetts

In Commonwealth v. Fatalo, the Supreme Judicial Court adopted the "general acceptance" test of Frye. For the most part, Massachusetts courts relied on the test in deciding whether evidence produced by a scientific theory or process was admissible. Over the years, however, the courts did not seem to apply the Frye test with any semblance of regularity. Some types of "scientific" evidence were subject to scrutiny, while others fell from the scope of Frye's analysis. By 1994, commentators noted that "no principle adequately explains or justifies the Massachusetts approach of subjecting some expert testimony to the rigors of Frye, while granting other testimony a 'free pass' to the jury."

These observations did not go unheeded, and in 1994 the Supreme Judicial Court adopted the Daubert "reasoning," acknowledging that "[i]n some instances, perhaps without adequately articulated reasons, we simply have decided that Frye principles do not apply in deciding the admissibility of expert testimony apparently based on a scientific theory or process." In an effort to clarify the standards for admissibility, the Court accepted "the basic reasoning of the Daubert opinion" in Commonwealth v. Lanigan ("Lanigan II").

In Lanigan I, a defendant charged with child sexual offenses filed motions in limine to prevent the Commonwealth from introducing evidence based on deoxyribonucleic acid (DNA) tests at trial. The Supreme Judicial Court upheld the exclusion of the evidence, ruling that the process used to estimate the frequency with which the defendant's "DNA profile" would have occurred in the population (known as the "product rule") had not been "generally accepted in the field of population genetics."

On remand, the Commonwealth offered evidence based on a different process for determining the likelihood of a DNA match. This test was ruled to be admissible by the trial judge, and the defendant was convicted on all counts.

Figure 16.4 Kelly / Frye Daubert (Cont.)

http://cyber.law.harvard.edu/daubert/about.htm. Page Last
Modified on May 6, 1999 by Dan Fridman - Copyright 1999.
All materials are the property of the Berkman Center for
Internet & Society and Harvard Law School. Materials may be
reproduced, distributed, or quoted as long as appropriate credit
and citation is given.

This article is culmination of materials selected from the
Berkman Center for Internet & Society and Harvard Law
School, by Daniel S. Fridman and J. Scott Janoe – Harvard
Law School '99, presented at the State Supreme Court Justices
Conference in Washington, D.C., January 19, 1999.

Figure 16.5 Admissibility: The Judge as Gatekeeper

**Title: National Conference on Science and the Law
Proceedings.**

Series: Research Forum

Author: National Institute of Justice

Published: NIJ, July 2000

Subject: Criminal justice system

The entire report can be viewed at:

http://www.ncjrs.org/txtfiles1/nij/179630.txt

Panel II. Admissibility: The Judge as Gatekeeper
Panelists: Edward J. Imwinkelried Professor of Law University of
California, Davis, School of Law Davis, California

The trial judge conducts his or her gatekeeping inquiry under
Daubert for the express purpose of answering that question. In
addition, under the jurisprudence governing the initial burden of
production, in determining whether the proponent is entitled to get to
the jury on a particular issue, the judge considers both the
proponent's evidence and the contrary evidence submitted by the
opponent.[13] The common denominator is that in Daubert, Judge
Blackmun made it clear that Rule 104(a) governs the issue of whether
the proponent's proffered testimony constitutes admissible
"scientific . . . knowledge" within the meaning of that expression in

> ### Figure 16.5 Admissibility: The Judge as Gatekeeper (Cont.)
>
> Rule 702.[14] Under Rule 104(a), the judge attempting to screen out "junk science" must consider the evidence on both sides, pro as well as con,[15] on the issue of whether the proponent's testimony qualifies for admission under Daubert. Finally, in both settings, the proponent and opponent progress through various stages. Under the initial burden of production, the proponent can: lose because his or her showing is too weak,[16] reach the trier of fact when the issue is rationally arguable,[17] or fail because the opponent's contrary showing is overpowering.[18] As we shall see, the scientific evidence cases suggest that the proponent and opponent of that type of testimony can work through comparable stages.

BEST EVIDENCE RULE

A best evidence rule means that the evidence presented is the 'real thing' or best existing evidence. For example, a copy of a contract may not stand up in court as evidence if there is an original signed contract available. Certified copies of certain documents such as government records or court documents may be acceptable

PHOTOGRAPHS AS EVIDENCE

Whether the photographs are film-based or digital there are two requirements they must meet in order to be admissible. First the photo must be relevant to the case at. Second the authenticity of the photographs must be proven. To prove the authenticity of the photographs the investigator or crime scene tech may be required to testify on the stand. They will attest to the fact that the photos are an accurate representation of the crime scene as they viewed it. Having a well documented photo-log will go a long way in establishing the validity of your photos.

Figure 16.6 Excerpt from the Kentucky State Police Physical Evidence Handbook

Kentucky State Police Physical Evidence Handbook

No matter how extensive the photographic efforts at the crime scene, photographs must stand the test of legal admissibility. The general standards used to review the credibility of the photographs are: 1. Accurate representations 2. Free of distortion 3. Material and relevant 4. Unbiased. If a photograph is deemed to depict only the gruesome nature of the scene to excite the emotions of the viewer, then its potential to prejudice the viewer may outweigh its value as a purveyor of truth. Additionally, the distortion represented in the photograph may be so prominent that the accuracy and reliability of the photograph is severely questioned. To contend with the issue of distortion in photographs, the best situation is to have the person who actually took the photograph testify concerning the inherent accuracy of the photographs.

THE ADMISSIBILITY OF DIGITAL PHOTOGRAPHS

Courts are much more lenient in admitting digital photos than they were in the past. It is still important to follow proper procedures to ensure they will be allowed. These proper procedures should include preservation of original image, a photo-log (date, time, and who took the image), chain of custody, security of image, any enhancements, and availability for release. Preservation of the image can be done by using image security software and saving the image file to a computer hard drive.

Review the following excerpts from the Federal Rules of Evidence and related notes. The rules and the ideas behind them give the investigator insight into the intent of the courts and an idea of what you may expect in a court. Most jurisdictions have similar rules for state and local cases. It is recommended that you familiarize yourself with the rules of evidence of the state in which you live.

Figure 16.7 Excerpt from the Federal Rules of Evidence

FEDERAL RULES OF EVIDENCE
TITLE 28—APPENDIX
FEDERAL RULES OF EVIDENCE - ARTICLE X.
CONTENTS OF WRITINGS, RECORDINGS, AND PHOTOGRAPHS
Rule 1001. Definitions

For purposes of this article the following definitions are applicable:

(1) Writings and recordings.—"Writings" and "recordings" consist of letters, words, or numbers, or their equivalent, set down by handwriting, typewriting, printing, photostating, photographing, magnetic impulse, mechanical or electronic recording, or other form of data compilation.

(2) Photographs.—"Photographs" include still photographs, X-ray films, video tapes, and motion pictures.

(3) Original.—An "original" of a writing or recording is the writing or recording itself or any counterpart intended to have the same effect by a person executing or issuing it. An "original" of a photograph includes the negative or any print there from. If data are stored in a computer or similar device, any printout or other output readable by sight, shown to reflect the data accurately, is an "original".

(4) Duplicate.—A "duplicate" is a counterpart produced by the same impression as the original, or from the same matrix, or by means of photography, including enlargements and miniatures, or by mechanical or electronic re-recording, or by chemical reproduction, or by other equivalent techniques which accurately reproduces the original. (Pub. L. 93-595, § 1, Jan. 2, 1975, 88 Stat. 1945.)

NOTES OF ADVISORY COMMITTEE ON PROPOSED RULES

In an earlier day, when discovery and other related procedures were strictly limited, the misleading named "best evidence rule" afforded substantial guarantees against inaccuracies and fraud by its insistence upon production of original documents. The great enlargement of the scope of discovery and related procedures in recent times has measurably reduced the need for the rule. Nevertheless important areas of usefulness persist: discovery of

Figure 16.7 Excerpt from the Federal Rules of Evidence (Cont.)

documents outside the jurisdiction may require substantial outlay of time and money; the unanticipated document may not practically be discoverable; criminal cases have built-in limitations on discovery. Cleary and Strong, The Best Evidence Rule: An Evaluation in Context, 51 Iowa L.Rev. 825 (1966).

Paragraph (1). Traditionally the rule requiring the original centered upon accumulations of data and expressions affecting legal relations set forth in words and figures. This meant that the rule was one essentially related to writings. Present day techniques have expanded methods of storing data, yet the essential form which the information ultimately assumes for usable purposes is words and figures. Hence the considerations underlying the rule dictate its expansion to include computers, photographic systems, and other modern developments.

Paragraph (3). In most instances, what is an original will be self-evident and further refinement will be unnecessary. However, in some instances particularized definition is required... While strictly speaking the original of a photograph might be thought to be only the negative, practicality and common usage require that any print from the negative be regarded as an original. Similarly, practicality and usage confer the status of original upon any computer printout. Transport Indemnity Co. v. Seib, 178 Neb. 253, 132 N.W.2d 871 (1965).

Paragraph (4). The definition describes "copies" produced by methods possessing an accuracy which virtually eliminates the possibility of error. Copies thus produced are given the status of originals in large measure by Rule 1003, infra. Copies subsequently produced manually, whether handwritten or typed, are not within the definition. It should be noted that what is an original for some purposes may be a duplicate for others. Thus a bank's microfilm record of checks cleared is the original as a record. However, a print offered as a copy of a check whose contents are in controversy is a duplicate. This result is substantially consistent with 28 U.S.C. § 1732(b). Compare 26 U.S.C. § 7513(c), giving full status as originals to photographic reproductions of tax returns and other documents,

Figure 16.7 Excerpt from the Federal Rules of Evidence (Cont.)

made by authority of the Secretary of the Treasury, and 44 U.S.C. § 399(a), giving original status to photographic copies in the National Archives.

NOTES OF COMMITTEE ON THE JUDICIARY, HOUSE REPORT NO. 93-650

The Committee amended this Rule expressly to include "video tapes" in the definition of "photographs."

Rule 1002. Requirement of Original

To prove the content of a writing, recording, or photograph, the original writing, recording, or photograph is required, except as otherwise provided in these rules or by Act of Congress.

(Pub. L. 93-595, § 1, Jan. 2, 1975, 88 Stat. 1946.)

NOTES OF ADVISORY COMMITTEE ON PROPOSED RULES

The rule is the familiar one requiring production of the original of a document to prove its contents, expanded to include writings, recordings, and photographs, as defined in Rule 1001(1) and (2), supra.

Application of the rule requires a resolution of the question whether contents are sought to be proved. Thus an event may be proved by nondocumentary evidence, even though a written record of it was made. If, however, the event is sought to be proved by the written record, the rule applies. For example, payment may be proved without producing the written receipt which was given. Earnings may be proved without producing books of account in which they are entered. McCormick § 198; 4 Wigmore § 1245. Nor does the rule apply to testimony that books or records have been examined and found not to contain any reference to a designated matter.

The assumption should not be made that the rule will come into operation on every occasion when use is made of a photograph in evidence. On the contrary, the rule will seldom apply to ordinary photographs. In most instances a party wishes to introduce the item and the question raised is the propriety of receiving it in evidence. Cases in which an offer is made of the testimony of a witness as to what he saw in a photograph or motion picture, without producing the

Figure 16.7 Excerpt from the Federal Rules of Evidence (Cont.)

same, are most unusual. The usual course is for a witness on the stand to identify the photograph or motion picture as a correct representation of events which he saw or of a scene with which he is familiar. In fact he adopts the picture as his testimony, or, in common parlance, uses the picture to illustrate his testimony. Under these circumstances, no effort is made to prove the contents of the picture, and the rule is inapplicable. Paradis, The Celluloid Witness, 37 U.Colo.L. Rev. 235, 249-251 (1965).

On occasion, however, situations arise in which contents are sought to be proved. Copyright, defamation, and invasion of privacy by photograph or motion picture falls in this category. Similarly as to situations in which the picture is offered as having independent probative value, e.g. automatic photograph of bank robber. See People v. Doggett, 83 Cal.App.2d 405, 188 P.2d 792 (1948) photograph of defendants engaged in indecent act; Mouser and Philbin, Photographic Evidence—Is There a Recognized Basis for Admissibility? 8 Hastings L.J. 310 (1957). records under Rule 803(6) commonly contain reports interpreting X-rays by the staff radiologist, who qualifies as an expert, and these reports need not be excluded from the records by the instant rule.

The reference to Acts of Congress is made in view of such statutory provisions as 26 U.S.C. § 7513, photographic reproductions of tax returns and documents, made by authority of the Secretary of the Treasury, treated as originals, and 44 U.S.C. § 399(a), photographic copies in National Archives treated as originals.

Rule 1003. Admissibility of Duplicates

A duplicate is admissible to the same extent as an original unless (1) a genuine question is raised as to the authenticity of the original or (2) in the circumstances it would be unfair to admit the duplicate in lieu of the original.

(Pub. L. 93-595, § 1, Jan. 2, 1975, 88 Stat. 1946.)

NOTES OF ADVISORY COMMITTEE ON PROPOSED RULES

When the only concern is with getting the words or other contents before the court with accuracy and precision, then a counterpart

Figure 16.7 Excerpt from the Federal Rules of Evidence (Cont.)

serves equally as well as the original, if the counterpart is the product of a method which insures accuracy and genuineness. By definition in Rule 1001(4), supra, a "duplicate" possesses this character.

Therefore, if no genuine issue exists as to authenticity and no other reason exists for requiring the original, a duplicate is admissible under the rule. This position finds support in the decisions, Myrick v. United States, 332 F.2d 279 (5th Cir. 1964), no error in admitting photostatic copies of checks instead of original microfilm in absence of suggestion to trial judge that photostats were incorrect; Johns v. United States, 323 F.2d 421 (5th Cir. 1963), not error to admit concededly accurate tape recording made from original wire recording; Sauget v. Johnston, 315 F.2d 816 (9th Cir. 1963), not error to admit copy of agreement when opponent had original and did not on appeal claim any discrepancy. Other reasons for requiring the original may be present when only a part of the original is reproduced and the remainder is needed for cross-examination or may disclose matters qualifying the part offered or otherwise useful to the opposing party. United States v. Alexander, 326 F.2d 736 (4th Cir. 1964). And see Toho Bussan Kaisha, Ltd. v. American President Lines, Ltd., 265 F.2d 418, 76 A.L.R.2d 1344 (2d Cir. 1959).

NOTES OF COMMITTEE ON THE JUDICIARY, HOUSE REPORT NO. 93-650

The Committee approved this Rule in the form submitted by the Court, with the expectation that the courts would be liberal in deciding that a "genuine question is raised as to the authenticity of the original."

Rule 1004. Admissibility of Other Evidence of Contents

The original is not required, and other evidence of the contents of a writing, recording, or photograph is admissible if—

(1) Originals lost or destroyed.—All originals are lost or have been destroyed, unless the proponent lost or destroyed them in bad faith; or

(2) Original not obtainable.—No original can be obtained by any available judicial process or procedure; or

Figure 16.7 Excerpt from the Federal Rules of Evidence (Cont.)

(3) Original in possession of opponent.—At a time when an original was under the control of the party against whom offered, that party was put on notice, by the pleadings or otherwise, that the contents would be a subject of proof at the hearing, and that party does not produce the original at the hearing; or

(4) Collateral matters.—The writing, recording, or photograph is not closely related to a controlling issue.

(Pub. L. 93-595, § 1, Jan. 2, 1975, 88 Stat. 1946; Mar. 2, 1987, eff. Oct. 1, 1987.)

NOTES OF ADVISORY COMMITTEE ON PROPOSED RULES

Basically the rule requiring the production of the original as proof of contents has developed as a rule of preference: if failure to produce the original is satisfactory explained, secondary evidence is admissible. The instant rule specifies the circumstances under which production of the original is excused.

The rule recognizes no "degrees" of secondary evidence. While strict logic might call for extending the principle of preference beyond simply preferring the original, the formulation of a hierarchy of preferences and a procedure for making it effective is believed to involve unwarranted complexities. Most, if not all, that would be accomplished by an extended scheme of preferences will, in any event, be achieved through the normal motivation of a party to present the most convincing evidence possible and the arguments and procedures available to his opponent if he does not. Compare McCormick § 207…

NOTES OF COMMITTEE ON THE JUDICIARY, HOUSE REPORT NO. 93-650

The Committee approved Rule 1004(1) in the form submitted to Congress. However, the Committee intends that loss or destruction of an original by another person at the instigation of the proponent should be considered as tantamount to loss or destruction in bad faith by the proponent himself.

Figure 16.7 Excerpt from the Federal Rules of Evidence (Cont.)

NOTES OF ADVISORY COMMITTEE ON PROPOSED RULES

The admission of summaries of voluminous books, records, or documents offers the only practicable means of making their contents available to judge and jury. The rule recognizes this practice, with appropriate safeguards. 4 Wigmore § 1230.

Rule 1007. Testimony or Written Admission of Party

Contents of writings, recordings, or photographs may be proved by the testimony or deposition of the party against whom offered or by that party's written admission, without accounting for the nonproduction of the original.

(Pub. L. 93-595, § 1, Jan. 2, 1975, 88 Stat. 1947; Mar. 2, 1987, eff. Oct. 1, 1987.)

NOTES OF ADVISORY COMMITTEE ON PROPOSED RULES

While the parent case, Slatterie v. Pooley, 6 M. & W. 664, 151 Eng. Rep. 579 (Exch. 1840), allows proof of contents by evidence of an oral admission by the party against whom offered, without accounting for nonproduction of the original, the risk of inaccuracy is substantial and the decision is at odds with the purpose of the rule giving preference to the original. See 4 Wigmore § 1255. The instant rule follows Professor McCormick's suggestion of limiting this use of admissions to those made in the course of giving testimony or in writing. McCormick § 208, p. 424. The limitation, of course, does not call for excluding evidence of an oral admission when nonproduction of the original has been accounted for and secondary evidence generally has become admissible. Rule 1004, supra.

A similar provision is contained in New Jersey Evidence Rule 70(1)(h).

NOTES OF ADVISORY COMMITTEE ON RULES— 1987 AMENDMENT

The amendment is technical. No substantive change is intended.

Rule 1008. Functions of Court and Jury

When the admissibility of other evidence of contents of writings, recordings, or photographs under these rules depends upon the

Figure 16.7 Excerpt from the Federal Rules of Evidence (Cont.)

fulfillment of a condition of fact, the question whether the condition has been fulfilled is ordinarily for the court to determine in accordance with the provisions of rule 104. However, when an issue is raised (a) whether the asserted writing ever existed, or (b) whether another writing, recording, or photograph produced at the trial is the original, or (c) whether other evidence of contents correctly reflects the contents, the issue is for the trier of fact to determine as in the case of other issues of fact.

(Pub. L. 93-595, § 1, Jan. 2, 1975, 88 Stat. 1947.)
http://www.gpoaccess.gov/uscode/title28a/28a_5_10_.html

COMPUTER RECORDS AND THE FEDERAL RULES OF EVIDENCE

Are you wondering where computer data and documents fall under the "Best Evidence Rule"? I'm sure you are curious just what the Federal Laws have to say regarding this matter. Well, you are in luck. We have provided a interesting article detailing the matter.

Figure 16.8 Computer Records and the Federal Rules of Evidence

U.S. Department of Justice
Executive Office for United States Attorneys
United States Attorneys' USA Bulletin
March 2001 Vol. 49, No.2

Computer Records and the Federal Rules of Evidence
Orin S. Kerr
USA Bulletin
(March 2001)

Orin S. Kerr
Trial Attorney

Computer Crime and Intellectual Property Section

This article explains some of the important issues that can arise when the government seeks the admission of computer records under the Federal Rules of Evidence. It is an excerpt of a larger DOJ manual entitled "Searching and Seizing Computers and Obtaining Electronic

Figure 16.8 Computer Records and the Federal Rules of Evidence (Cont.)

Evidence in Criminal Investigations", which is available on the internet at www.cybercrime.gov/ searchmanual.htm.

Most federal courts that have evaluated the admissibility of computer records have focused on computer records as potential hearsay. The courts generally have admitted computer records upon a showing that the records fall within the business records exception, Fed. R. Evid. 803(6):

Records of regularly conducted activity. A memorandum, report, record, or data compilation, in any form, of acts, events, conditions, opinions, or diagnoses, made at or near the time by, or from information transmitted by, a person with knowledge, if kept in the course of a regularly conducted business activity, and if it was the regular practice of that business activity to make the memorandum, report, record, or data compilation, all as shown by the testimony of the custodian or other qualified witness, unless the source of information or the method or circumstances of preparation indicate lack of trustworthiness. The term "business" as used in this paragraph includes business, institution, association, profession, occupation, and calling of every kind, whether or not conducted for profit.

See, e.g., United States v. Cestnik, 36 F.3d 904, 909-10 (10th Cir. 1994); United States v. Moore, 923 F.2d 910, 914 (1st Cir. 1991); United States v. Briscoe, 896 F.2d 1476, 1494 (7th Cir. 1990); United States v. Catabran, 836 F.2d 453, 457 (9th Cir. 1988); Capital Marine Supply v. M/V Roland Thomas II, 719 F.2d 104, 106 (5th Cir. 1983). Applying this test, the courts have indicated that computer records generally can be admitted as business records if they were kept pursuant to a routine procedure for motives that tend to assure their accuracy.

However, the federal courts are likely to move away from this "one size fits all" approach as they become more comfortable and familiar with computer records. Like paper records, computer records are not monolithic: the evidentiary issues raised by their admission should depend on what kind of computer records a proponent seeks to have admitted. For example, computer records that contain text often can be divided into two categories:

Figure 16.8 Computer Records and the Federal Rules of Evidence (Cont.)

computer-generated records, and records that are merely computer-stored. See People v. Holowko, 486 N.E.2d 877, 878-79 (Ill. 1985). The difference hinges upon whether a person or a machine created the records' contents. Computer-stored records refer to documents that contain the writings of some person or persons and happen to be in electronic form. E-mail messages, word processing files, and Internet chat room messages provide common examples. As with any other testimony or documentary evidence containing human statements, computer-stored records must comply with the hearsay rule. If the records are admitted to prove the truth of the matter they assert, the offeror of the records must show circumstances indicating that the human statements contained in the record are reliable and trustworthy, see Advisory Committee Notes to Proposed Rule 801 (1972), and the records must be authentic.

In contrast, computer-generated records contain the output of computer programs, untouched by human hands. Log-in records from Internet service providers, telephone records, and ATM receipts tend to be computer- generated records. Unlike computer-stored records, computer-generated records do not contain human "statements," but only the output of a computer program designed to process input following a defined algorithm. Of course, a computer program can direct a computer to generate a record that mimics a human statement: an e-mail program can announce "You've got mail!" when mail arrives in an inbox, and an ATM receipt can state that $100 was deposited in an account at 2:25 pm. However, the fact that a computer, rather than a human being, has created the record alters the evidentiary issues that the computer-generated records present. See, e.g., 2 J. Strong, McCormick on Evidence §294, at 286 (4th ed. 1992). The evidentiary issue is no longer whether a human's out-of-court statement was truthful and accurate (a question of hearsay), but instead whether the computer program that generated the record was functioning properly (a question of authenticity). See id.; Richard O. Lempert & Steven A. Saltzburg, A Modern Approach to Evidence 370 (2d ed. 1983); Holowko, 486 N.E.2d at 878-79.

Figure 16.8 Computer Records and the Federal Rules of Evidence (Cont.)

Finally, a third category of computer records exists: some computer records are both computer-generated and computer-stored. For example, a suspect in a fraud case might use a spreadsheet program to process financial figures relating to the fraudulent scheme. A computer record containing the output of the program would derive from both human statements (the suspect's input to the spreadsheet program) and computer processing (the mathematical operations of the spreadsheet program). Accordingly, the record combines the evidentiary concerns raised by computer-stored and computer-generated records. The party seeking the admission of the record should address both the hearsay issues implicated by the original input and the authenticity issues raised by the computer processing.

As the federal courts develop a more nuanced appreciation of the distinctions to be made between different kinds of computer records, they are likely to see that the admission of computer records generally raises two distinct issues. First, the government must establish the authenticity of all computer records by providing "evidence sufficient to support a finding that the matter in question is what its proponent claims." Fed. R. Evid. 901(a). Second, if the computer records are computer-stored records that contain human statements, the government must show that those human statements are not inadmissible hearsay.

A. Authentication

Before a party may move for admission of a computer record or any other evidence, the proponent must show that it is authentic. That is, the government must offer evidence "sufficient to support a finding that the [computer record or other evidence] in question is what its proponent claims." Fed. R. Evid. 901(a). See United States v. Simpson, 152 F.3d 1241, 1250 (10th Cir. 1998).

The standard for authenticating computer records is the same as for authenticating other records. The degree of authentication does not vary simply because a record happens to be (or has been at one point) in electronic form. See United States v. DeGeorgia, 420 F.2d

Figure 16.8 Computer Records and the Federal Rules of Evidence (Cont.)

889, 893 n.11 (9th Cir. 1969); United States v. Vela, 673 F.2d 86, 90 (5th Cir. 1982). But see United States v. Scholle, 553 F.2d 1109, 1125 (8th Cir. 1977) (stating in dicta that "the complex nature of computer storage calls for a more comprehensive foundation"). For example, witnesses who testify to the authenticity of computer records need not have special qualifications. The witness does not need to have programmed the computer himself, or even need to understand the maintenance and technical operation of the computer. See UnitedStates v. Moore, 923 F.2d 910, 915 (1st Cir. 1991) (citing cases). Instead, the witness simply must have first-hand knowledge of the relevant facts to which he or she testifies. See generally United States v. Whitaker, 127 F.3d 595, 601 (7th Cir. 1997) (FBI agent who was present when the defendant's computer was seized can authenticate seized files) United States v. Miller, 771 F.2d 1219, 1237 (9th Cir. 1985) (telephone company billing supervisor can authenticate phone company records); Moore, 923 F.2d at 915 (head of bank's consumer loan department can authenticate computerized loan data).

Challenges to the authenticity of computer records often take one of three forms. First, parties may challenge the authenticity of both computer-generated and computer-stored records by questioning whether the records were altered, manipulated, or damaged after they were created. Second, parties may question the authenticity of computer-generated records by challenging the reliability of the computer program that generated the records. Third, parties may challenge the authenticity of computer-stored records by questioning the identity of their author.

1. Authenticity and the Alteration of Computer Records

Computer records can be altered easily, and opposing parties often allege that computer records lack authenticity because they have been tampered with or changed after they were created. For example, in United States v. Whitaker, 127 F.3d 595, 602 (7th Cir. 1997), the government retrieved computer files from the computer of a narcotics dealer named Frost. The files from Frost's computer included detailed records of narcotics sales by three aliases: "Me"

Figure 16.8 Computer Records and the Federal Rules of Evidence (Cont.)

(Frost himself, presumably), "Gator" (the nickname of Frost's co-defendant Whitaker), and "Cruz" (the nickname of another dealer). After the government permitted Frost to help retrieve the evidence from his computer and declined to establish a formal chain of custody for the computer at trial, Whitaker argued that the files implicating him through his alias were not properly authenticated. Whitaker argued that "with a few rapid keystrokes, Frost could have easily added Whitaker's alias, 'Gator' to the printouts in order to finger Whitaker and to appear more helpful to the government." Id. at 602.

The courts have responded with considerable skepticism to such unsupported claims that computer records have been altered. Absent specific evidence that tampering occurred, the mere possibility of tampering does not affect the authenticity of a computer record. See Whitaker, 127 F.3d at 602 (declining to disturb trial judge's ruling that computer records were admissible because allegation of tampering was "almost wild-eyed speculation . . . [without] evidence to support such a scenario"); United States v. Bonallo, 858 F.2d 1427, 1436 (9th Cir. 1988) ("The fact that it is possible to alter data contained in a computer is plainly insufficient to establish untrustworthiness."); United States v. Glasser, 773 F.2d 1553, 1559 (11th Cir. 1985) ("The existence of an air-tight security system [to prevent tampering] is not, however, a prerequisite to the admissibility of computer printouts. If such a prerequisite did exist, it would become virtually impossible to admit computer-generated records; the party opposing admission would have to show only that a better security system was feasible."). Id. at 559. This is consistent with the rule used to establish the authenticity of other evidence such as narcotics. See United States v. Allen, 106 F.3d 695, 700 (6th Cir. 1997) ("Merely raising the possibility of tampering is insufficient to render evidence inadmissible."). Absent specific evidence of tampering, allegations that computer records have been altered go to their weight, not their admissibility. See Bonallo, 858 F.2d at 1436.

2. Establishing the Reliability of Computer Programs

Figure 16.8 Computer Records and the Federal Rules of Evidence (Cont.)

The authenticity of computer-generated records sometimes implicates the reliability of the computer programs that create the records. For example, a computer-generated record might not be authentic if the program that creates the record contains serious programming errors. If the program's output is inaccurate, the record may not be "what its proponent claims" according to Fed. R. Evid. 901.

Defendants in criminal trials often attempt to challenge the authenticity of computer-generated records by challenging the reliability of the programs. See, e.g., United States v. Dioguardi, 428 F.2d 1033, 1038 (2d Cir. 1970); United States v. Liebert, 519 F.2d 542, 547-48 (3d Cir. 1975). The courts have indicated that the government can overcome this challenge so long as "the government provides sufficient facts to warrant a finding that the records are trustworthy and the opposing party is afforded an opportunity to inquire into the accuracy thereof[.]" United States v. Briscoe, 896 F.2d 1476, 1494 (7th Cir. 1990). See also Liebert, 519 F.2d at 547; DeGeorgia, 420 F.2d. at 893 n.11. Compare Fed. R. Evid. 901(b)(9) (indicating that matters created according to a process or system can be authenticated with "[e]vidence describing a process or system used . . . and showing that the process or system produces an accurate result"). In most cases, the reliability of a computer program can be established by showing that users of the program actually do rely on it on a regular basis, such as in the ordinary course of business. See, e.g., United States v. Moore, 923 F.2d 910, 915 (1st Cir. 1991) ("[T]he ordinary business circumstances described suggest trustworthiness, .. . at least where absolutely nothing in the record in any way implies the lack thereof.") (computerized tax records held by the IRS); Briscoe, 896 F.2d at 1494 (computerized telephone records held by Illinois Bell). When the computer program is not used on a regular basis and the government cannot establish reliability based on reliance in the ordinary course of business, the government may need to disclose "what operations the computer had been instructed to perform [as well as] the precise instruction that had been given" if the opposing party requests. Dioguardi, 428 F.2d at 1038. Notably, once

Figure 16.8 Computer Records and the Federal Rules of Evidence (Cont.)

a minimum standard of trustworthiness has been established, questions as to the accuracy of computer records "resulting from . . . the operation of the computer program" affect only the weight of the evidence, not its admissibility. United States v. Catabran, 836 F.2d 453, 458 (9th Cir. 1988).

Prosecutors may note the conceptual overlap between establishing the authenticity of a computer-generated record and establishing the trustworthiness of a computer record for the business record exception to the hearsay rule. In fact, federal courts that evaluate the authenticity of computer-generated records often assume that the records contain hearsay, and then apply the business records exception. See, e.g., UnitedStates v. Linn, 880 F.2d 209, 216 (9th Cir. 1989) (applying business records exception to telephone records generated "automatically" by a computer); United States v. Vela, 673 F.2d 86, 89-90 (5th Cir. 1982) (same). As discussed later in this article, this analysis is technically incorrect in many cases: computer records generated entirely by computers cannot contain hearsay and cannot qualify for the business records exception because they do not contain human "statements." See Part B, infra. As a practical matter, however, prosecutors who lay a foundation to establish a computer-generated record as a business record will also lay the foundation to establish the record's authenticity. Evidence that a computer program is sufficiently trustworthy so that its results qualify as business records according to Fed. R. Evid. 803(6) also establishes the authenticity of the record. Compare United States v. Saputski, 496 F.2d 140, 142 (9th Cir. 1974).

3. Identifying the Author of Computer-Stored Records

Although handwritten records may be penned in a distinctive handwriting style, computer-stored records consist of a long string of zeros and ones that do not necessarily identify their author. This is a particular problem with Internet communications, which offer their authors an unusual degree of anonymity. For example, Internet technologies permit users to send effectively anonymous e-mails, and Internet Relay Chat channels permit users to communicate without disclosing their real names. When prosecutors seek the

Figure 16.8 Computer Records and the Federal Rules of Evidence (Cont.)

admission of such computer-stored records against a defendant, the defendant may challenge the authenticity of the record by challenging the identity of its author.

Circumstantial evidence generally provides the key to establishing the authorship and authenticity of a computer record. For example, in United States v. Simpson, 152 F.3d 1241 (10th Cir. 1998), prosecutors sought to show that the defendant had conversed with an undercover FBI agent in an Internet chat room devoted to child pornography. The government offered a printout of an Internet chat conversation between the agent and an individual identified as "Stavron," and sought to show that "Stavron" was the defendant. The district court admitted the printout in evidence at trial. On appeal following his conviction, Simpson argued that "because the government could not identify that the statements attributed to [him] were in his handwriting, his writing style, or his voice," the printout had not been authenticated and should have been excluded. Id. at 1249.

The Tenth Circuit rejected this argument, noting the considerable circumstantial evidence that "Stavron" was the defendant. See id. at 1250. For example, "Stavron" had told the undercover agent that his real name was "B. Simpson," gave a home address that matched Simpson's, and appeared to be accessing the Internet from an account registered to Simpson. Further, the police found records in Simpson's home that listed the name, address, and phone number that the undercover agent had sent to "Stavron." Accordingly, the government had provided evidence sufficient to support a finding that the defendant was "Stavron," and the printout was properly authenticated. See id. at 1250. See also United States v. Tank, 200 F.3d 627, 630-31 (9th Cir. 2000) (concluding that district court properly admitted chat room log printouts in circumstances similar to those in Simpson). But see United States v. Jackson, 208 F.3d 638 (7th Cir. 2000) (concluding that web postings purporting to be statements made by white supremacist groups were properly excluded on authentication grounds absent evidence that the postings were actually posted by the groups).

Figure 16.8 Computer Records and the Federal Rules of Evidence (Cont.)

B. Hearsay

Federal courts have often assumed that all computer records contain hearsay. A more nuanced view suggests that in fact only a portion of computer records contain hearsay. When a computer record contains the assertions of a person, whether or not processed by a computer, the record can contain hearsay. In such cases, the government must fit the record within a hearsay exception such as the business records exception, Fed. R. Evid. 803(6). When a computer record contains only computer-generated data untouched by human hands, however, the record cannot contain hearsay. In such cases, the government must establish the authenticity of the record, but does not need to establish that a hearsay exception applies for the records to be admissible.

1. Inapplicability of the Hearsay Rules to Computer-Generated Records

The hearsay rules exist to prevent unreliable out-of-court statements by human declarants from improperly influencing the outcomes of trials. Because people can misinterpret or misrepresent their experiences, the hearsay rules express a strong preference for testing human assertions in court, where the declarant can be placed on the stand and subjected to cross-examination. See Ohio v. Roberts, 448 U.S. 56, 62-66 (1980). This rationale does not apply when an animal or a machine makes an assertion: beeping machines and barking dogs cannot be called to the witness stand for cross-examination at trial. The Federal Rules have adopted this logic. By definition, an assertion cannot contain hearsay if it was not made by a human being. Can we just use the word person? See Fed. R. Evid. 801(a) ("A 'statement' is (1) an oral or written assertion or (2) nonverbal conduct of a person, if it is intended by the person as an assertion.") (emphasis added) ; Fed. R. Evid. 801(b) ("A declarant is a person who makes a statement.") (emphasis added).

As several courts and commentators have noted, this limitation on the hearsay rules necessarily means that computer-generated records untouched by human hands cannot contain hearsay. One state

Figure 16.8 Computer Records and the Federal Rules of Evidence (Cont.)

supreme court articulated the distinction in an early case involving the use of automated telephone records:

The printout of the results of the computer's internal operations is not hearsay evidence. It does not represent the output of statements placed into the computer by out of court declarants. Nor can we say that this printout itself is a "statement" constituting hearsay evidence. The underlying rationale of the hearsay rule is that such statements are made without an oath and their truth cannot be tested by cross-examination. Of concern is the possibility that a witness may consciously or unconsciously misrepresent what the declarant told him or that the declarant may consciously or unconsciously misrepresent a fact or occurrence. With a machine, however, there is no possibility of a conscious misrepresentation, and the possibility of inaccurate or misleading data only materializes if the machine is not functioning properly.

State v. Armstead, 432 So.2d 837, 840 (La. 1983). See also People v. Holowko, 486 N.E.2d 877, 878-79 (Ill. 1985) (automated trap and trace records); United States v. Duncan, 30 M.J. 1284, 1287-89 (N-M.C.M.R. 1990) (computerized records of ATM transactions); 2 J. Strong, McCormick on Evidence §294, at 286 (4th ed.1992); Richard O. Lempert & Stephen A. Saltzburg, A Modern Approach to Evidence 370 (2d ed. 1983). Cf. United States v. Fernandez-Roque, 703 F.2d 808, 812 n.2 (5th Cir. 1983) (rejecting hearsay objection to admission of automated telephone records because "the fact that these calls occurred is not a hearsay statement."). Accordingly, a properly authenticated computer-generated record is admissible. See Lempert & Saltzburg, at 370.

The insight that computer-generated records cannot contain hearsay is important because courts that assume the existence of hearsay may wrongfully exclude computer-generated evidence if a hearsay exception does not apply. For example, in United States v. Blackburn, 992 F.2d 666 (7th Cir. 1993), a bank robber left his eyeglasses behind in an abandoned stolen car. The prosecution's evidence against the defendant included a computer printout from a

Figure 16.8 Computer Records and the Federal Rules of Evidence (Cont.)

machine that tests the curvature of eyeglass lenses. The printout revealed that the prescription of the eyeglasses found in the stolen car exactly matched the defendant's. At trial, the district court assumed that the computer printout was hearsay, but concluded that the printout was an admissible business record according to Fed. R. Evid. 803(6). On appeal following conviction, the Seventh Circuit also assumed that the printout contained hearsay, but agreed with the defendant that the printout could not be admitted as a business record:

"the [computer-generated] report in this case was not kept in the course of a regularly conducted business activity, but rather was specially prepared at the behest of the FBI and with the knowledge that any information it supplied would be used in an ongoing criminal investigation. . . . In finding this report inadmissible under Rule 803(6), we adhere to the well-established rule that documents made in anticipation of litigation are inadmissible under the business records exception."

Id. at 670. See also Fed. R. Evid. 803(6) (stating that business records must be "made . . . by, or transmitted by, a person").

Fortunately, the Blackburn court ultimately affirmed the conviction, concluding that the computer printout was sufficiently reliable that it could have been admitted under the residual hearsay exception, Rule 803(24). See id. at 672. However, instead of flirting with the idea of excluding the printouts because Rule 803(6) did not apply, the court should have asked whether the computer printout from the lens-testing machine contained hearsay at all. This question would have revealed that the computer-generated printout could not be excluded on hearsay grounds because it contained no human "statements."

2. Applicability of the Hearsay Rules to Computer-Stored Records

Computer-stored records that contain human statements must satisfy an exception to the hearsay rule if they are offered for the truth of the matter asserted. Before a court will admit the records, the court must establish that the statements contained in the record were made

Figure 16.8 Computer Records and the Federal Rules of Evidence (Cont.)

in circumstances that tend to ensure their trustworthiness. See, e.g., Jackson, 208 F.3d at 637 (concluding that postings from the websites of white supremacist groups contained hearsay, and rejecting the argument that the postings were the business records of the ISPs that hosted the sites).

As discussed earlier in this article, courts generally permit computer-stored records to be admitted as business records according to Fed. R. Evid. 803(6). Different circuits have articulated slightly different standards for the admissibility of computer-stored business records. Some courts simply apply the direct language of Fed. R. Evid. 803(6). See e.g.,United States v. Moore, 923 F.2d 910, 914 (1st Cir. 1991); United States v. Catabran, 836 F.2d 453, 457 (9th Cir. 1988). Other circuits have articulated doctrinal tests specifically for computer records that largely (but not exactly) track the requirements of Rule 803(6). See, e.g., United States v. Cestnik, 36 F.3d 904, 909-10 (10th Cir. 1994) ("Computer business records are admissible if (1) they are kept pursuant to a routine procedure designed to assure their accuracy; (2) they are created for motives that tend to assure accuracy (e.g., not including those prepared for litigation); and (3) they are not themselves mere accumulations of hearsay.") (quoting Capital Marine Supply v. M/V Roland Thomas II, 719 F.2d 104, 106 (5th Cir. 1983)); United States v. Briscoe, 896 F.2d 1476, 1494 (7th Cir. 1990) (computer-stored records are admissible business records if they "are kept in the course of regularly conducted business activity, and [that it] was the regular practice of that business activity to make records, as shown by the testimony of the custodian or other qualified witness.") (quoting United States v. Chappell, 698 F.2d 308, 311 (7th Cir. 1983)). Notably, the printout itself may be produced in anticipation of litigation without running afoul of the business records exception. The requirement that the record be kept "in the course of a regularly conducted business activity" refers to the underlying data, not the actual printout of that data. See United States v. Sanders, 749 F.2d 195, 198 (5th Cir. 1984).

From a practical perspective, the procedure for admitting a computer-stored record pursuant to the business records exception is

Figure 16.8 Computer Records and the Federal Rules of Evidence (Cont.)

the same as admitting any other business record. Consider an e-mail harassment case. To help establish that the defendant was the sender of the harassing messages, the prosecution may seek the introduction of records from the sender's ISP showing that the defendant was the registered owner of the account from which the e-mails were sent. Ordinarily, this will require testimony from an employee of the ISP ("the custodian or other qualified witness") that the ISP regularly maintains customer account records for billing and other purposes, and that the records to be offered for admission are such records that were made at or near the time of the events they describe in the regular course of the ISP's business. Again, the key is establishing that the computer system from which the record was obtained is maintained in the ordinary course of business, and that it is a regular practice of the business to rely upon those records for their accuracy.

The business record exception is the most common hearsay exception applied to computer records. Of course, other hearsay exceptions may be applicable in appropriate cases. See, e.g., Hughes v. United States, 953 F.2d 531, 540 (9th Cir. 1992) (concluding that computerized IRS forms are admissible as public records under Fed. R. Evid. 803(8)).

C. Other Issues

The authentication requirement and the hearsay rule usually provide the most significant hurdles that prosecutors will encounter when seeking the admission of computer records. However, some agents and prosecutors have occasionally considered two additional issues: the application of the best evidence rule to computer records, and whether computer printouts are "summaries" that must comply with Fed. R. Evid. 1006.

1. The Best Evidence Rule

The best evidence rule states that to prove the content of a writing, recording, or photograph, the "original" writing, recording, or photograph is ordinarily required. See Fed. R. Evid. 1002. Agents and prosecutors occasionally express concern that a mere printout of a computer-stored electronic file may not be an "original" for the purpose of the best evidence rule. After all, the original file is merely

Figure 16.8 Computer Records and the Federal Rules of Evidence (Cont.)

a collection of 0's and 1's. In contrast, the printout is the result of manipulating the file through a complicated series of electronic and mechanical processes.

Fortunately, the Federal Rules of Evidence have expressly addressed this concern. The Federal Rules state that

[i]f data are stored in a computer or similar device, any printout or other output readable by sight, shown to reflect the data accurately, is an "original".

Fed. R. Evid. 1001(3). Thus, an accurate printout of computer data always satisfies the best evidence rule. See Doe v. United States, 805 F. Supp. 1513, 1517 (D. Hawaii. 1992). According to the Advisory Committee Notes that accompanied this rule when it was first proposed, this standard was adopted for reasons of practicality. While strictly speaking the original of a photograph might be thought to be only the negative, practicality and common usage require that any print from the negative be regarded as an original. Similarly, practicality and usage confer the status of original upon any computer printout. Advisory Committee Notes, Proposed Federal Rule of Evidence 1001(3) (1972).

2. Computer Printouts as "Summaries"

Federal Rule of Evidence 1006 permits parties to offer summaries of voluminous evidence in the form of "a chart, summary, or calculation" subject to certain restrictions. Agents and prosecutors occasionally ask whether a computer printout is necessarily a "summary" of evidence that must comply with Fed. R. Evid. 1006. In general, the answer is no. See Sanders, 749 F.2d at 199; Catabran, 836 F.2d at 456-57; United States v. Russo, 480 F.2d 1228, 1240-41 (6th Cir. 1973). Of course, if the computer printout is merely a summary of other admissible evidence, Rule 1006 will apply just as it does to other summaries of evidence.

ABOUT THE AUTHOR

Orin S. Kerr is a Trial Attorney, Computer Crime and Intellectual Property Section, Criminal Division, United States Department of Justice.

DEMONSTRATIVE EVIDENCE

Demonstrative evidence has a powerful appeal to juries. For example, if you are comparing two products to purchase and you are evaluating the qualities, what is more convincing, an interesting narrative, or a real life demonstration? Demonstrative evidence shows a jury the quality of the evidence in a dramatic way. Some evidence, by its nature is demonstrative. For example, store videos of robberies. Sometimes demonstrative evidence backfires, such as the infamous, OJ Glove demonstration. In that case, the investigators collected evidence that was properly recovered and documented, but was presented in an inappropriate manner, thus helping the defense and doing serious damage to the prosecutions credibility. Demonstrative evidence for the Courtroom will be covered in greater detail in Chapter 18 Visual Aids.

SUMMARY

Yes, the photo-logs are tedious, so are detailed sketches, final reports, articulating probable cause for a warrant, chain of custody logs, property receipts, evidence logs etc. It must be done this way in order for the evidence to be used in court. Your success as an investigator will be enhanced with the knowledge of evidence, and the State and Federal laws surrounding it.

DISCUSSION QUESTIONS

1. How do the Federal Rules of Evidence address the "originality" of computer data in relation to the best evidence rule?

2. Are the Hearsay Rules applied differently in cases of computer related evidence?

PRACTICAL EXERCISE

1. Research your states rule for admissibility of scientific evidence, has your state maintained Frye, adopted Daubert, or adapted its own rules? Many states rules can be found on the Center for Internet & Society and Harvard Law School website located at: http://cyber.law.harvard.edu/daubert/

2. Find out if your state had laws governing the admissibility of digital photographs, compare them with a couple other states.

ADDITIONAL READING

USA Today. "Bryant returns for pretrial hearing on admissibility of evidence". Posted 2/3/2004 11:07 AM. Located at: http://www.usatoday.com/sports/basketball/nba/2004-02-03-bryant-hearing_x.htm

Physical Evidence Handbook. Kentucky State Police Forensic Laboratories Section (Revised 6/01) www.firearmsid.com/Downloads/PHYSICAL%20EVIDENCE%20HAND BOOK%20Rev6-01.pdf

Evidence Based Prosecution: Protecting the Record Admissibility Issues. http://www.state.ga.us/cjcc/Handouts/13

ENDNOTES:

1. http://www.gpoaccess.gov/constitution/html/amdt5.html and http://www.gpoaccess.gov/constitution/html/amdt4.html

2. Ibid.

3. Ibid.

4. Ibid.

Chapter 17

Testimony

CHAPTER OVERVIEW

Eventually a crime scene investigator or technician will have to testify as to what he or she did regarding a crime scene. This chapter is designed to illustrate how the methods of crime scene documentation come into play during trial. This chapter will define discovery and the Federal Rules regarding it. We will demonstrate how this 'discovery' of documentation and crime scene procedures affects the testimony of the crime scene investigator.

OBJECTIVES

1. Summarize the different types of discovery.
2. Identify Federal Rules regarding discovery.
3. Compare and contrast proper and improper crime scene documentation methods and how they affect testimony.

INTRODUCTION

Hopefully your crime scene documentation efforts led to the identity and arrest of a suspect, and the evidence collected meets the rules of evidence. So, are you done?

Nope! Let's say your documentation led to an arrest, and your evidence is admitted into trial. Chances are you will have to now testify before the court regarding your evidence, collection and documentation. Sound like fun? Keep that question in mind when you read the article at the end of the chapter.

DISCOVERY

What is Discovery?

Discovery is a process in which the defense and prosecution in criminal cases, or the plaintiff and defendant in civil cases, lay their cards on the table. Unlike popular TV dramas, there are no "surprise witnesses" or unexpected evidence produced in trials. The discovery process means that both sides, under the supervision of the judge, disclose what witnesses and evidence will be used in the trial. This portion of the judicial process happens in the pretrial phase, early in the trial.

What is Discoverable?

Discoverable items include witnesses and demonstrative evidence. The other side is not only made aware of the intent to use this evidence, but has the right to examine it. Both parties have the right to interview potential witnesses, but the witnesses are not required to talk. For example, the following items may be included in discovery:

Types of Discovery

- Interrogatories
  - Written
  - Oral
- Examinations
  - Depositions
  - Affidavits
- Reports
- Photographs

- Witnesses
  - Witness statements
- 911 calls

Federal Rule 16 - Discovery and Inspection

(a) Government's Disclosure.

(1) Information Subject to Disclosure.

(A) Defendant's Oral Statement. Upon a defendant's request, the government must disclose to the defendant the substance of any relevant oral statement made by the defendant, before or after arrest, in response to interrogation by a person the defendant knew was a government agent if the government intends to use the statement at trial.

(B) Defendant's Written or Recorded Statement. Upon a defendant's request, the government must disclose to the defendant, and make available for inspection, copying, or photographing, all of the following:

(i) any relevant written or recorded statement by the defendant if:

the statement is within the government's possession, custody, or control; and the attorney for the government knows—or through due diligence could know—that the statement exists;

(ii) the portion of any written record containing the substance of any relevant oral statement made before or after arrest if the defendant made the statement in response to interrogation by a person the defendant knew was a government agent; and

(iii) the defendant's recorded testimony before a grand jury relating to the charged offense.

(C) Organizational Defendant. Upon a defendant's request, if the defendant is an organization, the government must disclose to the defendant any statement described in Rule 16(a)(1)(A) and (B) if the government contends that the person making the statement:

(i) was legally able to bind the defendant regarding the subject of the statement because of that person's position as the defendant's director, officer, employee, or agent; or

(ii) was personally involved in the alleged conduct constituting the offense and was legally able to bind the defendant regarding that conduct because of that person's position as the defendant's director, officer, employee, or agent.

(D) Defendant's Prior Record. Upon a defendant's request, the government must furnish the defendant with a copy of the defendant's prior criminal record that is within the government's possession, custody, or control if the attorney for the government knows—or through due diligence could know—that the record exists.

(E) Documents and Objects. Upon a defendant's request, the government must permit the defendant to inspect and to copy or photograph books, papers, documents, data, photographs, tangible objects, buildings or places, or copies or portions of any of these items, if the item is within the government's possession, custody, or control and:

(i) the item is material to preparing the defense;

(ii) the government intends to use the item in its case-in-chief at trial; or

(iii) the item was obtained from or belongs to the defendant.

(F) Reports of Examinations and Tests. Upon a defendant's request, the government must permit a defendant to inspect and to copy or photograph the results or reports of any physical or mental examination and of any scientific test or experiment if:

(i) the item is within the government's possession, custody, or control;

(ii) the attorney for the government knows—or through due diligence could know—that the item exists; and

(iii) the item is material to preparing the defense or the government intends to use the item in its case-in-chief at trial.

(G) Expert Witnesses. At the defendant's request, the government must give to the defendant a written summary of any testimony that the government intends to use under Rules 702, 703, or 705 of the Federal Rules of Evidence during its case-in-chief at trial. If the government requests discovery under subdivision (b)(1)(C)(ii) and the defendant complies, the government must, at the defendant's request, give to the defendant a written summary of testimony that the government intends to use under Rules 702, 703, or 705 of the Federal Rules of Evidence as evidence at trial on the issue of the defendant's mental condition. The summary provided under this subparagraph must describe the witness' opinions, the bases and reasons for those opinions, and the witness' qualifications.

(b) Defendant's Disclosure.

(1) Information Subject to Disclosure.

(A) Documents and Objects. If a defendant requests disclosure under Rule 16(a)(1)(E) and the government complies, then the defendant must permit the government, upon request, to inspect and to copy or photograph books, papers, documents, data, photographs, tangible objects, buildings or places, or copies or portions of any of these items if:

(i) the item is within the defendant's possession, custody, or control; and

(ii) the defendant intends to use the item in the defendant's case-in-chief at trial.

(B) Reports of Examinations and Tests. If a defendant requests disclosure under Rule 16(a)(1)(F) and the government complies, the defendant must permit the government, upon request, to inspect and to copy or photograph the results or reports of any physical or mental examination and of any scientific test or experiment if:

(i) the item is within the defendant's possession, custody, or control; and

(ii) the defendant intends to use the item in the defendant's case-in-chief at trial, or intends to call the witness who prepared the report and the report relates to the witness's testimony.

(C) Expert Witnesses. The defendant must, at the government's request, give to the government a written summary of any testimony that the defendant intends to use under Rules 702, 703, or 705 of the Federal Rules of Evidence as evidence at trial, if—

(i) the defendant requests disclosure under subdivision (a)(1)(G) and the government complies; or

(ii) the defendant has given notice under Rule 12.2(b) of an intent to present expert testimony on the defendant's mental condition.

This summary must describe the witness's opinions, the bases and reasons for those opinions, and the witness's qualifications [.]

Seized items must also be made available to the defense team to review even if the prosecution doesn't intend to use them in court.

The defense must ensure to request all pertinent discovery. The Federal Defender's Office of Eastern Washington and Idaho (http://www.fdewi.org/) uses a form letter that appears to be very thorough in requesting discovery. Take a look:

> *Author note / Carol Hawks:
>
> In a Federal fraud case in which I worked as an investigator for the criminal defense team, I had to deal with Federal agents who were reluctant to provide full access to evidentiary items. Like a lot of complicated fraud cases, there were quite a few boxes containing documents. Rather than allowing me to go through the documents to review what the government seized, the agent wanted me to only review what they were planning to use in trial.

Figure 17.1 Sample Discovery Letter

Re:

Dear :

This letter is to advise you that I will be representing _____ and to request that you provide discovery as soon as possible. We request production of the information required by the standing discovery order (SDO) and, specifically the following:

(1) Statements. All written and oral statements made by the defendant. This request includes, but is not limited to, any rough notes, records, reports, transcripts or other documents and tapes in which statements of the defendant are contained. The substance of oral statements which the government intends to introduce are discoverable under Fed. R.Crim. P. 16(a)(1)(A)(amended December 1, 1991) and Brady v. Maryland. (SDO, p.1 2)

(2) Documents, statements, reports, tangible evidence. Production of all documents, statements, agents' reports, and tangible evidence favorable to the defendant on the issue of guilt or which affects the credibility of the government's case. This evidence must be produced pursuant to Brady v. Maryland and United States v. Agurs, 427 U.S. 97 (1976). (SDO, p. 2-3)

(3) Prior record/other act evidence. All evidence, documents, records of judgments and convictions, photographs and tangible evidence, and information pertaining to any prior arrests and convictions or prior bad acts. Evidence of prior record is available under Fed. R. Crim. P. 16(a)(1)(B). Evidence of prior similar acts is discoverable under Fed. R. Crim. P. 16(a)(1)(C) and Fed. R. Evid. 404(b) (as amended December 1, 1991) and 609. This request also includes the defendant's "rap" sheet and/or NCIC computer check on the defendant. (SDO, p. 2, 4)

(4) Seized evidence. All evidence seized as a result of any search, either warrantless or with a warrant, in this case. This is available under Fed. R. Crim. P. 16(a)(1)(C). (SDO p. 2) In addition, it is requested that copies of all search and arrest warrants issued in connection with this prosecution, including any supporting affidavits or telephonic transcriptions, be provided.

(5) Agent's reports, notes, memos. All arrest reports, investigator's notes, memos from arresting officers, sworn statements, and prosecution reports pertaining to the defendant. These reports are available under Fed. R.Crim. P. 16(a)(1)(B) and (C); and Fed. R. Crim. P. 26.2 and 12(i). In addition, it is requested that any witness interview notes that could be considered to be statements attributable to the witness be provided. See Goldberg v. U.S., 425 U.S. 94 (1976). (SDO p. 4 requires preservation of notes)

Figure 17.1 Sample Discovery Letter (Cont.)

(6) Other documents/tangible objects. All other documents and tangible objects, including photographs, books, papers, documents, or copies or portions thereof which are material to the defense or intended for use in the government's case-in-chief or were obtained from or belong to the defendant. Specifically requested are all documents, items and other information seized pursuant to any search. This is available under Brady and Fed. R. Crim. P. 16(a)(1)(C). (SDO p. 4)

(7) Bias of government witnesses. Any evidence that any prospective government witness is biased or prejudiced against the defendant or has a motive to falsify or distort her/her testimony. See Pennsylvania v. Ritchie, 480 U.S. 39 (1987); United States v. Strifler, 851 F.2d 1197 (9th Cir. 1988). (SDO p. 3)

(8) Prior record/other acts of government witnesses. Any evidence that any prospective government witness has engaged in any criminal act whether or not resulting in a conviction. See F.R.E. Rule 608(b) and Brady.

(9) Investigation of witnesses. Any evidence that any prospective witness is under investigation by federal, state or local authorities for any criminal or official misconduct. United States v. Chitty, 760 F.2d 425 (2d Cir.), cert. denied, 474 U.S. 945 (1985).

(10) Evidence regarding ability to testify. Any evidence, including any medical or psychiatric reports or evaluations, tending to show that any prospective witness's ability to perceive, remember, communicate, or tell the truth is impaired; and any evidence that a witness has ever used narcotics or other controlled substance, or has ever been an alcoholic. United States v. Strifler, 851 F.2d 1197 (9th Cir. 1988); Chavis v. North Carolina, 637 F.2d 213, 224 (4th Cir. 1980); United States v. Butler, 567 F.2d 885 (9th Cir.1978).

(11) Personnel files. It is requested that the government review each agent's personnel file for review for information requested in paragraphs (7) - (10) above and determine whether there is any impeaching information contained in the files, see United States v. Henthorn, 931 F.2d 29 (9th Cir. 1991).

(12) Government witnesses. The name and last known address of each prospective government witness. See United States v. Neap, 834 F.2d 1311 (7th Cir. 1987); United States v. Tucker, 716 F.2d 583 (9th Cir. 1983) (failure to interview government witnesses by counsel is ineffective); United States v. Cook, 608 F.2d 1175, 1181 (9th Cir. 1979) (defense has equal right to talk to witnesses). (SDO p. 3-4)

(13) Evidence of failed polygraph of government witness(es). Disclosure that any government witness has taken and failed a polygraph is requested. See Bartholomew v. Wood, 34 F.3d 870 (9th Cir. 1994).

Figure 17.1 Sample Discovery Letter (Cont.)

(14) Other witnesses. The name and last known address of every witness to the crime or crimes charged (or any of the overt acts committed in furtherance thereof) who will not be called as a government witness. United States v. Cadet, 727 F.2d 1469 (9th Cir. 1984).

(15) Favorable testimony. The name of any witness who made an arguably favorable statement concerning the defendant or who could not identify him or who was unsure of his identity or participation in the crime charged. Jackson v. Wainwright, 390 F.2d 288 (5th Cir. 968); Chavis v. North Carolina, 637 F.2d 213, 223 (4th Cir. 1980); James v. Jag, 575 F.2d 1164, 1168 (6th Cir. 1978); Hudson v. Blackburn, 601 F.2d 785 (5th Cir. 1975). (SDO p. 3)

(16) Rule 26.2 Material/Timing of production. It is requested that the government provide all material available pursuant to Fed. R. Crim. P. 26.2, sufficiently in advance of trial or motion hearings so as to avoid unnecessary delay prior to cross examination.

(17) Experts/resumes. The curriculum vitae of any and all experts the government intends to call at trial, including any and all books, treatises or other papers written by the expert which is relevant to the testimony.

(18) Expert's reports and summaries. Production of any and all reports of any examinations or tests, is requested pursuant to Rule 16(a) (1)(D). In addition, it is requested that the government disclose a written summary of testimony the government intends to use under FRE 702, 703 or 705. As required by Rule 16(a)(1)(E), the summaries must describe the witnesses' opinions, the bases and the reasons therefor and the witnesses' qualifications. See Fed. R. Crim. P. 16(a)(1)(E) (added December 1,1993).

(19) Confidential Informant(s) and related information. It is requested that the government reveal the identity of any and all confidential informants who were percipient witnesses to the charges in this case and information regarding any promises made to the CI and the information provided by the CI.

(20) Promises made or "deals" with government witnesses. Under Giglio v. United States, 405 U.S. 150 (1972), the government must provide all promises of consideration given to witnesses. See also United States v. Shaffer, 789 F.2d 682 (9th Cir. 1986). This request includes cooperation agreements with witnesses who are not called as government witnesses. See United States v. Kojayan, 8 F.3d 1315 (9th Cir. 1993).

(21) Specific inquiries of agents. It is requested that the government make specific inquiry of each government agent connected to the case for discovery requested above. See Kyles v. Whitley, 115 S.Ct. 1555 (1995) ("no one doubts that police investigators sometimes fail to inform a prosecutor of all they know" but "neither is there any serious doubt that

> ## Figure 17.1 Sample Discovery Letter (Cont.)
>
> procedures and regulations can be established to carry [the prosecutor's] burden and to insure communication of all relevant information on each case to every lawyer who deals with it").
>
> (22) Minutes of Grand Jury Proceedings. Production of the minutes of the grand jury proceedings is requested in order to determine whether there has been compliance with Rule 6 with regard to attendance and the number of grand jurors voting on this indictment. See Rule 6(b)-(d).
>
> (23) Grand Jury transcripts. All grand jury transcripts are requested in accordance with SDO p. 4-5.
>
> (24) Statement by government of refusal to provide. The government is requested to advise if it has any of the above-requested items or the items required by the SDO but refuses to provide them to the defense.
>
> (25) Statement of existence of other information. (a) It is requested that the United States state whether the defendant was identified in any lineup, showup, photo spread or similar identification proceeding, and produce any pictures utilized or resulting from such procedure and the names of any identifying witnesses. (b) It is requested that the United States state whether the defendant was an aggrieved person, as defined in 18 U.S.C. 2510(11), or any electronic surveillance, and if so, set forth in detail the circumstances of such surveillance.
>
> Thank you for your attention to these requests.
>
> Sincerely,

What Happens if You Don't Disclose?

If you fail to provide the disclosure information, then you can't use the evidence in trial. The other side has the right to object to the admission of the evidence or the testimony of the witness and the objection will probably be sustained.

Federal Rule 16 - Discovery and Inspection - Regulating Discovery

(e) Regulating Discovery.

(1) Failure to Comply. If a party fails to comply with this rule, the court may:

(A) order that party to permit the discovery or inspection; specify its time, place, and manner; and prescribe other just terms and conditions;

(B) grant a continuance;

(C) prohibit that party from introducing the undisclosed evidence; or

(D) enter any other order that is just under the circumstances.

What is Not Discoverable?

The notes and conversations of counsel are not discoverable. These are examples of protected items:

- Counsel notes
- Attorney - client conversations/correspondence
- Polygraphs and voice stress analyzer

Federal Rule 16 - Discovery and Inspection - Government's Disclosure

(a) Government's Disclosure.

(2) Information Not Subject to Disclosure. Except as Rule 16(a)(1) provides otherwise, this rule does not authorize the discovery or inspection of reports, memoranda, or other internal government documents made by an attorney for the government or other government agent in connection with investigating or prosecuting the case. Nor does this rule authorize the discovery or inspection of statements made by prospective government witnesses except as provided in 18 U.S.C. sec. 3500.

(3) Grand Jury Transcripts. This rule does not apply to the discovery or inspection of a grand jury's recorded proceedings, except as provided in Rules 6, 12(h), 16(a)(1), and 26.2.

Federal Rule 16 - Discovery and Inspection - Defendant's Disclosure

(b) Defendant's Disclosure.

(2) Information Not Subject to Disclosure. Except for scientific or medical reports, Rule 16(b)(1) does not authorize discovery or inspection of:

(A) reports, memoranda, or other documents made by the defendant, or the defendant's attorney or agent, during the case's investigation or defense; or

(B) a statement made to the defendant, or the defendant's attorney or agent, by:

    (i)   the defendant;

    (ii) a government or defense witness; or

    (iii) a prospective government or defense witness.

FEDERAL RULES OF EVIDENCE

Article IV. Relevancy and its Limits

Rule 404. Character Evidence Not Admissible To Prove Conduct; Exceptions; Other Crimes

(a) Character evidence generally-Evidence of a person's character or a trait of character is not admissible for the purpose of proving action in conformity therewith on a particular occasion, except:

> (3) Character of witness.-Evidence of the character of a witness, as provided in rules 607, 608, and 609. *(As amended Mar. 2, 1987, eff. Oct. 1, 1987; Apr. 30, 1991, eff. Dec. 1, 1991; Apr. 17, 2000, eff. Dec. 1, 2000.)

Rule 405. Methods of Proving Character

(a) Reputation or opinion.-In all cases in which evidence of character or a trait of character of a person is admissible, proof may be made by testimony as to reputation or by testimony in the form of an opinion. On cross-examination, inquiry is allowable into relevant specific instances of conduct.

(b) Specific instances of conduct.-In cases in which character or a trait of character of a person is an essential element of a charge, claim, or defense, proof may also be made of specific instances of that person's conduct.

Article VI. Witnesses

Rule 601. General Rule of Competency

Every person is competent to be a witness except as otherwise provided in these rules. However, in civil actions and proceedings, with respect to an element of a claim or defense as to which State law supplies the rule of decision, the competency of a witness shall be determined in accordance with State law.

Rule 602. Lack of Personal Knowledge

A witness may not testify to a matter unless evidence is introduced sufficient to support a finding that the witness has personal knowledge of the matter. Evidence to prove personal knowledge may, but need not, consist of the witness' own testimony. This rule is subject to the provisions of rule 703, relating to opinion testimony by expert witnesses. (As amended Mar. 2, 1987, eff. Oct. 1, 1987; Apr. 25, 1988, eff. Nov.1, 1988.)

Rule 603. Oath or Affirmation

Before testifying, every witness shall be required to declare that the witness will testify truthfully, by oath or affirmation administered in a form calculated to awaken the witness' conscience and impress the witness' mind with the duty to do so. (As amended Mar. 2, 1987, eff. Oct. 1, 1987.)

Rule 607. Who May Impeach

The credibility of a witness may be attacked by any party, including the party calling the witness. (As amended Mar. 2, 1987, eff. Oct. 1, 1987.)

Rule 608. Evidence of Character and Conduct of Witness

(a) Opinion and reputation evidence of character.-The credibility of a witness may be attacked or supported by evidence in the form of opinion or reputation, but subject to these limitations:

 (1) the evidence may refer only to character for truthfulness or untruthfulness, and

 (2) evidence of truthful character is admissible only after the character of the witness for truthfulness has been attacked by opinion or reputation evidence or otherwise.

(b) Specific instances of conduct.-Specific instances of the conduct of a witness, for the purpose of attacking or supporting the witness' character for truthfulness, other than conviction of crime as provided in rule 609, may not be proved by extrinsic evidence. They may, however, in the discretion of the court, if probative of truthfulness or untruthfulness, be inquired into on cross-examination of the witness

 (1) concerning the witness' character for truthfulness or untruthfulness, or

 (2) concerning the character for truthfulness or untruthfulness of another witness as to which character the witness being cross-examined has testified.

The giving of testimony, whether by an accused or by any other witness, does not operate as a waiver of the accused's or the witness' privilege against self-incrimination when examined with respect to matters that relate only to character for truthfulness. (As amended Mar. 2, 1987, eff. Oct. 1, 1987; Apr. 25, 1988, eff. Nov. 1, 1988; Mar. 27, 2003, eff. Dec. 1, 2003.)

Rule 611. Mode and Order of Interrogation and Presentation

(a) Control by court-The court shall exercise reasonable control over the mode and order of interrogating witnesses and presenting evidence so as to (1) make the interrogation and presentation effective for the ascertainment of the truth, (2) avoid needless consumption of time, and (3) protect witnesses from harassment or undue embarrassment.

(b) Scope of cross-examination-Cross-examination should be limited to the subject matter of the direct examination and matters affecting the credibility of the witness. The court may, in the exercise of discretion, permit inquiry into additional matters as if on direct examination.

(c) Leading questions-Leading questions should not be used on the direct examination of a witness except as may be necessary to develop the witness' testimony. Ordinarily leading questions should be permitted on cross-examination. When a party calls a hostile witness, an adverse party, or a witness identified with an adverse ·party, interrogation may be by leading questions. (2, 1987, eff. Oct. 1, 1987.)

Rule 612. Writing Used To Refresh Memory

Except as otherwise provided in criminal proceedings by section 3500 of title 18, United States Code, if a witness uses a writing to refresh memory for the purpose of testifying, either-

(1)   while testifying, or

(2)   before testifying, if the court in its discretion determines it is necessary in the interests of justice, an adverse party is entitled to have the writing produced at the hearing, to inspect it, to cross-examine the witness thereon, and to introduce in evidence those portions that relate to the testimony of the witness. If it is claimed that the writing contains matters not related to the subject matter of the testimony the court shall examine the writing in camera, excise any portions not so related, and order delivery of the remainder to the party entitled thereto. Any portion withheld over objections shall be preserved and made available to the appellate court in the event of an appeal. If a writing is not produced or delivered pursuant to order under this rule, the court shall make any order justice requires, except that in criminal cases when the prosecution elects not to comply, the order shall be one striking the testimony or, if the court in its discretion determines that the interests of justice so require, declaring a mistrial. (As amended Mar. 2, 1987, eff. Oct. 1, 1987.)

Rule 613. Prior Statements of Witnesses

(a) Examining witness concerning prior statement-In examining a witness concerning a prior statement made by the witness, whether written or not, the statement need not be shown nor its contents disclosed to the witness at that time, but on request the same shall be shown or disclosed to opposing counsel.

(b) Extrinsic evidence of prior inconsistent statement of witness-Extrinsic evidence of a prior inconsistent statement by a witness is not admissible unless the witness is afforded an opportunity to explain or deny the same and the opposite party is afforded an opportunity to interrogate the witness thereon, or the interests of justice otherwise require. This provision does not apply to admissions of a party-opponent as defined in rule 801(d)(2). (As amended Mar. 2, 1987, eff. Oct. 1, 1987; Apr. 25, 1988, eff. Nov.1, 1988.)

Ah, but what does all this mean to you? Instead of spelling it out in boring detail we have provided the following example:

Figure 17.2 "The Tape"

Rachel was 9 years old and routinely went roller-skating along the beach service road. This day was no different, bright, warm, and clear with thousands of other beach goers in sight. Except this day she would not return home. Almost a week passed before her remains were discovered, 50 miles away on a wooded mountaintop.

The investigation was intense and a suspect was developed. Randy was a parolee with a long history of kidnap and rape. He was a suspect in several homicides, but there had never been a witness to connect him to the actual scene. Rachel's case would be different.

Two months into the case a part time forestry worker, Donna, came forward, saying that she had witnessed Randy pushing a young girl into the forest, near where Rachel's body had been found. A short time later she saw Randy coming out of the forest, alone, with blood covering his shirt. Donna knew that the young girl was in trouble as she was being pushed out of sight, but Donna did nothing. She had spent the last two months trying to force the images out of her mind.

One of the lead detectives solicited the aid of a friend and forensic psychologist to help him interview Donna. It took weeks to arrange the interview with her. She demanded that they "only talk", no notes were to be taken, no recordings made. They knew that they would probably only have one chance to talk to her and that she would probably refuse to testify. So the detective hid a tape recorder in his jacket pocket with the tiny microphone running down his sleeve.

Each answer had to be pulled from Donna, but after two hours they had gotten her statement and she identified Randy from the photo-line-up. The detective and the psychologist waited until they were back in the car and the tape was turned off, before they started to celebrate. They had finally gotten that "m——f——" and spent the hour's drive back to the station discussing how glorious it would be to see that "m——f—— burn in the electric chair".

"The Tape" (Cont.)

Unfortunately, the detective had pushed the pause button instead of record when he started the interview. And to make things worse, he managed to record the conversation between the two on the drive back. None of this was discovered until the case was coming up for trial and the defense had a copy of the tape.

Donna did take the stand, but claimed she had no memory of the suspect and victim, nor could she remember talking to the detective. The defense had a "field day" with the detective and the psychologist.

Enough additional evidence had been developed to convict Randy; however, the conviction was overturned, twice, and he is now awaiting his third trial for this murder. In the many years since this case DNA testing has become routine and has finally linked Randy to one other murder, with more certainly to follow. The story of "the tape" will have to be told again and again.

Courtesy of Don Howell

NOTE-TAKING

Your field notes may be discoverable. Agencies vary in their policies regarding the retention of officer notes. Many have a strict policy requiring officers to destroy their notes upon completion of a final report. On the other side of the spectrum, some departments require officers to submit their handwritten or tape recorded field notes with the final report. Either way, be consistent with your department's policy. If you tell a judge you "never keep your notes" but later testify in a different trial that you have notes, you could be in risk of losing credibility with the court.

On another note (pardon the pun) you may want to reconsider what you put in your notes now that you know they can be subject to discovery

Figure 17.3 Dan Byram on Note-taking

Retired police lieutenant Daniel Byram
MA Human Behavior
23 years law enforcement
17 years experience post secondary education
Graduate of DEA Drug Unit Commander Academy
Member of CALI and ASIS

Retired Lieutenant Byram gives some valuable pointers for note-taking in his book "Lieutenant Byram's Investigative Handbooks: Crime Scenes".

1) Always use the same type of ink pen to avoid being accused of changing the content after the time you claim the notes were written.

2) Never use profanity or cute codes such as "Mr. Smith (AH) reported the burglary". In this example, if the officer was truthful on the stand, he would have to testify that "AH" is police shorthand for the word a—hole. That cute attempt at literary handiwork and cryptography is going to make someone an AH on the stand and it isn't Mr. Smith.

3) The notes should be in a loose leaf binder so individual pages can be removed for court. You do not want to hand over your whole notebook to a prominent defense attorney. They have no need to see anything except the case notes for the particular investigation in file.

4) Don't put personal notes in the notebook. Your shopping list doesn't need to be subject t o the discovery process.

5) If you make a mistake, do not erase, white out or draw through. Merely make a single line through the error so it can still be read. Making an error isn't a problem, having something blanked out in your notebook is!

Consider the kind of information collected and documented from the crime scene. On the stand you will give testimony to the physical evidence and your interpretation of what that evidence means. If you made notes, took photos and drew sketches you will be able to convince the jury or judge of the facts that support you interpretation. Offer only the facts, as you know them.

Figure 17.4 A Personal Interview with Retired Lt. Dan Byram

I worked a lot of narcotics and vice cases over the years; as an undercover cop and as a narc unit commander. There were a lot of times when we did cases that were very similar in nature, for example, multiple drug buys at the same location with the same suspect. Rookie narcs often failed to take notes, and often waited until the end of the work week to write their reports and suddenly found that the time, date, and exact conversations became cloudy. In other cases, they would write a 'quick report' and not go into great detail. Later, sometimes much later, they would take the stand in court and face cross- examination with an experienced drug attorney who would attack their recollection and confuse them, thereby bringing their credibility into question. The fundamentals that apply to any typical investigation, like a burglary or theft, also apply to special operations cases; detailed, contemporaneous, thorough note-taking is critical to successful case development.

Another issue for narc officers regarding evidence is that in many cases, the narc must be his or her own crime scene tech. They are responsible for collecting, preserving, and presenting their own physical evidence and often must conduct basic analysis on the evidence they collect. They do this by photographing, weighing, conducting chemical tests, and packaging the evidence from their buys.

You may ask "why is this so important"? Without the accurate documentation of the evidence, the agent risks accusations of corruption, or the embarrassment of buying "bunk" and subsequently losing credibility with the criminal element that the agent has infiltrated. Further, weak documentation will cause untold grief for the investigator in court.

Figure 17.5 National Conference on Science and the Law Proceedings

Title: National Conference on Science and the Law Proceedings.
Series: Research Forum
Author: National Institute of Justice
Published: NIJ, July 2000
Subject: Criminal justice system
The entire report can be viewed at: http://www.ncjrs.org/txtfiles1/nij/179630.txt

Panel VII. Expert Witnesses: Is Justice Ruined by Expertism?

—E. Michael McCann

In trial testimony, a competent, adequately trained officer testified about a palm print matching the defendant's which the officer had recovered from one of the walls in one of the slaying scenes. The officer, in testifying, said that the palm print was "fresh." This testimony was of double importance, supporting the prosecution theory of guilt and

Figure 17.5 National Conference on Science and the Law Proceedings

indirectly addressing the potential defense argument that the defendant had been in the house at an earlier date for some other reason than slaying the deceased. The defense attorney, a very capable lawyer, did not attack this testimony.

Overnight, I thought about that testimony. I had never heard testimony of "fresh fingerprints." I thought, "has there been a new development?" I called the technician at his home and asked, "you testified that the palm prints were 'fresh'. Is there new technology that can date palm prints?" He responded, "no, I was in error; it was a mistake."

I put the technician on the stand the next morning to recant his own testimony that the palm print was "fresh." I firmly believe that the error was inadvertent in that the technician's keen desire to support the prosecution and anticipate the defense caused him to subconsciously put the word "fresh" before the words "palm print."

REAL LIFE EXAMPLE

In the beginning of the chapter we pondered whether testifying was "fun". We don't know if anyone describes it as fun, but it certainly can be bearable if the person testifying has done their job correctly. Consider the information provided in this textbook concerning proper methods in documenting and processing a crime scene; records and evidence management, note-taking, photos, sketches, and reports. Now consider what would happen if you ignored these lessons. The article below summarizes all the key aspects that this book has been describing, take them to heart.

Article 17.1 Crime Scene Tactics Faulted

Crime Scene Tactics Faulted

By Demorris Lee and Aisling Swift, Staff Writers

DURHAM — For nearly two days in December 2001, Durham crime-scene technicians combed the home of Mike Peterson looking for evidence that the death of his wife Kathleen was more than the result of a fall down a wooden staircase.

They videotaped the home, took notes about where drops of blood were found, looked for fingerprints. When blood wasn't visible to the naked eye, senior crime-scene technician Eric Campen sprayed Luminol, a solution that exposes it. As a result of that testing, Campen said during a recent court hearing, "we found what we needed."

But for now, only Campen, a 15-year veteran, knows the details of what Luminol testing exposed. He testified late last month that he took no notes, that he didn't draw a diagram of the foot pattern the Luminol testing revealed, that he has yet to complete a report of his findings — and that 16 months later, his report was being created from memory.

Article 17.1 Crime Scene Tactics Faulted (Cont.)

After the evidence was gathered from the home in Durham's upscale Forest Hills neighborhood, a grand jury indicted Peterson on a murder charge. As the May 5 trial approaches, however, the latest disclosure of evidence-gathering practices by Durham crime-scene technicians has allowed defense attorneys David Rudolf and Thomas Maher to question the accuracy of the crucial Luminol report.

And it will attract more scrutiny of the forensic services unit, a frequent target of defense lawyers.

"The supervision in the whole department was lacking because they didn't think the ... unit was important," said Warren Allred, a former evidence technician who left the department in 2000 to work as a public defenders' office investigator in Kentucky. "I don't think they know the importance of evidence collection."

Some examples:

* In 2000, Superior Court Judge Orlando Hudson dismissed rape charges against Bryant Von Strothers. Former technician Bruce Preiss had collected evidence in the case, but instead of turning it over to the department's property room, he kept it in the trunk of his car for seven months before throwing it away.

* In the 2001 murder trial of Eric Crutchfield, public defender Bob Brown mounted a defense for his client highlighting the work of Preiss, again the crime-scene technician. With the word "errors" written in capital letters on a flip chart, Brown took Preiss through every mistake he made collecting evidence. Preiss admitted listing the wrong date, time and location of a shell casing and failing to check the house for fingerprints. Crutchfield was convicted nonetheless.

* Last month, defense attorney Karen Bethea-Shields questioned why forensics technicians did not lift a bloody fingerprint from the scene while investigating the murder of Paul Muwanga, 41. Shields' client, Kelvin Gerald Butler, was found not guilty of the 2001 stabbing death. Shields said the fingerprint could have made the trial unnecessary.

Tom Loflin, a defense lawyer who works with Shields, says he has seen no improvements in recent years.

The forensics work has gotten "worse and worse up until now, when it is often really a joke," Loflin said. "What would any reasonable person think? A bloody fingerprint that the forensics team didn't bother to lift? And that's just one example of the kind of work they do."

Staffing and training

The 12-member Forensic Services Unit, headed by Ann Saccoccio, consists of 11 unsworn civilians supervised by a police sergeant. They gather, process and preserve crime-scene evidence for the Durham Police Department, the county sheriff's office, fire departments, Veterans Affairs police, the N.C. Highway Patrol and the campus police for Duke and N.C. Central universities. The unit responded to 4,700 crime scenes in the 12 months ending April 1.

To qualify to work in the department, applicants must have an associate's degree in criminal justice or a related field from a technical institute or community college, or comparable work knowledge or experience.

Some forensics technicians have come from the city sanitation department and the 911 communications center. In the past, many lacked crime-scene experience.

After the problems with Preiss' work came to light, Durham police conducted an internal review of the unit, but what it turned up was not disclosed. An April 2001 audit by the State Bureau of Investigation called the unit "highly efficient" and "professional" but cited some problems and suggested changes.

It recommended increasing training, having a supervisor review technicians' notes and reports before they are disseminated, and testing technicians' knowledge.

Police said Saccoccio, who was hired because of her extensive training and experience, made those and other improvements. Many recent hires have law enforcement backgrounds and receive additional training when hired.

But police said the unit remains understaffed and pay is low. To reduce the workload, the duty of responding to vehicle break-ins was shifted from technicians to officers. That has cut the number of cases handled annually from roughly 6,300 cases to 4,700.

"The Durham Police Department stands behind the work of its Forensics Services Unit," said Chief Steve Chalmers, calling employees well-trained professionals.

He declined further comment.

Maj. Lucy Zastrow of the sheriff's office called technicians "well-trained" investigators and attributed past or current problems to human error. "Everybody makes a mistake sometime," she said. "That doesn't mean they are not good."

The coming spotlight

In the Peterson case, prosecutors have no eyewitness and no known motive or murder weapon, so the crime-scene work and forensics evidence will be important. In his testimony last month, however, Campen conceded that he didn't follow the basic tenets of forensics: writing notes at the scene, taking photos and videotapes of Luminol tests, and writing reports quickly.

In other testimony, technician Dan George, a five-year veteran, acknowledged that police officers did not follow proper protocol when they allowed Peterson and his son, Todd, to cradle Kathleen Peterson; when they allowed at least six people to walk through the crime scene, tracking blood; and when Mike Peterson was allowed to sit on a nearby couch, to which he transferred blood from Kathleen Peterson's body.

Allred, the former evidence technician, said technicians are often swamped, running from crime scene to crime scene, which can lead to mistakes.

A contributing problem, he said, is that police officers often fail to secure crime scenes.

"We would arrive there and we were not sworn; we were not the bosses," he said. "Sometimes, someone would bring a rookie in to look at a body. They would just be allowed to let anyone wander through, in and out, in and out, and that's wrong."

Police said those problems have been addressed.

Robert Gaensslen, director of graduate studies for forensic science at the University of Illinois in Chicago, said not documenting results is "a big no-no."

"Documentation is the most important thing you do at a crime scene," he said. "Document the scene. Document the evidence. This is the kind of thing you do contemporaneously."

Durham police written procedures don't set deadlines for reports by crime-scene technicians, but say they should be "working on the prompt completion of their major crime reports and necessary follow-up." Police said major case reports generally are to be completed within four weeks, and supervisors are held responsible.

The SBI requires that its crime-scene investigators document all aspects of a crime scene and evidence, and turn in reports within 15 days, according to the SBI's Field Procedure Manual.

Brown, the public defender, said he has always had questions about the Durham forensic unit's ability to "thoroughly do a crime scene."

"They don't do a very good job," he said. "It's not just one or two officers. It happens over a period of time. There is always a greater probability of an innocent person being convicted on the basis of sloppy work."

SUMMARY

No matter what type of agency you work for; small or rural, big city police department, federal, and/or private, implementation of accurate and complete documentation skills will be required. When you are working a crime scene or a case always keep in mind that what you do can be "discovered" and that you will have to testify to it. Your reputation depends on it. It starts at the crime scene and ends in the courtroom. We hope that you have gained an appreciation for the painstaking and important job documenting a crime scene can be.

DISCUSSION QUESTIONS

1. Explain discovery and give examples of what types of things are discoverable.

2. What things are not subject to discovery?

3. Imagine you are the defense attorney in the above mentioned Mike Peterson case, applying what you have learned thus far, explain how would you handle your cross examination of senior crime-scene technician Eric Campen? What rules and issues would you bring up?

Chapter 18

Visual Aids

CHAPTER OVERVIEW

"A picture is worth a thousand words." How true if you consider researchers estimate we retain only 15% of what we hear but a whopping 80% of what we see and hear. This chapter points out types of visual aids and demonstrative evidence (along with some do's and don'ts), Federal Rules regarding them, and just how it applies to the crime scene investigator. The chapter focuses on the increasing use of computers and visual aids.

CHAPTER OBJECTIVES

1. Identify different types of courtroom visual aids.
2. Illustrate the best methods for presenting visual aids.
3. Explain the benefits of using visual aids.

HOW VISUAL AIDS / DEMONSTRATIVE EVIDENCE RELATES TO THE INVESTIGATOR

Public prosecutors typically have several cases they are working on at one time. Because the attorney is pressed for time the investigator may be required to prepare much of the visual evidence to support his or her testimony.

Figure 18.1 Reasons to Use Visual Aids

In a criminal trial, in many jurisdictions, the prosecution and defense are allowed to have a designated investigator assigned to them who is not included in the 'rule' when it is invoked. In other words, they may be a witness, but they are allowed to sit at the attorney's side throughout the trial.

According to the U.S. Bureau of Justice Statistics, police and detectives employed by local governments primarily worked in cities with more than 25,000 inhabitants. Some cities have very large police forces, while thousands of small communities employ fewer than 25 officers each. Forty-six local, special, and State agencies employed 1,000 or more full-time sworn officers, while approximately 7,000 departments employed fewer than 10 each.

In light of the number of criminal justice systems that are small, perhaps less than ten officers on the PD, maybe one local superior court judge, and just one prosecutor, then the local officer may be wearing many hats. The first responder, initial investigator, crime scene technician and chief investigator may be the same police officer.

This is why it is critical in most jurisdictions, that well-rounded officers be developed who are capable of handling every aspect of a criminal investigation.

Conversely, the defense may have limited assets and be able to afford one investigator, if they are fortunate enough to have that. Therefore the private investigator must be able to evaluate and respond to every aspect of the investigation as well.

The well-rounded investigator must have working knowledge of the rules of evidence, courtroom procedures, forensic procedures, and investigative techniques to survive in the majority of jurisdictions. Bottom line, no one else is there to do it!

Retired Lt. Dan Byram

Courtroom presentations can be enhanced with visual aids. They can make verbal arguments physically powerful and more persuasive. Humans are multi-sensory beings, the more senses that are engaged the more we learn. According to the U.S. Office of Naval Research "studies show that we retain much more of what we see than what we hear. Studies further show that we retain best what we see and hear together. A scientific [courtroom testimony] talk is an opportunity to show and tell. If done properly, it provides your audience with knowledge presented in a way that best enables them to absorb and retain it. Oral presentations are interactive experiences between the audience and the speaker. The speaker presents himself or herself, as well as the talk, to the audience. The speaker and the audience exchange signals. A speaker brings the subject to life for the audience through personal involvement and familiarity with it. Good interaction with the audience helps the delivery and aids the retention of the material by the audience.

Types of Demonstrative Visuals

The types of items that can be used as visual demonstrative evidence depend largely on the nature of the case. The visual items selected should be relevant to the case and enhance the verbal testimony. Below are some descriptions as to how visual aids can help in a particular case.

- An officer verbally describes to a jury the brutal details of the murder scene. Then the jury is given a *color photo* of the actual scene.

- Have you ever had someone try to explain a traffic accident to you? It is difficult to describe to the listener the details about which lanes the drivers were in, what direction the cars were traveling, the conditions of the road, weather, speeds, street signs, etc. Imagine how helpful it would be if the listener could see a *map overview* of the intersections, a *video* of the path traveled, or a *computer reenactment* depicting the speeds traveled.

- In a complicated murder case the defense claimed the defendant could not have had time to commit the murders in the time frame they supposedly occurred. A defense team could show a *time line* of events in a visual way either by using a poster board, flip chart, overhead projection, etc.

- Sometimes a scene is too complex to be understood by photo, video or drawings. At times the jury is brought to the site in question to view for themselves as was the case in the O.J. Simpson trial.

Examples of Demonstrative Visual Aids

- Graphs
- Photos
- Explanations
- 3 Dimensional Models
- Time lines
- Maps
- Medical drawings
- Reenactments
- Charts
- Videos
- Overhead Transparencies
- PowerPoint Presentations
- Sketches
- X-rays
- Document Enlargements
- Field trips to the crime scene

Mediums for Demonstrative Visuals

There are a number of mediums (or tools) available to demonstrate visual aids. Overhead projectors allow the user to place a transparency (clear plastic sheet with writing or pictures) on a reflective lens and project a much larger image onto a wall or screen.

Documents such as crime scene sketches, handwriting exemplars, police or medical reports, birth certificates, rap sheets, etc., can be enlarged or "blown up" and mounted to large poster boards.

The use of computers in the courtroom for demonstrating visual evidence has blossomed with the advent of software such as PowerPoint, Computer Aided Drafting (CAD), and 3-D animations.

Examples of Demonstrative Mediums

- Overhead Projector
- Computer
- Flip Charts
- Poster Boards
- Handouts

Descriptions of Some Demonstrative Aids

Overhead Transparencies

To help the audience comprehend intricate information, try the overlay technique. The first transparency contains the title or starting point. The second transparency is laid on top and fills in more detail. The third transparency is laid on top and contains more data and so on and so on. This helps the audience from becoming overwhelmed with a lot of material at once and allows you to control the rate of speed. Another method is to print all the data on one transparency, and place a piece of paper over top. Slide the paper down one line or point at a time. This allows you to reveal the information in the same controlled format.

PowerPoint

PowerPoint presentations are much like overhead transparencies in that the material can be laid out one step and a time; however PowerPoint is much easier and more powerful (as the name implies). PowerPoint is a Microsoft program that allows the user to create a computerized slide show. A wide spectrum of colors for background and fonts are available. Music or sound bytes can be added. Clip art or photos can be pasted in.

PowerPoint presentations are easy to use. The transition between slides can be controlled by a mouse click or automatically set. Changes to an overhead transparency can cost time and money, a PowerPoint slide can be changed with a few keystrokes.

Poster Boards

Documents can be enlarged to fit the poster board. Photographs can be enlarged to aid the jury in viewing minute details. They are useful, for example, in a forgery case when an expert is trying to show the jury the subtle differences in signatures. The documents in question can be blown up or enlarged allowing the jury to view highlighted areas.

Below are examples of courtroom graphics; these images can be presented with overhead projectors, poster boards, and computer generated PowerPoint slides.

[Samples courtesy of Robina Royer, Esq. & Gavin Gregory, Decision Quest
www.decisionquest.com]

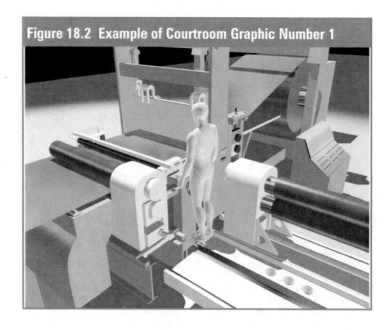

Figure 18.2 Example of Courtroom Graphic Number 1

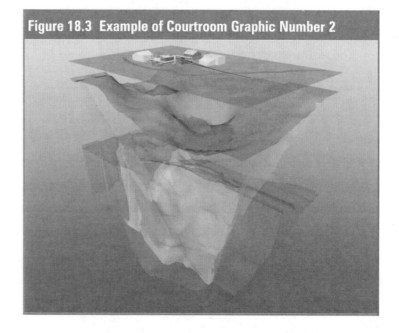

Figure 18.3 Example of Courtroom Graphic Number 2

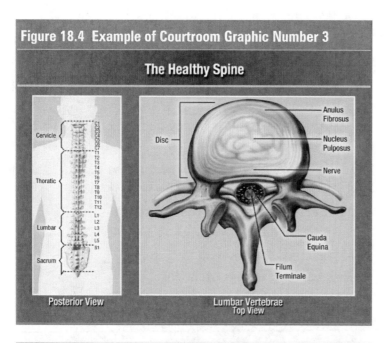

Figure 18.4 Example of Courtroom Graphic Number 3

The Healthy Spine

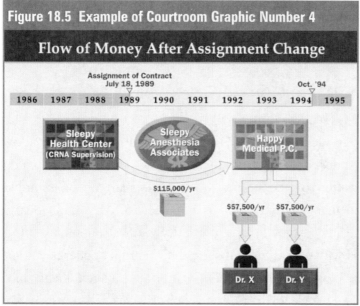

Figure 18.5 Example of Courtroom Graphic Number 4

Flow of Money After Assignment Change

Do's and Don'ts for Presenting Demonstrative Visual Aids

Be careful not to go over the top with visual aids, they should add to you presentation, not be the presentation. Don't use fancy graphics, charts or overheads if they don't help streamline your message. Basically don't use them just for the sake of using them. You don't want the judge or jury to forget you and focus on the visuals.

- Do familiarize yourself with the courtroom. Ask yourself:
  - How is the room setup?
  - How far will the audience or jurors be from the visual aids?
  - Will the farthest person away be able to read the aids?

- Do keep the focus on the key points.
    - Don't put too much information on one page or chart
- Do keep it simple.
    - Don't distract with too many colors or typefaces (limit each to two or three).
    - Do use bright colors if they help highlight key points.
- Do a practice run.
    - Walk through your presentation for a peer to evaluate.
    - Identify and work out any kinks.
- Don't get spellbound by your presentation
    - Speak to the jury, not your visual aids.
    - Make eye contact with the jurors.
- Observe the reactions of the jury
    - Do they look confused or are they taking notes?
    - Give them enough time to study the material.

FEDERAL RULES FOR USING VISUAL AIDS

Federal Rules of Appellate Procedure

Title VII. General Provisions

Rule 34. Oral Argument

(a) In General; Local Rule. Oral argument shall be allowed in all cases unless pursuant to local rule a panel of three judges, after examination of the briefs and record, shall be unanimously of the opinion that oral argument is not needed. Any such local rule shall provide any party with an opportunity to file a statement setting forth the reasons why oral argument should be heard. A general statement of the criteria employed in the administration of such local rule shall be published in or with the rule and such criteria shall conform substantially to the following minimum standard:

(g) Use of Physical Exhibits at Argument; Removal. If physical exhibits other than documents are to be used at the argument, counsel shall arrange to have them placed in the courtroom before the court convenes on the date of the argument. After the argument counsel shall cause the exhibits to be removed from the courtroom unless the court otherwise directs. If exhibits are not reclaimed by counsel within a reasonable time after notice is given by the clerk, they shall be destroyed or otherwise disposed of, as the clerk shall think best.

Federal Rule of Evidence 1006

In United States of America v. Oberkampf Supply Of Lubbock, Inc. Criminal No. 5-95CR-074-C the court states:

> The contents of voluminous writings, recordings, or photographs, which cannot conveniently be examined in court, may be presented in the form of a chart, summary, or calculation. The originals, or duplicates, shall be made available for examination or copying, or both, by other parties at a reasonable time and place. The government submits that the reasonable time and place required by the Rule should allow the government sufficient time, in advance of trial, to examine and analyze such material in preparation for trial. Early production of such material obviates the need to request a recess during the trial for the purpose of examining such material. The government therefore requests that the Court set a date for the disclosure of all material, the contents of which defendants intend to introduce into evidence in summary form. In this regard, the Court should be aware that the government already has disclosed to defendants such available material that it intends to introduce in this matter.

> If defendants call an expert witness during trial, the government undoubtedly will inquire as to the basis for any opinion proffered by the expert witness during his direct testimony. The government then will be forced to request a recess to review the underlying material before meaningful cross- examination can proceed. To avoid this potential delay, the government requests that such notice and materials be provided to the government at least one day prior to such testimony. The advance notice is also necessary to ensure that the government will have an opportunity to schedule a comparable expert, if necessary, to hear and evaluate such expert testimony and material prior to cross-examination.

Conclusion:

For the foregoing reasons, the government respectfully requests this Court set a date by which all discovery shall be provided to the government.

COMPUTERS AND VISUAL AIDS

There is little doubt that computers have changed our lives. They are used in retail stores, banks, airports, police cars, advertising agencies, and schools, even elementary schools. Computers are now becoming very common in the courtroom. Digital imaging, 3-D animation, graphic recreations, and various trial software programs are changing the face of the courtroom and testimony. Along with the positive changes come lessons, complications, and questions. These issues are addressed intelligently and thoroughly in a captivating dialogue captured in the National Conference on Science and the Law Proceedings.

The following text is taken from the National Institute of Justice National Conference on Science and the Law Proceedings. The material has been edited down to fit the topics and issues relevant to this chapter. The full text is available at http://www.ncjrs.org/txtfiles1/nij/179630.txt

---

Figure 18.6 Scientific & Demonstrative Evidence: Is Seeing Believing?

Title: National Conference on Science and the Law Proceedings.
Series: Research Forum
Author: National Institute of Justice
Published: NIJ, July 2000
Subject: Criminal justice system
Panel IV. Scientific and Demonstrative Evidence: Is Seeing Believing?

Moderator Ronald Reinstein Associate Presiding Judge Superior Court of Arizona Phoenix, Arizona

Panelists Robert J. Humphreys The Commonwealth's Attorney City of Virginia Beach, Virginia

Samuel A. Guiberson President Guiberson Law Offices, P.L.C. Houston, Texas

Mark Garcia Litigation Graphics Consultant FTI/Consulting Los Angeles, California

Mark Garcia : ...Before I show you some portfolio samples using the FTI's proprietary TrialMax software, I want to point out that there are off-the-shelf visual presentation software packages that, while less robust, may be more cost efficient and effective in telling the litigant's story in the courtroom. Microsoft's PowerPoint is one such user-friendly application and this software is typically bundled with MS Word. PowerPoint is limited, however, to very tight and very linear presentations. On the other hand, the FTI TrialMax application offers more control of multimedia formatted graphic evidence. Irrespective of whether the trial lawyer is in opening, direct, cross, or closing mode, any type of digitized exhibit can be retrieved, annotated, and brought back with those annotations in seconds.

The most dominant application of TrialMax is in the area of discovery document management and presentation. With most types of complex civil litigation there are usually many documents that need to be shown at trial. Many times the courtroom becomes a war of the exhibit boards, which are very cumbersome to manipulate for most trial teams, even when they are mounted on flip boards. In terms of economics, the average cost of an exhibit board will range between $200 and $500. That adds up quickly over a dozen to 20 exhibit boards, at which point you could purchase the laptop

Figure 18.6 Scientific & Demonstrative Evidence: Is Seeing Believing? (Cont.)

and presentation software that I am using today. So, the economies of computerized presentation of litigation graphics are now clearly evident for even small-scale litigation. Of greater significance are the user-friendly exhibit format tools that a program like TrialMax offers. Document presentation treatments involving text highlights, callouts, font changes, blocking, redacting, and so on can now all be manipulated digitally by the trial lawyers themselves. The user can work with these tools either with the icon-marked keys on the toolbar or via "hot" keys. While FTI will often counsel clients on creating exhibits that maximize juror perceptions of color, text, and illustrated terms and concepts, trial attorneys themselves are now capable via TrialMax to make modifications even minutes before trial. In the example you are now viewing, I am using a tool that offers a "John Madden" like approach to circle, underscore, or annotate a chart or graph.

Now that we are on the topic of charts and illustrations, I am now showing you features like magnification and split-screen, which can help jurors better focus on key discussion points and relate illustrated concepts to text in key documents or deposition transcripts. By the way, the user can also load and display videotaped deposition testimony or animation into these screen windows.

All of this presentation technology expands the range of graphic evidence preparation options for trial lawyers. The most commonly used exhibit to teach jurors facts of a case is the timeline. Some of you may be familiar with this case, which dealt with the issue of a high-level auto executive who left GM and went to VW and who was accused of trade-secret misappropriation of GM marketing data. This interactive timeline takes key points in the story and matches them with key evidentiary documents and other graphic exhibits, which the presenter can retrieve instantly, inclusive of all of their prepared highlights. The stylized use of certain color and text treatments in this timeline further highlight the defense's key themes.

Another popular use of evidentiary graphics is with respect to presenting damage estimates to a jury. This example is taken from the Francis Ford Coppola case, which involved a copyright dispute on a scripted treatment for an animated feature film adaptation of Pinocchio. Here, FTI developed visual analogies that broke down the different types of damages that would have accrued if the scheduled production had been put in actual distribution. Many times our firm is presented with voluminous accounting or statistical data related to damage estimates, often developed right before trial and in handwritten form. We will respond with a cleaner, more comprehensible version.

Figure 18.6 Scientific & Demonstrative Evidence: Is Seeing Believing? (Cont.)

Now, I would like to move away from the area of two-dimensional static graphics and address the world of videotaped deposition testimony and animation. Here, I can use the same TrialMax platform and instantly program and present segments or clips of video deposition testimony that have been converted to digitized MPEG files. In this example, I can even trim frames from either the beginning or end. FTI has earned a reputation for producing high-impact, cost-efficient animation to support expert witness testimony in all types of civil litigation. Advances in computer processor technology and the proliferation of competitive animation authoring programs have driven down the per minute production cost of 3-D animation to make these motion graphics affordable for use in even small scale cases.

Ronald Reinstein: While he's sitting up here, does anybody have any questions of Mark?

Mr. Mark Garcia: ...First of all, this technology that you saw today is actually provided to our clients for free. We actually give the software, in fact even the hardware, and frequently you'll have to make arrangements for, like, video monitors, although a lot of the Federal courts now are buying pools of monitors and providing them free to counsel.

...So, there are lots and lots of documents. I find the same kind of mindset in the legal field usually flows through in the kinds of graphics they will create. They'll try to put into a graphic, into a screen on an art board, so many items, so much complexity, so much text, that what they don't realize is that, while it makes sense to the trial advocate, it's overwhelming to the juror. And that's where we try to simplify it and pull out those [inaudible].

Judge Ronald Reinstein: Robert?

Mr. Robert J. Humphreys: ...the notion that what we're all about in a courtroom is to persuade, to communicate, which is the prerequisite to persuasion. That is, the trier of fact, whether it's the judge or the jury, and persuade them through the witness and, hopefully, of what that evidence is in a way the jury can understand, can digest and apply to the laws, and to the other facts that might exist in the case.

...diagrams, photographs, and physical evidence generally can be very, very powerful. In some ways it can even overshadow the live witness.

And of course, in this day and age, we're dealing with Generation X, we're dealing with folks who cut their teeth on multimedia— television, the movies, you know, Star Wars, special effects, Titanic, you name it. These are the folks that are out there, that we're grabbing off the streets and plopping down into our jury boxes to decide cases. And we need to understand that, both as practitioners, such as Sam and myself, trial court

Figure 18.6 Scientific & Demonstrative Evidence: Is Seeing Believing? (Cont.)

judges, appellate court judges, and above all, experts who also have to communicate and get their usually esoteric points across to that jury.

But those of you, who have been practitioners, or experts in this particular field, probably know about the explanation of reaction time. In a case like a drunk driving case, a motor vehicle manslaughter case or something like that, you have the scientist up there spouting formulas about hydroplaning, or how far you'd travel at a given speed in a given length of time. And, you know, the jury's eyes are glazing over at some point. But you can show it very simply.

The old adage is that a picture is worth 1,000 words. Even talking about something like DNA—just those three magic letters make most people's eyes glaze over right away. There is the notion that the DNA molecule is approximately 2 feet long, when you stretch it all out, and that every living thing, on this planet at least, has DNA, and that there are some parts of the DNA molecule that all living things have in common, other parts that just mammals have in common, and then certain parts that scientists say are unique to each one of us except for maybe our identical twin.

So, how do you get all that across to a jury? Well, of course the experts can get up there and talk about it, and if they're a good expert, they'll talk about it. By the way, some experts, I think, get paid by the syllable. And maybe they do, I don't know, but the ones that, in my experience, work well with juries are the ones that can break it down, convince the jury. In fact, you know the best expert, the ideal expert, at least in my experience, that I would want to use—and I'm dating myself—is Mr. Wizard. Or, for you younger folks, Bill Nye the Science Guy. Because they can explain pretty complex stuff in a very easily understood way that your average 9-, 10-, 11-, and 12-year-old can understand.

Expert witnesses are witnesses, after all, and witnesses, like lay witnesses, are there to communicate, to impart information, and you can do it diagrammatically. I mean a photograph, crime scene photograph such as the two represented here, on a diagram, that simply shows the point of view, that helps the trier of fact orient itself to where this crime occurred, how it occurred, generally where the parties were standing when it occurred, or just before it occurred. That sort of thing can be very, very helpful. And you could, of course, take that to the next level and actually diagram the whole crime using PowerPoint... the point is, that's how you communicate visually; not visually alone but orally combined with the visual representation.

Taking something like how gunpowder residue gets on someone's hand, you can simply take them right out of a ballistics text, as the photograph at the top there from Hill's Homicide Events Reconstruction.

Figure 18.6 Scientific & Demonstrative Evidence: Is Seeing Believing? (Cont.)

[http://home.revealed.net/whill/]You simply slap it on a copier, copy it, and blow it up a little bit so the jury can understand it. Below are simply photographs taken under strobe light conditions showing basically the same thing but, in connection with a particular case, the blowback, deposits—gun powder residue—on the individual's hand who's holding the weapon, and where it comes from. It doesn't just come from the barrel, it comes from the receiver area as well, that sort of thing. And unless you happen to have some firearms expert sitting on your jury, they're probably not going to understand this stuff very well without some graphic representation.

The alternative, as happened in one location in North Carolina, is the jury's going to do their own ballistics test in the jury room. If you let the ammunition go back with them, which is what happened there, and they shot it out the window.

Blood pattern interpretation, using Luminal, if necessary, to bring the blood patterns out. This is from a case: Can you find the bloody hammer impression? Well, your expert is going to testify about it, but imagine if you were the jury, how much more helpful it would be if, along with that testimony, there were some photographs showing exactly how the head of that hammer fits a particular impression.

So, why bother with these visuals? You know, why do you do all this? You've all heard the old proverb, "To hear is to forget, to see is to remember, to do is to understand." Well, except for the jury doing their own ballistics test back in the jury room, it's pretty difficult for them to actually do what you or your experts are going to be talking about in the course of the trial. But the next best thing, of course, is to let them see how something occurred. Or see how a concept can be brought to fruition in the case of a scientific expert. Jurors, as we've already talked about, are more accustomed to visuals, they've grown up with them, they see them all the time. They're bombarded by Madison Avenue and Steven Spielberg. Juror retention is increased. Your average human being, according to every study I've ever seen, will retain something on the order of 80 percent of what they see, versus only about 15 percent of what they hear.

Less chance of misperception, that a juror who maybe was daydreaming or is hard of hearing, or didn't hear the modifiers or the adjectives that the witness used when they described whatever it was they were describing.

And from our perspective as practitioners, visuals can also enhance or disguise your witness. Maybe your witness isn't the best witness in the world, maybe they're soft-spoken, maybe they don't communicate very well, but the visuals can help enhance their credibility or, to put it another way, overcome or disguise to some degree all of that. Now, if I'm offending any public defenders out there, I'm sorry, but I mean it works both ways. And because jurors assess and process all of this information when they're assessing credibility, it's certainly all fair game to put in front of them.

Judge Ronald Reinstein: You know, Robert, as Sam's getting up, have you ever heard the argument that what you do is too persuasive?

Mr. Robert J. Humphreys: [Inaudible.] I was telling him earlier about a conversation I had last week. I got a call out of the blue from the Attorney General of South Dakota, who was in the middle of a trial. He's the first attorney general I know that's actually ever set foot in a courtroom, apparently. But he was in the middle of a trial, he was using PowerPoint in the trial, and during his closing argument, the defense objected. And the stated reason for the objection was, "Your Honor, that is too persuasive." And the judge stopped the trial and said, "I'm going to take a recess of several hours and I want some law on this.".

So, they called me to ask me if I could provide them maybe with some guidance to some law on how it's okay to be too persuasive. Off the top of my head, I couldn't think of anything, but I did give them some case citations. About every State in the union except New York approves the use of visuals like this throughout the trial, certainly in opening and closing arguments. And the same law basically applies to exhibits. I can boil it all down to, "If you can say it, you can show it." "What the ear may hear, the eye may see," as one of the judges put it.

Mr. Samuel A. Guiberson: What I really like about what's happened so far is that you're seeing a panorama of the ways in which technology is applied to court, to the experience of being an advocate. Let's look at what we've done. We've had a lawyer talking, he made you laugh, showed you pictures, you have seen videos, you've seen stills, you've heard sound. What have you done? You've been part of a total communication experience.

...Technology has become integrated with the way we express ourselves in the courtroom—not because we want to show off, not because we believe that a PowerPoint presentation like this one has any value if your point has no power. It doesn't. It's not just about special effects. It's about being especially effective... One of the problems we encounter is that the threshold of scrutiny for digital exhibits... has become greater as it becomes more interpretive; that is, as it is employed by an expert to state expert opinions about an unwitnessed event, accident, or crime.

The more interpretive exhibit is simple because the courts are familiar with predicates for expert testimony. And then, of course, the expressive exhibit is simply that one which extends the expression of the witness,

Figure 18.6 Scientific & Demonstrative Evidence: Is Seeing Believing? (Cont.)

"Now Miss Jones, the video you're about to see, you've seen it, does it accurately depict the night the accident occurred?" It is an extension of the expression, the testimony of a particular witness.

What we've got to recognize is, as lawyers and their media are integrated, so witnesses and their media are integrated. The exhibit, the demonstrative exhibit, is not something apart from the witness; the exhibit is the witness. The witness is that exhibit. The exhibit on the screen is an extension of the words and recollections of that witness.

Now, let me show you that this is not always—you know we think of this being computer animation. It also applies to photographs. When I say "down in the digits," it means how to interpret what the infirmities of the photographic exhibit might be. Now, we all know that photographs, you know, are routinely admitted. What you're looking at, of course, is a digital rendering of a photograph. That photograph—a digital photograph can, of course, in some instances today, and certainly more so tomorrow, photographic images are going to be, in their origin, digital. And that subjects us to a lot of potential manipulation. This, of course, has been treated digitally to make it appear a little darker than it actually might have been.

There's your actual photograph. Look at the sign—we're going to sort of invent a scenario here. Under the Mojave Motel there, there's a sign. Let's say this is a case about somebody driving their 14-foot-high Winnebago through a 7-foot sign.

Pretty obvious. Clearance, seven. "Well, did you see the 7-foot clearance sign?" "No, sir, I couldn't see a thing."

But you could see it here, you see. Those subtle variations that the digital process permits can really vary the reality that is being described without truly varying the image of the exhibit. I think we'd all agree this doesn't have to be something diabolical. We'd all agree, if I were the proprietor of the Mojave Motel, "Is this a photograph of your motel?" Yes, sir. You see, because we are not trained, we haven't evolved in our media-wise sensibilities to understand, "Yes, sir, but on that kind of day, in those kind of conditions, you could see that sign." The subtleties, the very small, down in the details, digital manipulations, are not things that we usually associate with photographic exhibits.

So, we have a problem in how we approach these different forms of digital evidence. Are they expressive in that they allow an individual to vouch for the way the animation portrays the actual event; or, are they interpretive in the sense that we have only select data points of factual knowledge about how an event took place—that either a computer or an expert or a combination of the two has, shall we say, interstitially

Figure 18.6 Scientific & Demonstrative Evidence: Is Seeing Believing? (Cont.)

extrapolated a reality, going between the existing data points to create probabilities that would create a reality out of only a partial reality.

So, our risk is that courts and attorneys don't know how to deconstruct the digital into its programming parts. To see that it is really less than the sum of its parts, you have to understand how it's composed, how artful, what the art of the programming is, and what components of reality underlie the illusion, the apparent reality of the computer exhibit.

So, the virtually real—the animated, digital reality that seems perfect, dinosaurs with scales on their feet, everything we witness in the contemporary cinema, of course—shows us the virtually real. Is it more admissible because it's real? Does how authentic it is really underlie its admissibility? Or, is something like a digital exhibit that is very realistic simply like a more articulate lawyer, or a lawyer who simply paints a picture a little more artfully than another lawyer? The reality, the physical appearance of the digital exhibit does not dictate its quality. Its entertainment value is not its probative value.

And, in this sense, it's important to recognize that we are often lulled, by the very fancy Star Wars animated exhibits, into respecting them more as evidence than we would respect the stick figures that another lawyer might use on a low budget—a witness expresses the relative physical positions of people during a shoot-out. They're both equally expressive and equally valid as evidence. One simply is more articulate, because it uses a higher level of digital virtual reality. Be wary of aesthetic value pretending evidentiary value.

Like the devil, the digital is in the details. How do you confront the evidence if it's so obscure in its encoding that you have no way to reach down to that level, that particular granular level, at which it becomes either the truth or a lie? And that, of course, is a part of the way in which we must change our court procedures to recognize that digital exhibits require a level of scrutiny much more subtle, and in some ways more complex, than other forms of exhibits. We ought to talk about having digital discovery conferences early on in a case, where the court can come as an arbiter of what the parties intend to do as far as their expression in terms of the discovery and in terms of their trial exhibits. If the court can stimulate people to think whether or not they can use these methods, and if they have time to learn to use them effectively, and once deciding that they can use them effectively, each party can judge the reliability underlying the digital evidence that comes forth.

But the reality we have to accept and the courts need to recognize, all lawyers certainly do, is that truth comes to the court in words, it comes in

Figure 18.6 Scientific & Demonstrative Evidence: Is Seeing Believing? (Cont.)

sounds, and it comes in images, and the media itself is not the message, it is the message's messenger.
 	
    Where I think this visual stuff can be far more effective is in what I would refer to as simple illustrations of witnesses' testimony, such as, the crime scene diagram where the parties were positioned and what route they took based on their testimony. They can diagram it themselves right from the witness stand.
 	
    Participant: I know there was a judge here earlier this morning from Maryland, I don't know if he's still here, but last year, Maryland's Court of Appeals adopted proposed model rules governing the admissibility of computer-generated evidence specifically as to simulations, animations, and digital camera productions, but nothing else other than that as far as regular cameras.
 	
    Judge Ronald Reinstein: Several years ago, I had a prison murder trial. One prisoner was accused of killing another. A third prisoner, the State witness, who said that he saw the whole thing, testified on direct examination as to what he saw. The defense presented photographs of the scene, and because of the light that was used and the angles that were used, it made it seem like the prison witness could not have seen what he said he did, which was crucial to the State's case. The jury was a hung jury, 10 to 2 for acquittal.
 	
    Well, the State decided to try the case again. The second time they asked for a jury view of the scene. They did view the scene at the prisons. We took the jurors out there. And sure enough, there was no doubt, I think, in anybody's mind, that the prisoner witness could see the murder scene, and the jury came back in about an hour-and-a-half with a guilty verdict. That was the only difference in the two trials. So, images change.

DISCUSSION QUESTIONS

1. What are some of the mediums or tools for displaying visual aids?

2. Can visual aids be over used or out-do the testimony? Explain.

3. What is PowerPoint and how has it changed courtroom presentations?

IN-CLASS EXERCISE

Create a topic or testimony of an incident you would like to relate to a jury (students). Using the knowledge from this chapter and lecture, make a visual aid to support your testimony. Initially present your testimony with only a verbal explanation. Then repeat it utilizing your visual aid. Have the jury (students) discuss the differences and aspects of the two.

ADDITIONAL READING AND WEBSITES

It is difficult to present the strong effects visual aids can produce through a textbook. There are many companies that specialize in courtroom visual aids that now advertise on the web. Conduct an online search using the terms or combinations such as: visual aids, courtroom visual aids, demonstrative evidence.

Wayne N. Hill Sr.:
   http://home.revealed.net/whill/
Stephen Mancusi:
   http://www.forartist.com/forensic/demonstrative/demonstratvepg.htm
Legal Imaging:
   http://www.legalimaging.com/index.html
Visual Evidence Center;
   http://www.visevidence.com/ee.asp
Nimmer Legal Graphics:
   http://www.nimmer.net/legalgraphics/index.HTM